THE ILLUSTRATED GUIDE TO
MARINE FiSH
OF THE WORLD

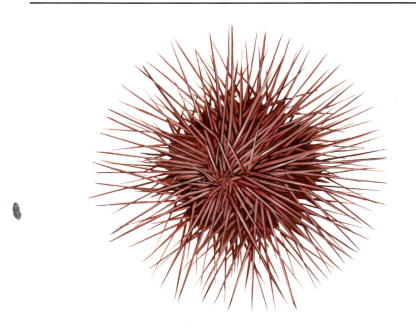

THE ILLUSTRATED GUIDE TO
MARINE FISH
OF THE WORLD

A visual directory of sea life featuring more than 450 fabulous species

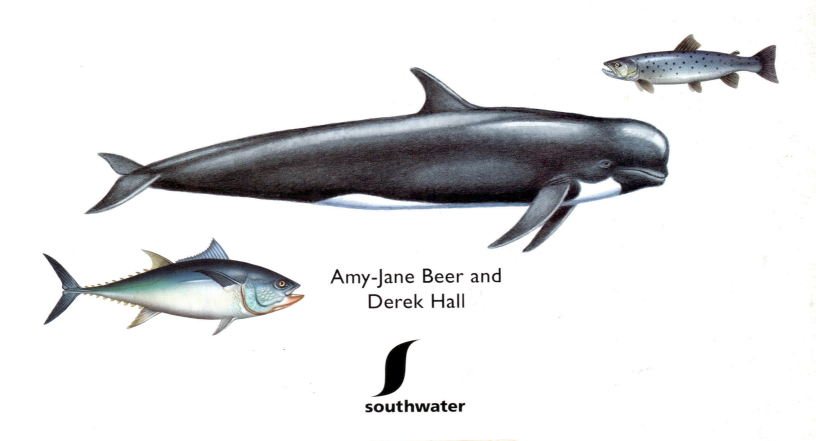

Amy-Jane Beer and
Derek Hall

southwater

 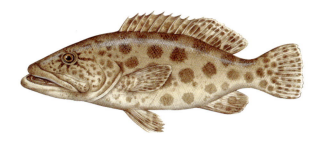 

This edition is published by Southwater, an imprint of Anness Publishing Ltd, Hermes House, 88–89 Blackfriars Road, London SE1 8HA; tel. 020 7401 2077; fax 020 7633 9499

www.southwaterbooks.com; www.annesspublishing.com

If you like the images in this book and would like to investigate using them for publishing, promotions or advertising, please visit our website www.practicalpictures.com for more information.

UK agent: The Manning Partnership Ltd; tel. 01225 478444; fax 01225 478440; sales@manning-partnership.co.uk
UK distributor: Grantham Book Services Ltd; tel. 01476 541080; fax 01476 541061; orders@gbs.tbs-ltd.co.uk
North American agent/distributor: National Book Network; tel. 301 459 3366; fax 301 429 5746; www.nbnbooks.com
Australian agent/distributor: Pan Macmillan Australia; tel. 1300 135 113; fax 1300 135 103; customer.service@macmillan.com.au
New Zealand agent/distributor: David Bateman Ltd; tel. (09) 415 7664; fax (09) 415 8892

Publisher: Joanna Lorenz
Editorial Director: Helen Sudell
Project Editors: Catherine Stuart, Melanie Hibbert
Production Manager: Claire Rae
Book and Jacket Design: Nigel Partridge ar
Artists: Mike Atkinson, Peter Bull, Peter Ba
Rose Cole, Julius Csotonyi, Anthony Duke

ETHICAL TRADING POLICY
At Anness Publishing we believe that busin   )gically
sustainable way, with respect for the enviro   of the
natural resources we employ. Because of ou   ou, as our
customer, can have the pleasure and reassur
on your behalf to naturally replace the mate
For further information about this scheme,

Previously published as part of a larger volume, *The Illustrated World Encyclopedia of Marine Fish & Sea Creatures*

PUBLISHER'S NOTE
Although the information in this book are believed to be accurate and true at the time of going to press, neither the authors nor the publisher can accept any legal responsibility or liability for any errors or omissions that may be made.

Frontispiece: Red lionfish emerge at night to hunt for prey.

PICTURE ACKNOWLEDGEMENTS
Note: t= top; m=middle; b=bottom; l=left; r=right
Illustrations
The illustrations appearing on the jacket, and on pages 1–7 and 8–160 of this book, were supplied by the following artists: Mike Atkinson, Peter Barrett, Penny Brown, Jim Channell, Felicity Rose Cole, Julius Csotonyi, Stuart Jackson Carter and Denys Ovenden. In addition, Anthony Duke created all maps appearing on pages 12–160.
Photographs
The following photographs were taken by Rowan Byrne, www.marinecreatures.com All jacket photographs except dolphin.
Inside pages: 6tr, 6bl, 7b. The following photographs were supplied by photographers (as credited), courtesy of www.imagequestmarine.com:
2: Roger Steene; 55: Carlos Villoch; 105: Masha Ushioda; 115: Peter Parks; 143 (panel): Johnny Jensen.

CONTENTS

INTRODUCTION

The marine creatures illustrated in this book are as complex and mysterious as the saltwater world they inhabit. From sponges, corals, jellyfish, worms, crustaceans, molluscs and echinoderms to fish, reptiles and mammals, profile species are described in detail, with a guide to habitat, size, breeding and feeding behaviour.

The inhabitants of an underwater environment face quite a different set of challenges to those met by plants and animals on dry land. But, in marvelling at the many ways marine organisms find to cope, it is easy to forget that, in fact, an aquatic life is the norm. Life on Earth originated in the seas, and it is quite strange to think of this existence as being more difficult or alien than one reliant upon air. And, while the means of carving out an existence may differ dramatically between habitats, the laws of survival remain basically the same for all living organisms.

The principles of life

Life itself is a complex series of chemical reactions, but these reactions do not take place without the necessary chemical ingredients and expenditure of energy. Obtaining these essentials is the most immediate

*Below: Blackbar soldierfish (*Myripristis jacobus*) belong to a family group known as squirrelfish. As with a large number of creatures, their common name is based on a distinguishing physical characteristic: an oblique black bar behind the head.*

problem for any living thing. Plants, including most algae, derive their energy requirements directly from the sun – absorbing packets of light energy called photons using special pigments, mainly chlorophyll, in a process known as photosynthesis. They use solar energy to convert water and carbon dioxide (simple chemical compounds available to them in abundance) into more complex ones known as carbohydrates.

These carbohydrates can be stored within the plant and broken down

*Above: Corals and sponges, such as this azure vase sponge (*Callyspongia plicifera*), may look rather like plants, but their reliance upon the consumption of other organisms to obtain energy means that they are classed as animals.*

later to release the energy required to make other reactions happen – either inside the original plant or within the body of any creature that eats it. For it to occur, this process of energy release requires the presence of another vital ingredient – oxygen. Animals cannot make use of the sun's energy directly – all their fuel ultimately comes from the consumption of other living organisms, such as plants, that act as fuel to be 'burned' in the presence of oxygen.

Throughout its life, the principal aims of any organism are to obtain fuel, take in the oxygen with which to make use of the fuel, and to dispose of the waste products that result from this process. Of course, if its life is to be a successful one, the organism must live long enough to reproduce, and this means avoiding being eaten or otherwise destroyed. These aims apply to every organism, but the adaptations needed by marine life depend upon a number of important environmental factors.

The challenges of marine life

Oxygen is 30 times more abundant in air than it is in water. Some areas of the ocean are more oxygen deficient than others – warm water contains less oxygen than does cold water, and some regions of the deep oceans have extremely low levels. Typically, animals living in these habitats compensate by having low-energy lifestyles and enhanced oxygen-gathering abilities – such as enlarged gills.

Below: Porcupinefish belong to the order Tetradontiformes, which also includes pufferfish. These inhabitants of coral reefs can inflate their body by gradually filling their stomach with water. Once puffed out, spines set deep in the skin also become erect, helping to thwart attacks by predators.

Above: Although the anatomy of a dolphin (Delphinidae) enables it to swim very fast, for much of the time it is comfortable cruising at a speed of around 6–8kmph/3.75–5mph.

A further difficulty encountered by aquatic creatures is the relative density of water: moving through it simply requires more energy than moving through air, so marine organisms that need to move quickly are typically streamlined and hydrodynamic in shape. But the viscosity of water also has its compensations – it offers many times more support than air. Terrestrial organisms, for example, need to invest

significant resources in both skeletal and muscular tissues in order just to support the weight of their own body on land. The ocean-dwellers are spared this expense, and many marine organisms invest bodily resources very differently. For example, they may become extremely large, or supremely athletic or well armoured. Where light and food are in short supply, as in some deep-sea habitats, still further adaptations are required.

A diverse world

The aim of this book is to feature some of the major animal groups in the marine community. You will learn about the speed of predatory sharks and billfish, the ethereal beauty of corals and glass sponges, and deep sea squid so monstrous that their very existence was once believed to be a seafaring myth.

This informative guide will introduce you to more than 450 fish and sea creatures from around the world and from every type of marine habitat: seashore, coastline and estuary; shallow seas and coral reefs, open ocean and deep water. Each habitat section contains detailed profiles of a large variety of species. The main profile entries include in-depth species descriptions as well as quick-reference indentification guides.

SEASHORES, COASTS AND ESTUARIES

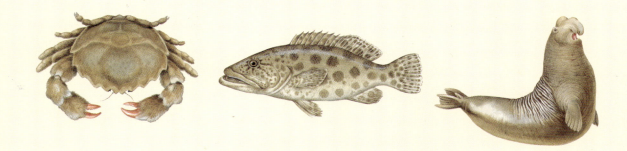

Many of the animals in these pages will be familiar to anyone that has spent time beside the sea. But despite their relative accessibility, these habitats are among the toughest in the marine environment, indeed in the world. Nowhere else on the planet do animals and plants have to deal with such dramatically fluctuating environmental conditions on a routine basis. Such conditions exert powerful selective forces. These have led to the evolution of a remarkable guild of diverse but outstandingly robust forms of animal life, which occupy habitats that are neither fully land nor sea.

The marginal habitats between land and sea also draw a range of visitors. Birds including waders, gulls and even certain eagles make a living from the sea and its shores and terrestrial mammals such as rats, foxes, and even elephants visit beaches to scavenge from the heaps of debris that wash up on every tide. These animals are beyond the scope of this book, but depending on where you are in the world, a visit to a seashore can always bring surprises.

Above, left to right: Sponge crab (Dromia personata); potato cod (Epinephelus tukula); northern elephant seal (Mirounga angustirostris).

Right: Australian sea lion (Neophoca cinerea) on the shore at Kangaroo Island, Australia.

SEA ANEMONES

Although they often resemble flowers, sea anemones are, in fact, true animals. Most attach themselves to rocks and other hard substrates – sometimes even to the shells of living animals – and catch their prey using stinging tentacles. Some species burrow in sand or mud. As with sponges, many species can reproduce by budding and fragmentation, as well as sexually.

Black coral

Antipathes subpinnata

Despite its common name and appearance, the black coral is, in fact, a type of sea anemone belonging to the class Anthozoa. It consists of a thin, blackish-brown branching skeleton forming a tree- or bush-like shape overlaid with greyish-white tissue in which are embedded numerous tiny polyps. The polyps have tentacles armed with stinging cells that capture small marine creatures. These are then transferred to the polyps' mouths to be digested, although anthozoan polyps cannot retract their tentacles. The black coral is found on stony substrates. Black coral is sometimes harvested for making into jewellery, and in the past it has also been used medicinally and in religious ceremonies. In addition, there is a small trade in live specimens for aquaria. Most black coral is exported from Taiwan, but significant quantities also come from Hawaii.

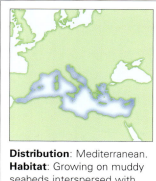

Identification: Hard, horny, tree-like skeleton, blackish-brown with tiny polyps embedded in overlying tissue and attached to the stony substrate. The pinhead-sized polyps feed by immobilizing their prey with stinging cells.

Distribution: Mediterranean.
Habitat: Growing on muddy seabeds interspersed with stones, from 10–250m/ 33–813ft.
Food: Tiny planktonic creatures.
Size: Skeleton up to 1m/ 3.25ft high; polyps about 1mm/0.04in high.
Breeding: Can reproduce asexually by division or sexually by producing eggs and sperm.
Status: Listed in CITES appendix II in 1981.

Beadlet anemone

Actinia equina

Identification: Smooth column with adhesive basal disc. About 200 tentacles arranged in five or six circlets around the mouth. Distinct ring of blue spots visible when tentacles retracted. Colour ranges from brown, red, orange or green; sometimes red with yellow-green spots.

The beadlet anemone is a common species, often seen as a dark, jelly-like blob a few centimetres high nestling in rocky crevices or at the base of breakwaters at low tide. However, it is very variable in colour, and is found in other hues, such as green or even red with yellow-green spots – the strawberry variety. Like many other anemones, the beadlet has a strong, sucker-like base, which it uses to attach itself firmly on to the substrate. The top of the column is densely packed with about 200 stinging tentacles, arranged in five or six circlets, or whorls, around the mouth. If disturbed, or when exposed at low tide, the tentacles retract, showing the ring of 24 blue spots that surrounds the oral disc.

Distribution: Atlantic Ocean, Mediterranean Sea.
Habitat: On rocks and in crevices from middle shore down to 8m/26ft.
Food: Tiny marine creatures.
Size: Column up to 7cm/ 2.8in high and 6cm/2.4in across; tentacles about 2cm/0.8in long.
Breeding: Can reproduce asexually by division or sexually by producing eggs and sperm.
Status: Not listed by IUCN.

Cerianthus lloydii: 15cm/6in long; tentacle span up to 7cm/2.8in
Like others in the order Ceriantharia, this species lives permanently within a long, soft tube buried in the sand or mud with only its tentacles exposed. The animal quickly withdraws its body and tentacles into the tube if threatened. Around the mouth are 60 or so long, brownish, green or white tentacles, surrounding a ring of shorter tentacles. It occurs from low water down to about 40m/131ft in the Atlantic Ocean.

Dahlia anemone (*Tealia felina*): 15cm/6in high
A variable anemone with a warty column often covered with fragments of gravel and shells; when closed it may be quite inconspicuous. Base strongly adhesive and sucker like. Between 80 and 160 robust, retractable stinging tentacles surround mouth. Colour is blue, grey or green with blotches. Mouth is pink, green or blue. Translucent tentacles often banded with various colours. From Atlantic middle shore downward.

Plumose anemone (*Metridium senile*): 10cm/4in high
The column is smooth with a well-defined collar below the tentacles. The tentacles are short and fine, giving a feather duster appearance. It attaches to rocks and underwater structures, such as pier supports, down to about 3m/10ft in the Atlantic Ocean and Mediterranean Sea. Its various colour forms include pink, orange and cream.

Opelet
Anemonia viridis

Also known as the snakelocks anemone because of its long, flexuous tentacles, the opelet is a large, attractive species, variably coloured and with violet tinges on the tips of its stinging tentacles. On the seashore, it is usually encountered in rockpools and in water-filled rocky crevices. The opelet rarely withdraws its tentacles, and so these anemones are quite easy to spot. The base of the column is only weakly adhesive and sucker-like and is wider than the column. Although the opelet is found mainly in places such as intertidal rockpools, it is sometimes encountered growing on the sea grass. This species often lives in the more intense light found in shallow waters.

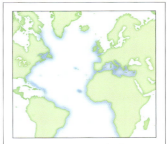

Distribution: Atlantic Ocean, Mediterranean Sea.
Habitat: In rockpools and in crevices from middle shore down to the sublittoral.
Food: Tiny marine creatures.
Size: Column up to 10cm/4in high; base about 7cm/2.8 in across; tentacles about 15cm/6in long.
Breeding: Can reproduce asexually by division or sexually by producing eggs and sperm.
Status: Not listed by IUCN.

Identification: Column with weakly adhesive basal disc. Approximately 170 tentacles arranged in about six circlets around the mouth. Colour ranges from brown, grey or bright green; fleshy tentacles have violet-tips – most apparent in green variety.

Red-speckled pimplet anemone
Anthopleura balli

This anemone, like several others, occurs in more than one colour variety. In this species, the most common colours are hues of yellow-green and orange-pink. The column is characterized by its distinctly warty appearance, with the warts becoming larger near the top. The tentacles are translucent, but attractively marked with varying tinges of colour. It tends to shun strong light conditions, and so prefers to live in shady places, such as under rocky overhangs or in dark holes. Like other anemones, it feeds by extending its column and waving its tentacles about in the water, waiting to ensnare any small animals that blunder into them.

Identification: Warty column with weakly adhesive basal disc. There are about 50 tapering tentacles around the mouth. Colour of column usually yellow-green or orange-pink. Translucent tentacles tinged with hues of grey, brown, pink or green.

Distribution: Atlantic Ocean, Mediterranean Sea.
Habitat: In crevices of rocks or under rocky overhangs where light levels are low from middle shore downwards.
Food: Tiny marine creatures.
Size: Column up to 5cm/2in high.
Breeding: Can reproduce asexually by division or sexually by producing eggs and sperm.
Status: Not listed by IUCN.

CORALS AND RELATIVES

Corals are distinguished from sea anemones because the polyps secrete around themselves a hard calcareous or limestone cup into which they can almost, or completely, retreat if threatened by a predator. Some species of corals may form enormous aggregations, known as coral reefs. The closely related Corallimorpharia, such as the Jewel 'anemone' below, lack a calcareous cup.

Scarlet-and-gold star coral

Balanophyllia regia

The scarlet-and-gold star coral is a brightly coloured, solitary species that sometimes occurs at the extreme low water mark on the seashore attached to rocks or in caves, although it is more commonly found in shallow sublittoral zones. The polyp is surrounded by a cylindrical calcareous exoskeleton into which it can only partially withdraw. Each polyp has about 48 tentacles armed with cells called nematocysts that fire venomous threads to subdue unwary creatures that blunder into them, before being transferred to the mouth. These nematocysts are fluid-filled capsules containing a barbed, hollow thread that is shot out delivering a paralyzing sting. They are used for both defence and to capture food.

Identification:
Calcareous, spongy skeleton broad and low. About 48 short, tapering tentacles arranged in rows around the mouth; tentacles lack terminal knobs. Polyp are yellow, orange or scarlet; tentacles translucent yellow.

Distribution: Atlantic Ocean.
Habitat: On rocks and in caves at lower shore and down to 10m/33ft.
Food: Tiny marine creatures.
Size: Skeleton 1cm/0.4in high.
Breeding: Can reproduce asexually by division or sexually by producing eggs and sperm.
Status: Not listed by IUCN.

Jewel 'anemone'

Corynactis viridis

Identification: Column smooth and low with broad, adhesive base. About 100 tentacles arranged in three circlets; tentacles terminate in small knob. Brightly coloured – green, pink, orange, white – with column and tentacles often in contrasting colours. Tentacles contain stinging cells to immobilize prey.

The common name of this coral is derived from its anemone-like appearance. The species does not have a hard skeleton. It occurs on rock faces, inside caves or under overhangs where the light is not strong, and may be found in large numbers. Low and squat and with a smooth column, the jewel 'anemone' is a solitary species (in other words, each individual consists of a single polyp) that is encountered in a wide variety of contrasting, often vivid colours. Each of the 100 or so tentacles terminates in a small knob, and, like other cnidarians, are armed with stinging cells.

Distribution: Atlantic Ocean, Mediterranean Sea.
Habitat: On rocks and in caves at lower shore and down to 100m/330ft.
Food: Tiny marine creatures.
Size: Body about 5mm/0.2in across.
Breeding: Can reproduce asexually by division or sexually by producing eggs and sperm.
Status: Not listed by IUCN.

Devonshire cup coral
(*Caryophyllia smithi*):
1.5cm/0.6in high
A solitary coral with a
stout, ridged skeleton
into which the polyp might
retreat (as here). The polyps
may be various colours –
white, pink, green or
brown. The tentacles,
also variable in colour, terminate in a small knob.
This Atlantic species on the extreme lower shore
and in water down to about 100m/328ft.

Balanophyllia italica: 2.5cm/1in high
The cylindrical skeleton forms an inverted cone
that is oval at the top. The polyps are iridescent
and may be colourless or brownish-yellow. It is
found on rocks and stones from about 1m/3.25ft
to 100m/330ft in the Atlantic and Mediterranean.

Cladocora cespitosa: 10cm/4in high
This species forms low, stony colonies and has
tubular skeletons. The polyps are brown and are
found on shells and rocks from 1–70m/
3.25–230ft in the Mediterranean.

Red sea fingers (*Alcyonium glomeratum*):
30cm/12in high
Found in gullies and caves in the Atlantic from
about 10m/33ft down, this species is similar to
dead man's fingers (*Alcyonium digitatum*), but
the lobes are more slender and often branched.
The colour is red, orange or yellow. The polyps,
each with eight tentacles, are white.

Dead man's fingers

Alcyonium digitatum

Each retractable polyp bears a number of
branching tentacles and is embedded in a
fleshy mass whose skeleton is composed of
unattached calcareous ossicles, resulting in a
soft and pliable coral. The thick, fleshy mass
forms erect, branching, finger-like lobes that
give rise to the coral's common name. When
disturbed, the polyps retreat inside the
skeleton. The coral colonizes rocks, stones
and shells, especially where weak light
prevents seaweeds from growing. It
sometimes also colonizes the shells of living
crabs and gastropod molluscs.

Identification: Mature colonies form stout, fleshy,
finger-like branching masses about
20cm/8in high and 20cm/8in across.
Colours are white,
pink, yellow
or orange.

Distribution: Atlantic Ocean.
Habitat: On rocks, stones
and shells from lower
shore down to 150m/165ft
or more.
Food: Tiny marine creatures.
Size: Polyps about 1cm/
0.4in tall.
Breeding: Can reproduce
asexually by division or
sexually by producing eggs
and sperm.
Status: Not listed by IUCN.

Red coral

Corallium rubrum

Red coral, or precious coral as it is also
known, is a colonial species. The retractable
polyps are embedded in tissue that is
supported by a skeleton made up of
needle-like calcium-carbonate rods fused
together and covered with a horn-like material.
The colony is firmly fixed to hard substrates,
such as rocks. Depending on environmental
conditions, the colony may form branching
shapes or may be fan-like or bushy. It can
look spectacular when the small polyps
extend their white tentacles into the
water to hunt for food. Red coral is one
of several species of coral that is prized
for making into jewellery and ornaments.
When cut, polished and waxed, it takes
on a brilliant lustre.

Identification: Colonial, with variable branching
shape. Colour of main skeleton red, pink, brown, black
or white. Polyps with white tentacles.

Distribution: Mediterranean.
Habitat: On rocks or other
firm substrates from about
50m/164ft.
Food: Tiny marine creatures.
Size: Colony up to 50cm/
19.7in high.
Breeding: Can reproduce
asexually by division or
sexually by producing eggs
and sperm.
Status: Not listed in CITES,
however the species may be
subject to local legislation
controlling the collection of,
or trade in, both red and
pink corals.

CHITONS AND GASTROPOD MOLLUSCS

The chitons are molluscs whose bodies are protected by a shell formed from overlapping plates. They creep about on the rocks grazing algae. The gastropods are a large and important group of molluscs represented by some of the best-known of all marine creatures. Many species live inside elaborate, coiled shells, although a few have no shell and are active swimmers.

Lepidochitona cinereus

Like other chitons, this small species has a shell composed of eight transverse, overlapping calcareous plates. The slightly articulated nature of the shell gives rise to the chitons' other common name: coat-of-mail shells. In living specimens, the edge of the shell is fringed with a fleshy girdle. The shell of this chiton is slightly less flattened than it is in many species and has a granular appearance. One of the most common chitons, it is found on rocks and under stones on the shore, where it creeps slowly about searching for algal films to graze on.

Identification: Shell consists of eight, slightly convex calcareous plates forming an elongated oval shape. Shell is granular in appearance and may be encrusted. Colour ranges from grey-olive to dull red; underside of shell plates is blue-green.

Distribution: Atlantic Ocean, Mediterranean and Baltic seas.
Habitat: Mainly on and under rocks and stones on the seashore; also on stones in rock pools.
Food: Algal films.
Size: 2cm/0.8in.
Breeding: Reproduces sexually by producing eggs and sperm.
Status: Not listed.

Pinto abalone

Haliotis kamtschatkana

Identification: Thin, flattened shell with lumpy or wavy pattern on exterior surface; three to six raised holes along one edge of shell. Exterior of shell mottled green or brown; interior white.

The pinto abalone is one of a group of primitive gastropod molluscs with flattened, whorled shells; the low profile of the shell is an adaptation to help it minimize resistance to the action of the waves and to protect it against predators. Water, waste products and gametes (reproductive cells) pass through a series of holes along one edge of the shell. This species lives on rocks and seaweeds, where it grazes on algae. It often occurs in groups. In the northern parts of its range it is found in the intertidal zone, but further south it is subtidal only. Its predators include the sea otter (*Enhydra lutris*) – for which it is a favourite food – as well as starfish. When confronted by a starfish the pinto abalone may respond by jerking away from the danger. Once heavily harvested for food, numbers are still declining, probably due to illegal poaching.

Distribution: Pacific Ocean: Alaska to California, US; northern Japan and Siberia.
Habitat: On seaweeds on rocky exposed coasts and in water down to about 15m/50ft.
Food: Algae.
Size: About 15cm/6in, sometimes larger.
Breeding: Reproduces sexually by producing eggs and sperm.
Status: Listed as Threatened by IUCN.

Common limpet

Patella vulgata

Distribution: North-eastern Atlantic around northerly Scandinavian coasts and British Isles to southern Icelandic shore; also western Atlantic off Nova Scotia.
Habitat: On rocks and in rockpools on middle and upper shore.
Food: Algae.
Size: 7cm/2.8in long.
Breeding: Reproduces sexually by producing eggs and sperm.
Status: Not listed by IUCN.

Throughout its range, the distinctive conical shell of the common limpet is a familiar sight on rocky shores, clamped firmly down to help retain moisture and to prevent predators plucking the creature from its resting place. However, during feeding, the limpet leaves the safety of its niche to graze on algae with its rasping tongue. Once it has fed, it returns unerringly to the same spot, the lower edge of its shell snugly fitting the folds of the rock on which it rests. The height of limpet shells varies according to location: those in sheltered places are relatively tall, whereas those found in exposed areas are lower to help reduce resistance to the pounding waves. Spawning is usually induced by inshore winds and accompanying rough seas.

Identification: Rough, irregularly ribbed conical shell with apex lying towards the front. Top of shell slightly rounded and flattened. Exterior of shell generally blue-green to grey, often with encrusting barnacles. Interior of shell white or yellow with visible muscle scar left by animal.

Gem chiton (*Acanthopleura gemmata*): 9cm/3.5in
A large, round-backed chiton with eight sculptured shell plates fringed by a girdle bearing long, calcareous spines. The spines may be curved, straight, blunt or sharp. Shell colour ranges from grey-green to grey-brown. Found in the Indo-Pacific from Africa to Australia, it occurs among rocks in the intertidal zone down to about 2m/6.6ft, where it feeds on algae.

Marbled chiton (*Chiton marmoratus*): 6cm/2.4in
This somewhat flattened species has smooth shell plates with almost parallel sides. Colours vary from grey to brown to olive-green. The girdle is narrow and covered in scales. This species of chiton is quite common throughout its entire Caribbean range, which stretches from the coastal waters of Florida down to the West Indies.

Common ormer (*Haliotis lamellosa*): 7cm/2.8in
Only a few of the hundred or so species in the family Haliotidae are represented in the Mediterranean region, this being one of them. The flattened, ear-shaped shell has a creased appearance to its outer surface and bears a row of holes on one edge, and is often encrusted with worm tubes and other debris. The inner surface is nacreous. It is found among rocks on the lower shore and in shallow water.

Blue-rayed limpet

Patina pellucida

The blue-rayed limpet is an attractive species, and it is characterized by the beautiful, electric-blue streaks, or rays, that radiate outwards from the apex of the shell to the margins. These markings are especially vivid in young specimens; they tend to fade in older animals, when the shell often darkens as well. This species generally lives on the fronds and holdfasts of seaweeds, such as laminarians, on the lower shore and in shallow water, where it feeds by rasping algae.

Identification: Smooth, semi-transparent shell with slightly off-centre apex. In young specimens, shell typically light brown or beige in colour with well-defined electric-blue streaks radiating from the apex to the margins; in older specimens, rays may become less distinct and shell may turn a generally darker, horn-like colour.

Distribution: North-eastern Atlantic around northerly Scandinavian coasts and British Isles to southern Icelandic shore; also western Atlantic off Nova Scotia.
Habitat: On the fronds and holdfasts of seaweeds on lower shore and in shallow water.
Food: Algae.
Size: 1.5cm/0.6in long.
Breeding: Reproduces sexually by producing eggs and sperm.
Status: Not listed by IUCN.

BIVALVE MOLLUSCS

Bivalve molluscs have a shell composed of two halves, or valves. In some species, both valves are similar, and in others they differ. Occasionally the valves are extremely reduced. Many bivalves live a sedentary life on or in the sand, but some can swim by clapping their valves together. Others attach themselves firmly to rocks and other substrates. A few bore into wood and rock.

Common mussel

Mytilus edulis

Throughout its range, clumps of the common mussel are a familiar sight festooning rocks, piers and crevices, although the species is also grown commercially in special beds as a source of food. The shell, roughly triangular in shape, consists of two similar valves. Common mussels are filter feeders, drawing in oxygen-rich water and tiny particles of food via their tube-like siphons when submerged by sea water. Once the tide recedes, the valves clamp shut again. A gland in the animal's foot secretes thin, silky filaments called byssal threads which anchor the mussel to the substrate; a single mussel may have hundreds of these threads.

Identification: Roughly triangular shell consisting of two valves, but shape varies according to environmental conditions. Shell smooth with pattern of radiating lines. Inconspicuous ligament with almost straight ligamental region. Terminal beak. Colour varies from purple to blue or brown. Inside of shell pearly with dark border.

Distribution: Coasts and estuaries worldwide.
Habitat: On rocks, stones, piers and breakwaters from middle shore downwards. Also found in estuarine waters.
Food: Tiny food particles filtered from the water.
Size: Variable: usually from 1–10cm/0.4–4in, sometimes larger than this.
Breeding: Reproduces sexually; eggs are shed and fertilized externally; larval phase follows.
Status: Not listed by IUCN.

Queen scallop

Aequipecten opercularis

This species is found from the intertidal zone down to 200m/660ft, sometimes in great numbers. The two shell valves are convex, although the lower one is less so, and sculpted with radiating ribs. The colour of this shell is quite variable and is often encrusted with sponges. When young, the queen scallop often attaches itself to the substrate with fine byssal threads for safety, often in the company of horse mussels. However, the adult scallop swims freely by rapidly clapping the two shell valves together. In this way, it can travel over quite considerable distances.

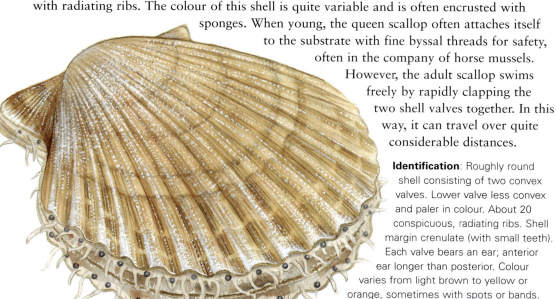

Identification: Roughly round shell consisting of two convex valves. Lower valve less convex and paler in colour. About 20 conspicuous, radiating ribs. Shell margin crenulate (with small teeth). Each valve bears an ear; anterior ear longer than posterior. Colour varies from light brown to yellow or orange, sometimes with spots or bands.

Distribution: Atlantic Ocean, Mediterranean Sea.
Habitat: Attaches to sand and gravel on seabed; found at depths of up to 200m/660ft.
Food: Tiny food particles filtered from the water.
Size: 9cm/3.5in.
Breeding: Reproduces sexually; eggs are shed and fertilized externally; larval phase follows.
Status: Not listed by IUCN.

European thorny oyster

Spondylus gaederopus

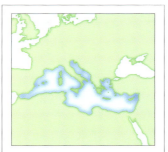

Distribution: Mediterranean.
Habitat: Attaches to rocks and other firm surfaces on the seabed.
Food: Tiny food particles filtered from the water.
Size: 10cm/4in long.
Breeding: Reproduces sexually; eggs are shed and fertilized externally; larval phase follows.
Status: Not listed by IUCN.

The thorny oysters are characterized by having shells covered with irregularly positioned spines of various lengths – although these are sometimes absent. The European thorny oyster, like other thorny oysters, cements itself to the rocky seabed or to some other firm object by one of its valves and remains there for life, relying on its thorny outgrowths for both physical protection and camouflage. The permanence of the oyster's existence is often underlined by the growth of worm tubes and barnacles that encrust the shell's outer surface.

Identification: Oval-shaped shell slightly longer than it is wide. Lower valve convex, upper valve flatter. Shell surface usually bears long, sharp spines – especially on upper valve. Colour of external shell surface purple, crimson or brown; lower valve usually paler. Interior of shell white.

Date mussel (*Lithophaga lithophaga*): 7cm/2.8in long
Elongated, smooth-edged shell consisting of two equal-sized valves. Fine sculptured lines on exterior shell surface. The exterior of the shell is brownish in colour and the interior is blue-white. This mussel lives in shallow waters in the Mediterranean Sea where it bores into limestone rock and coral skeletons.

Common European oyster
(*Ostrea edulis*): 10cm/4in long
The shape of this greyish mollusc can be variable, but it is often oval in outline or pear-shaped and the surface is rough or scaly. The two valves are dissimilar: the lower one is concave and fixed to the substrate, while the upper one is flatter and fits inside. Found down to about 80m/262ft in the Atlantic Ocean and Mediterranean Sea and in commercial oyster beds.

American oyster (*Crassostrea virginica*): 15cm/6in long
Shells of this oyster are typically flat, ribbed and elongate in shape but, as with several other oyster species, they can be variable in their appearance. The lower valve is securely fixed to hard objects. The exterior is dirty white in colour or grey and the inside is white. The American oyster is found in estuaries and bays from the Gulf of St Lawrence, in Canada, south to Brazil.

Mediterranean jewel box

Chama gryphoides

The bivalve molluscs in the family Chamidae are known as jewel boxes and are confined mostly to tropical waters, although the Mediterranean jewel box is, as its common name suggests, found in temperate waters. They resemble the thorny oysters in so far as the shells are often adorned with protective spines or other outgrowths, and they live by attaching themselves firmly to the substrate. The Mediterranean jewel box has two dissimilar valves. One valve is cup-shaped and attached to the substrate, while the other valve is smaller and opens like a lid, complete with hinge.

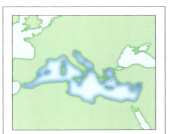

Distribution: Mediterranean.
Habitat: Attaches to rocks and other firm surfaces on the seabed.
Food: Tiny food particles filtered from the water.
Size: 4cm/1.6in long.
Breeding: Reproduces sexually; eggs are shed and fertilized externally; larval phase follows.
Status: Not listed by IUCN.

Identification: Shell comprises two dissimilar valves: lower valve cup-shaped and cemented to rocks or other firm surfaces on seabed; upper valve smaller and opens with a hinge mechanism. Shell displays series of ridged, radiating growth lines. Colour of external surface grey-white; inner surface brownish.

PRAWNS AND SHRIMPS

The true prawns and shrimps have light exoskeletons and their bodies are usually slightly flattened sideways. One of their two pairs of antennae is much longer than the other. Various species of prawns and shrimps are found in every part of the world's oceans and seas, from tidal pools and estuaries to coral reefs and the deepest trenches.

Snapping prawn (Pistol shrimp)

Alpheus ruber

Identification: Bulky prawn with a very short rostrum – the part of the carapace that is drawn out and projects between the animal's eyes. Long, jointed antennae. First pair of walking legs bear one 'normal' claw and one enlarged and modified claw. Second walking legs bear tiny pincers. Rich, almost luminous red colour.

This is one of many species of snapping prawns or pistol shrimps in the family Alpheidae, many of which occur on coral reefs. It owes its name to the snapping sound that it produces with a modified claw or pincer – usually the right claw. The movable part of the claw has a bulb at the base that fits into a socket when the claw is shut. When the prawn opens the claw wide, a sticky pad on the bulb locks against another pad on the socket, holding it open like the hammer of a cocked pistol. If the prawn then pulls on the big adductor muscle that closes the claw, the locking pads give way and the claw snaps shut with a report that can stun nearby animals. The animal uses this technique to immobilize and then capture its prey.

Distribution: North-eastern Atlantic; Mediterranean Sea.
Habitat: Crevices in rocky reefs and sand, and cavities in sponges.
Food: Small marine animals such as shrimps, small crabs and small fish.
Size: 2.5–3.5cm/1–1.4in.
Breeding: Reproduces sexually; females carry eggs beneath their bodies; these hatch into swimming larvae.
Status: Not listed by IUCN.

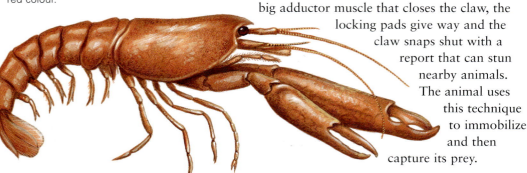

Common prawn

Leander serratus (Palaemon serratus)

The virtually transparent body of the common prawn makes it hard to see as it picks its way delicately over the bottom of a rockpool. It feeds by gathering small edible items with the pincers on its first two pairs of legs, while monitoring the water movement with its very long, sensitive antennae. At any hint of danger it propels itself backwards through the water into a nearby refuge with a quick flick of its tail. It can also swim slowly by beating the small limbs, or swimmerets, beneath its abdomen.

Identification: Elongated body; downturned tail with leaf-like structures at the end. Long, upcurved, toothed rostrum and two pairs of long antennae, the inner pair each divided in two. Small pincers at the tips of the first two pairs of walking legs. Body almost transparent, with a pinkish brown tint and reddish spots and lines.

Distribution: North-eastern Atlantic; Mediterranean and Black seas.
Habitat: Sandy and rocky shores, including rockpools, to depths of about 40m/130ft.
Food: Edible debris and small animals.
Size: Up to 10cm/4in.
Breeding: Reproduces sexually; females carry up to 4,000 eggs attached to hairs on their swimmerets, for around four months. They hatch into planktonic larvae.
Status: Not listed by IUCN.

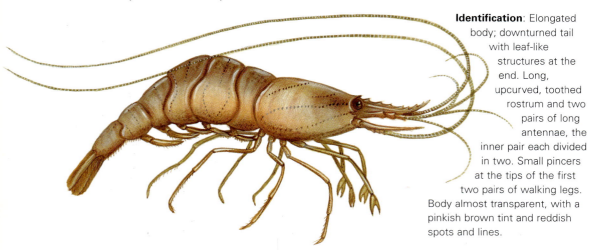

Opossum shrimp

Neomysis integer

Distribution: North-eastern Atlantic Ocean, as far south as Spain.
Habitat: Upper reaches of estuaries, and some tidal pools.
Food: Detritus, diatoms, algae and small crustaceans.
Size: Up to 1.7cm/0.7in.
Breeding: Reproduces sexually; females carry up to 100 larvae in a brood pouch for about two months before releasing them into the water.
Status: Not listed.

One of several different species of opossum shrimp that live in a variety of aquatic habitats, this small, free-swimming crustacean is adapted for life in the brackish waters of estuaries. It lives in groups, gathering microscopic food particles from the water. Like many marine organisms, it feeds near the surface at night, seeking the protection of deeper water in daylight. It has a well-developed instinct for dealing with the ebb and flow of the tide, retreating to the deep main channels as the tide level falls to avoid being stranded, but swimming against the current to prevent itself being swept out to sea. The name 'opossum shrimp' refers to the female's brood pouch, in which the young larvae spend their first weeks after hatching from their eggs.

Identification: Slender, almost transparent shrimp, with a carapace bulkier than its abdomen, and a short, pointed rostrum protruding between the eyes. Large stalked eyes and long antennae, feathery limbs adapted for swimming. Brood pouch for carrying up to about 100 larvae after hatching.

Common shrimp (*Crangon vulgaris*): 5cm/2in long
Varying from grey to dark brown in colour, this bottom-dwelling shrimp lives in shallow coastal waters to depths of 20m/66ft, in clean or muddy sand. It spends the day buried, emerging at night to creep over the sand in search of food. It uses its short, stout pincers to tackle worms, young fish and other crustaceans, as well as any edible debris it can find.

Aesop prawn
(*Pandalus montagui*): 15cm/6in long
This Arctic and North Atlantic species of prawn lives mainly on hard seabeds at depths of down to about 20m/66ft. Looking very like the common prawn, but with bright orange stripes on its mainly transparent body, it has a long, slightly upturned rostrum. It is one of the species that is commonly fished for food.

Chameleon prawn (*Hippolyte varians*): 3cm/1.2in long
This small prawn owes its common name to the way its colour varies and adapts to its habitat – an effective means of camouflage. During the day it may appear in hues of red, yellow, brown, green or blue, depending on the colour of the environment it finds itself in. At night, when the water turns darker, it always reverts to a bluish-green colour as it grazes on marine algae. It usually lives in shallow Mediterranean and Atlantic coastal waters, and may also be found in brackish estuarine habitats.

Banded coral shrimp

Stenopus hispidus

Sometimes known as the banded boxer shrimp because of its pugnacious, territorial behaviour – it will attack and even kill other trespassing shrimps – this colourful shrimp obtains most of its food by 'cleaning' other marine animals such as fish. It stays in one place on the reef and solicits for customers, which recognize the shrimp by its banded pattern and allow it to pick parasites and dead tissue from their skin. It will even valet particularly voracious fish such as moray eels, but it is occasionally eaten by opportunist triggerfish, large angelfish, wrasses and groupers.

Distribution: Tropical coral seas worldwide.
Habitat: Coral reefs, to depths of 30m/100ft.
Food: Parasites and dead skin removed from fish, plus other small animals and debris.
Size: Up to 7.5cm/3in.
Breeding: Reproduces sexually; females carry green eggs beneath the body. When hatched, the young live attached to the female for about six weeks, then swim to the surface to live among plankton.
Status: Not listed by IUCN.

Identification: A spiny shrimp, vividly patterned with dark red and white bands, and deep blue bases to its very long, enlarged front limbs, which are equipped with powerful pincers. Long, slender white legs, with small pincers on the first two pairs. Six long white antennae. Black eyes.

LOBSTERS, SQUAT LOBSTERS AND HERMIT CRABS

The lobsters and crayfish are powerfully built crustaceans with pincers on the first pair of walking legs. The last part of the abdomen forms a telson. The squat lobsters and hermit crabs often have their abdomen folded under the body. Hermit crabs protect their abdomens with the shells of dead molluscs.

Common lobster

Homarus gammarus

One of the largest of all crustaceans, the common lobster is also prized as a delicacy. When lobsters are cooked they turn red, but in life they are blue-black. The common lobster lives in the sublittoral zone, hiding under rocks or in caves and large crevices. It scavenges for much of its food, but also preys on creatures such as mussels. It first crushes the shell with its larger claw, or pincer, and then uses its smaller claw to remove the mollusc.

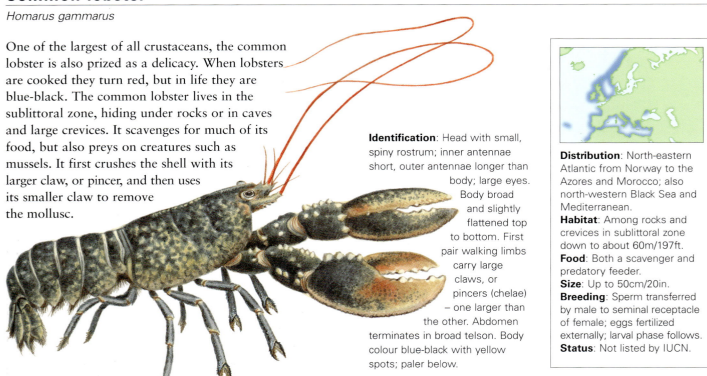

Identification: Head with small, spiny rostrum; inner antennae short, outer antennae longer than body; large eyes. Body broad and slightly flattened top to bottom. First pair walking limbs carry large claws, or pincers (chelae) – one larger than the other. Abdomen terminates in broad telson. Body colour blue-black with yellow spots; paler below.

Distribution: North-eastern Atlantic from Norway to the Azores and Morocco; also north-western Black Sea and Mediterranean.
Habitat: Among rocks and crevices in sublittoral zone down to about 60m/197ft.
Food: Both a scavenger and predatory feeder.
Size: Up to 50cm/20in.
Breeding: Sperm transferred by male to seminal receptacle of female; eggs fertilized externally; larval phase follows.
Status: Not listed by IUCN.

Squat lobster

Galathea strigosa

The often colourful and attractively marked squat lobsters are immediately recognizable because of their blue stripes, short, almost oval body shape (caused by the abdomen being folded underneath the thorax and so accounting for their common name of 'squat') and their long appendages bearing pincers. This species hides away under rocks or in crevices during the day, but emerges at night to hunt other marine creatures and to scavenge for food. Despite its relatively small size, it can be an aggressive species if handled and so needs to be treated with a degree of caution. Although they are called lobsters, squat lobsters are in fact more closely related to hermit crabs.

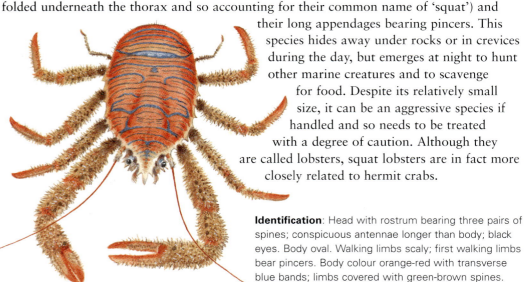

Identification: Head with rostrum bearing three pairs of spines; conspicuous antennae longer than body; black eyes. Body oval. Walking limbs scaly; first walking limbs bear pincers. Body colour orange-red with transverse blue bands; limbs covered with green-brown spines.

Distribution: North Atlantic from North Cape, Scandinavia to Spain and Canaries; also Mediterranean and Red Seas.
Habitat: Among rocks and crevices in lower shore and down to about 35m/115ft.
Food: Both a scavenger and predatory feeder.
Size: Up to 12cm/4.7in.
Breeding: Sperm transferred to seminal receptacle; eggs shed and fertilized externally.
Status: Not listed by IUCN.

Long-clawed porcelain crab
Porcellana longicornis

Distribution: North-eastern Atlantic; Mediterranean.
Habitat: Under stones and among laminarian seaweed holdfasts on lower shore.
Food: Small edible particles filtered from the water.
Size: 1cm/0.4in.
Breeding: Sperm transferred by male to seminal receptacle of female. Female sheds eggs which are then fertilized externally and held until they hatch into larvae.
Status: Not listed by IUCN.

Some members of the family Porcellanidae bear a superficial resemblance to true crabs (see later in this section), but porcelain crabs are actually more closely related to squat lobsters (Galatheidae) and hermit crabs (Paguridae). A few porcelain crab species do, however, resemble lobsters or prawns in shape, having long abdomens. They possess very long antennae (whereas those of true crabs are usually very short), which originate at the front of the head. They also have a very reduced fourth pair of walking legs. This species has particularly long claws that are made more conspicuous by being so disproportionate in size to the rest of the body; these are used for fighting rather than feeding. The long-clawed porcelain crab can be found under rocks and stones on the lower shore downwards, but it is also often associated with the root-like holdfasts of laminarian seaweeds (those of the genus Laminaria), among which the crab can hide from predators.

Identification: A small creature with long antennae. Carapace roundish and smooth. First walking legs are also smooth and bear long, slender pincers. Colour is reddish-brown. Claws are much longer than the rest of the body.

Slipper lobster (*Parribacus antarcticus*): 18cm/7in long
Sometimes called a bulldozer lobster, this crustacean has a flattened body and short antennae and claws. It relies on its blue-grey mottled colouring and bristly outline to help it remain concealed in holes by day. At night, it scavenges and also preys on small invertebrates and fish. Indo-Pacific and tropical Atlantic Ocean.

Crawfish (*Palinurus vulgaris*): 40cm/16in long
Also called the spiny lobster, the red-brown crawfish is recognized by the apparent lack of pincers on its walking legs – although females have a small pair on their fifth walking legs. The abdomen bears sharp spines. Found among rocks and in crevices in the Atlantic Ocean and Mediterranean Sea.

Galathea intermedia: 1cm/0.4in long
This little squat lobster bears a superficial resemblance to *Galathea strigosa*, although it is smaller and its legs are the same bright red colour as the rest of the body. Among stones and rocks on the lower shore downwards in the Atlantic Ocean and Mediterranean Sea.

Diogenes pugilator: 2.5cm/1in long
This small hermit crab has hairy antennae and white tips to its pincers. Like other hermit crabs, it lives in shells of dead gastropod molluscs to protect its abdomen. Found in shallow water in the Atlantic Ocean and Mediterranean Sea.

Common hermit crab
Eupagurus bernhardus

Instead of having their soft, vulnerable abdomens enclosed within a hard carapace, as the true crabs do, the hermit crabs have evolved a way of protecting this part of their body by living inside the shell of a dead gastropod, such as those of whelks. With its abdomen safely inside the shell, the hermit crab can move about the substrate with just the head, thorax and legs – which are encased in a hard exoskeleton like other crabs – protruding. Like many other hermit crabs, this species discards its shell for a bigger one as it grows. The hermit crab often shares its shell with certain species of anemones, sponges and marine worms.

Identification: First pair of walking legs end with big, granulated unequal pincers (the crab's right-hand pincer is the larger one). Second and third pairs of walking legs end in spiny claws; fourth and fifth pairs of walking legs are reduced. Colour of carapace red, orange or grey; pincers brown.

Distribution: Temperate Atlantic coasts of Europe; Mediterranean and Baltic.
Habitat: On the seabed from the lower shore downwards.
Food: Both a scavenger and predatory feeder.
Size: 10cm/4in.
Breeding: Sperm transferred by male to seminal receptacle of female. Female sheds eggs which are then fertilized externally and held until they hatch into larvae.
Status: Not listed by IUCN.

TRUE CRABS

True crabs are familiar animals of seashores and estuaries, and they make up a widespread and fascinating group of crustaceans. Typically robust with broad, flattened shells, or carapaces, true crabs also have reduced tails and powerful anterior pincers for dealing with prey and for defending themselves. The spider crabs get their common name from their long limbs and relatively smaller bodies.

Sponge crab

Dromia personata

This somewhat squat, broad crab has short, dark-brown, hairlike growths covering almost all of its carapace and legs, enhancing this impression still further. A small, fifth pair of legs is raised, and appears itself to be carried on the crab's back. The crab is sometimes encountered grasping a sponge on its back, using its rear-most pairs of legs – a method of concealment against predators such as octopuses. The sponge may eventually dwarf the crab's carapace in size, although it never becomes attached to it. In fact, if in some danger, the crab may abandon the sponge and flee without it. At night, the sponge crab feeds mainly by scavenging on the remains of other marine animals.

Distribution: Atlantic range is from southern North Sea and British Isles to Western Sahara, Azores and Canaries; all of Mediterranean Sea.
Habitat: On sandy and rocky shores and among pilings, down to about 30m/100ft.
Food: Scavenges.
Size: 8cm/3.25in.
Breeding: Eggs are fertilized externally.
Status: Not listed by IUCN.

Identification: Carapace broad and domed. Fourth and fifth pairs of walking legs are displaced and may be used to grasp items such as sponges for shelter. Carapace and legs brown; pincers pink.

Spider crab

Macropodia tenuirostris

Identification: Carapace triangular; longer than it is wide, and tapering severely at front. Carapace usually smooth or slightly granular but may be encrusted with seaweeds or other growths. Long, prominent rostrum with hooked hairs. Eyes on prominent stalks at side of rostrum. First pair of walking legs with pincers. Second and third pairs of walking legs long and straight; fourth and fifth pairs end in curved claws. Body colour red-brown or yellow-red.

The spider crabs are characterized by having small bodies in relation to their long, slender limbs, giving them a rather spider-like appearance – hence the common name. Some species can grow very large indeed – measuring 3.7m (12ft) across their outstretched legs. The species here is one of the smaller varieties, but it clearly shows the typical body form of these crabs. It is found among seaweeds in water varying in depth from about 9–97m/30–320ft, but also occasionally down to 300m/1,000ft. The spider crab scavenges edible food matter as well as hunting other marine animals.

Distribution: North Sea and British Isles south to Western Sahara and Cape Verde Is.
Habitat: Among seaweeds, usually from about 9m/30ft.
Food: Scavenger and also predatory on small marine creatures.
Size: 2cm/0.8in or less.
Breeding: Reproduces sexually. Some evidence that sperm may be stored in the receptacles of female crabs to fertilize further broods.
Status: Not listed by IUCN.

Velvet swimming crab

Macropipus puber

Distribution: Atlantic coasts of north-western Europe.
Habitat: Among rocks and stones from lower shore down to 10m/33ft or more.
Food: Varied diet, including seaweed, molluscs and crustaceans.
Size: 8cm/3.2in or less.
Breeding: Reproduces sexually; fertilization is external.
Status: Not listed by IUCN.

In addition to the typical scuttling action that most crabs employ when moving around on the substrate, some species have specially adapted limbs to enable them to swim. The various species of swimming crabs, found in many of the world's oceans, have their fifth pair of limbs modified to form flattened, paddle-like structures to allow them to swim rapidly backwards. The velvet swimming crab puts on an impressive display when threatened; it rises up on its legs and holds its claws apart in an attempt to make itself appear bigger. It feeds on a variety of food items from seaweeds to other crustaceans. When mating, the male velvet crab may cling on to the female for several days.

Identification: Front of carapace serrated with five teeth either side of the eyes and ten smaller teeth between the eyes. First pair of walking legs bears pincers. Flat, paddle-like back legs. Carapace and limbs covered with hairy bristles. Colour of carapace red-brown. Eyes are red.

Common shore crab (*Carcinus maenas*): 5cm/2in long
Characteristic sideways walking action when seen on the estuaries and salt marshes it favours. Can tolerate a wide range of salinities, and is abundant in brackish conditions. This opportunist scavenger eats seaweeds and preys on other invertebrates, especially bivalve molluscs such as mussels and cockles, using its powerful pincers to break open their shells.
A native of Europe and North Africa, it has also been introduced to other parts of the world.

Ghost crab (*Ocypode albicans*): 7cm/2.8in long
This stalk-eyed shore crab occurs on warm sandy beaches, from the Carolinas in the eastern USA to Brazil, where it scavenges for dead animals on the strandline. It lives in a burrow in the sand, emerging to feed in large numbers at low tide. It owes its common name to its cryptic sandy coloration, which makes it seem to disappear when it stops moving.

Spiny spider crab (*Maia squinado*): 18cm/7in long
A long-legged and spider-like species of the Atlantic and Mediterranean, the red-brown carapace of this crab is approximately triangular with a tapering front, and is covered with bristles and spines. Powerful pincers on its first walking legs. Found from lower shore down to about 50m/165ft.

Chinese mitten crab

Eriocheir sinensis

This species' common name comes from the bristly covering on the pincers, which gives the impression that the animal is wearing mittens. This crab is a native of the coastal and estuarine regions of the Yellow Sea in Asia. However, it has long been naturalized in parts of the European Atlantic, where it quickly established itself, and is now found in parts of California in the US. The Chinese mitten crab is an omnivorous species that eats a range of food from marine plants to worms and small molluscs. Sometimes members of this species will clamber over dry land if dams or other obstructions impede their migration – even turning up in swimming pools and on roads. This crab may have a harmful effect on native marine life.

Distribution: Indigenous to China; also found Yellow Sea; estuarine habitats in northern Europe and North America.
Habitat: In mud and sand, often burrowing.
Food: Seaweeds, molluscs and crustaceans.
Size: 7cm/2.8in.
Breeding: Reproduces sexually; females carry between 250,000 and 1 million eggs until hatching, and both sexes die soon after reproduction.
Status: Not listed by IUCN.

Identification: Carapace squarish in shape, with four teeth between the eyes. First pair of walking legs bears equal-sized pincers covered in 'hairy' bristles. Other legs long and also hairy. Colour of carapace olive-green; lower parts of legs and claw tips paler.

TRUE CRABS, HORSESHOE CRABS AND SEA SPIDERS

Horseshoe crabs are not true crabs, despite their common name. These ancient, shallow-water arthropods are the sole survivors of a group of invertebrates that flourished millions of years ago. Their relatives, the sea spiders, are small, curious marine animals found in shallow water and the ocean deeps.

Mud fiddler crab

Uca pugnax

Identification: Carapace squarish with an H-shaped depression in the middle. Eyes born on long, thin, prominent stalks. Males have one claw hugely enlarged and covered in granules. Other walking legs banded. Females and young crabs have claws of equal size. Colour of carapace brown to yellowish; claws yellowish to white.

Fiddler crabs are so called because males have an enlarged claw they use to protect their burrows, and which they wave to attract females when mating. This claw may account for 65 per cent of the crab's body weight. Males also engage in ritualized arm waving when confronting rivals, although serious injury is rare. The smaller of the two claws is used to collect and sift mud and other material when looking for decaying plant and animal matter to eat. Fiddler crab burrows may be 30cm/12in deep, and provide a safe haven from predators and a site for mating. At low tide, fiddlers leave their burrows to look for food, quickly returning to them – or to any other convenient burrow – if any danger should threaten.

Right: Aerial view of the mud fiddler crab, illustrating the disproportionally large claw.

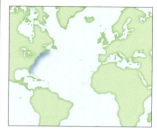

Distribution: Mid-Atlantic US coast.
Habitat: Muddy and sandy estuaries and shores.
Food: Detritus and algae.
Size: 2.5cm/1in.
Breeding: Reproduces sexually; fertilization of eggs is external.
Status: Not listed by IUCN.

Horn-eyed ghost crab

Ocypode ceratophthalma

Identification: Carapace squarish and robust. First pair of walking legs bear large, but unequal-sized, pincers. Other legs relatively long. Large, erect oblong eyes on stalks with prominent horn above; larger in males. Colour cream-brown with greyish markings and traces of yellow.

This species of ghost crab hides in conspicuous burrows, which it digs in the sand of the upper shore of sheltered beaches, with only its large eyes protruding above the surface on stalks. Special hairs growing on its legs help it to absorb moisture from wet sand through capillary action, which reduces the amount of time it needs to spend near water. The ghost crab is both a scavenger and an active hunter, emerging at dusk to prey on small marine animals it encounters near the water's edge. Good vision and the ability to run quickly make the horn-eyed ghost crab an efficient hunter. A prominent horn situated above each of the stalked eyes of this species gives rise to its common name.

Right: Aerial view of the horn-eye ghost crab, illustrating the protrusion of the eyes.

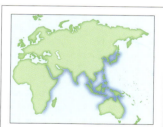

Distribution: East Africa and Red Sea to Japan, Hawaii and Tahiti. Also Australian tropics.
Habitat: Sandy shores.
Food: Scavenger; also preys on small marine animals.
Size: 7cm/2.8in.
Breeding: Reproduces sexually; fertilization of eggs is external.
Status: Not listed by IUCN.

Horseshoe crab

Limulus polyphemus

Distribution: Eastern US coastline from Maine to Gulf of Mexico.
Habitat: Sandy and muddy substrates down to 30m/98ft or more.
Food: Worms, molluscs, crustaceans.
Size: 60cm/24in.
Breeding: Reproduces sexually; females lay between 2,000 and 20,000 eggs.
Status: Listed as Low Risk by IUCN.

The horseshoe crabs in the class Merostoma are primitive marine arthropods, whose ancestors arose in the Silurian Period, more than 400 million years ago. In fact, the horseshoe crabs, or king crabs as they are also known, are more closely related to the extinct trilobites and to modern spiders and ticks than they are to true crabs and crustaceans. The body is covered by a protective, hinged carapace, and a long caudal spine extends from the back. The caudal spine can be used to right the animal if it is accidentally turned over. Under the carapace are the chelicerae and five pairs of walking legs. The horseshoe crab burrows in sand and mud, although it can swim. Worms and other invertebrate food are crushed by the pincer-like chelicerae on either side of the mouth. During mating, these crabs congregate in the intertidal zone, where the female lays her eggs in holes in the sand. The horseshoe crab can live for about 20 years.

Identification: Horseshoe-shaped carapace broad, domed and hinged, back of carapace bears spines. Long, tapering caudal spine. One pair each of pedipalps (mouth appendages) and chelicerae (modified fangs). Five pairs of walking legs. Colour of carapace dark-brown.

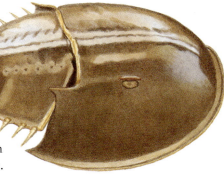

Hairy crab (*Pilumnus hirtellus*): 2cm/0.8in long
With almost all of its red-brown, spiny upper carapace and legs covered in dense bristles, this crab is sometimes very hard to spot, especially when silt collects between the hairs. The pincers have dark-brown tips and are stout and powerful, with one being larger than the other. Found on seaweeds, stones, rocks and in crevices on the lower shore and in shallow Atlantic and Mediterranean waters down to 80m/262ft.

Masked crab (*Corystes cassivelaunus*): carapace 4cm/1.6in long
Recognized by its slender, oval carapace with four teeth on each lateral margin and a further two teeth between the eyes.
First pair of walking legs (chelipeds) twice as long as the carapace in males, but much shorter in females. Long, hairy antennae held together in front – when the animal is buried in sand they form a tube enabling water to reach the gills. Carapace brown to yellow in colour. Found in sand on lower shore and shallow water in the Atlantic Ocean.

Sea spider (*Nymphon gracile*): 1cm/0.4in long
Looking very much like a small terrestrial spider, this species is found on rocky shores and in shallow waters in the Atlantic Ocean and Mediterranean Sea. The eight long, thin legs are about three or four times the length of the body. Although the body is translucent, the gut is visible, giving the animal a pinkish tinge. Like terrestrial spiders, it has chelicerae (fang-like appendages close to the mouth) and palps (members used as sensory and feeding aids) for cutting off small pieces of prey and transferring them to the mouth at the end of the proboscis. Both sexes have ovigerous (egg-bearing) legs, although the eggs are brooded by the male. This species may live for a year.

Sea spider

Pycnogonum littorale

Like other sea spiders, this species is characterized by the head and thorax being fused to form a narrow, elongated structure called a cephalothorax. It also bears the legs, into which the digestive system extends and, in females, also the ovaries. The abdomen is tiny, consisting of a single segment. As well as the walking legs, males have an extra pair of 'ovigerous' legs, held under the body. As the female lays her eggs, they are collected by the male and held on the ovigerous legs where they are brooded until they hatch. The sea spider feeds by sucking up body tissues through its proboscis.

Distribution: Common around coasts of Great Britain and Ireland; not present in north-east Scotland.
Habitat: Under stones and on seaweed on the lower shore and in shallow water.
Food: Sucks body tissues from marine organisms, such as sea anemones.
Size: 2cm/0.8in.
Breeding: Reproduces sexually; after mating, males brood the eggs.
Status: Not listed by IUCN.

Identification: Heavily built body with short, thick legs. No palps or chelicerae present. Cephalothorax terminates in a narrow, conical proboscis. Four pairs of walking legs and one pair of ovigerous legs in males. Males pale brown in colour; females white or cream.

STARFISH

With no front or back and able to change direction without turning, starfish are most unusual creatures. These echinoderms are immediately recognizable from their shape, which basically consists of a body drawn out to form distinct arms, or rays. There are usually five or six arms present, although some species have considerably more – perhaps as many as 20. The mouth is found on the underside.

Common starfish

Asterias rubens

Identification: Robust body drawn out into five arms; body highest in the middle, tapering to ends of arms. Body covered with spines and bears tiny, pincer-like structures (pedicellariae) that help remove parasites. Underside of body bears rows of tube feet; arms grooved on underside. Colour is yellow-brown above, paler on the underside.

One of the most familiar images of the seaside, the common starfish has a body covered in small spines and drawn out into five broad arms, or rays. Like other starfish, it moves by means of tube feet – small, fluid-filled structures on the underside of the arms that expand and contract, pulling the animal along. The tube feet may also be used to grip prey when feeding. The common starfish is predatory, tracking down its food mainly by smell. Once it finds a suitable prey item, such as a bivalve mollusc, it engulfs it with its arms, everts its stomach over the prey, or into the shell in the case of many molluscs, and digests it before absorbing the contents. The common starfish is found among rocks and in mussel beds, often in large congregations.

Distribution: North Atlantic.
Habitat: Among rocks and in mussel and oyster beds from lower shore to sublittoral.
Food: Crustaceans, molluscs, worms; predator as well as scavenger.
Size: 50cm/19.7in across, though usually smaller.
Breeding: Eggs are fertilized externally and develop into planktonic larvae.
Status: Not listed by IUCN.

Blue star

Linckia laevigata

Identification: Body consists of five finger-like, radiating arms; arms are almost same thickness along their whole length and have rounded tips. Underside of body bears rows of tube feet, and mouth. Colour usually bright blue; some starfish of this species also bear prominent white spots, as shown here.

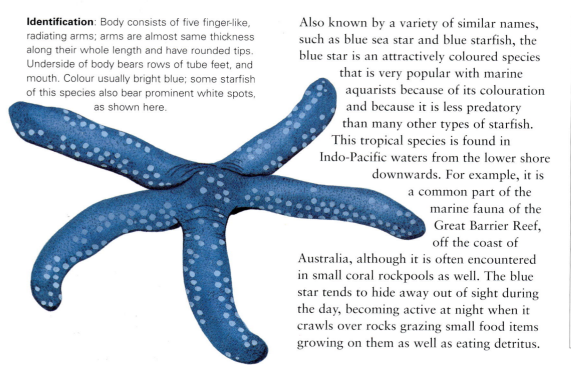

Also known by a variety of similar names, such as blue sea star and blue starfish, the blue star is an attractively coloured species that is very popular with marine aquarists because of its colouration and because it is less predatory than many other types of starfish. This tropical species is found in Indo-Pacific waters from the lower shore downwards. For example, it is a common part of the marine fauna of the Great Barrier Reef, off the coast of Australia, although it is often encountered in small coral rockpools as well. The blue star tends to hide away out of sight during the day, becoming active at night when it crawls over rocks grazing small food items growing on them as well as eating detritus.

Distribution: Tropical coasts of Indian Ocean and Indo-Pacific region.
Habitat: Among rocks on reefs from lower shore down to 60m/197ft.
Food: Detritus and small organisms encrusting rocks.
Size: 30cm/12in across.
Breeding: Eggs are fertilized externally and develop into planktonic larvae.
Status: Not listed by IUCN.

Common sunstar

Crossaster papposus

Distribution: North-eastern Atlantic; Pacific seaboard of USA down to Gulf of Maine; population also found at Budget Sound, Alaska.
Habitat: Among rocks, on sand and in mussel and oyster beds in shallow water from about 10–40m/33–130ft.
Food: Echinoderms, molluscs, sea pens.
Size: 25cm/10in across.
Breeding: Eggs are fertilized externally and develop into planktonic larvae.
Status: Not listed by IUCN.

This highly distinctive and attractive starfish, sometimes called the rose sea star, is immediately recognizable by its large, round disc and its array of between 8 and 16 arms, or rays, each of which is shorter than the width of the disc itself. The body of this species is further characterized by the very prominent spines that cover the disc and the arms. The common sunstar is found in sheltered locations, often in the company of other echinoderms, such as brittlestars. It feeds by everting its stomach on to its prey and digesting it. Among its food items are other, smaller starfish, such as cushion stars. The common sunstar is itself preyed on by other starfish, such as *Solaster dawsoni*.

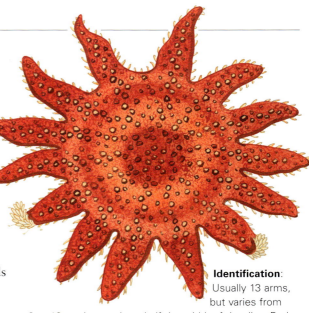

Identification: Usually 13 arms, but varies from 8 to 16; each arm about half the width of the disc. Body covered in conspicuous spines. Colour varies from purple, brownish-red, yellow or red above; yellowish-white below. Patterning also variable – combinations of colours or a single colour with a concentric white ring.

Giant sea star (*Pisaster giganteus*): 30cm/12in across
This large, five-armed species has a brown body covered with short, white spines, each encircled by a blue-coloured ring. Because of its appearance, it is sometimes called the jewelled star. Found in Pacific Ocean waters among sand and rocks at the low-water mark and in shallow water, it is carnivorous, feeding on invertebrates such as mussels.

Spiny starfish (*Marthasterias glacialis*): 30cm/12in across
This species has a body with five stiff arms, each of which bears three rows of prominent spines, each encircled by small, pincer-like pedicellariae. It is mainly brown or green-grey with purple arm tips above, and yellow-white below. The spiny starfish can sometimes grow as large as 70cm/27.5in across. It is found from low water down to about 200m/660ft in the Atlantic Ocean and Mediterranean Sea.

Porania pulvillus: 10cm/4in across
A cushion-like starfish with short arms and a fleshy body, which feels somewhat greasy to the touch. White papillae (small bumps) cover the upper surface. The colour ranges from scarlet to orange, with a pattern of white streaks and lines above; paler coloured below. This species is found on rocks and sponges from about 10–250m/33–800ft in Atlantic Ocean waters.

Goosefoot star

Anseropoda placenta

This species gets its common name because its body bears a resemblance to a goose's webbed foot. The goosefoot star's body is thin, almost pentagonal in shape, with slightly ragged, concave edges between the five arms. It has no pedicellariae – tiny, pincer-like organs on some echinoderms that keep the body clean and free from parasites. The upper surface has short spines, and the underside of the arms bear tube feet that can expand and contract to enable the echinoderm to move about. This species frequents sandy and muddy substrates.

Distribution: North-eastern Atlantic Ocean; US Pacific population at Gulf of Maine.
Habitat: On or in sand and muddy gravel in shallow water down to 100m/330ft.
Food: Small crustaceans.
Size: 20cm/8in across.
Breeding: Eggs are fertilized externally and develop into planktonic larvae.
Status: Not listed by IUCN.

Identification: The body is thin and flat and its shape is almost pentagonal. Bears five arms. Body colour is mainly white, with a vivid red centre and five radiating red lines – one running along the centre of each arm. The perimeter of the body is also red. Distribution of this colour is variable between individuals. Underside of body tends to be yellowish.

SEA URCHINS, HEART URCHINS AND SEA CUCUMBERS

These echinoderms are among the oldest surviving marine creatures on Earth. Sea urchins are round-bodied with conspicuous, moveable spines, while the heart urchins, which include the sea potatoes, are covered in shorter bristles. The sea cucumbers are sac-like species lacking obvious arms.

Black sea urchin

Arbacia lixula

Identification: Test roughly rounded, slightly flattened below, with a dense covering of short spines with sharp, pointed tips that totally obscure it. Colour of spines brownish-black. Colour of test pink with red lines indicating position of pores that allow water to enter the tube feet.

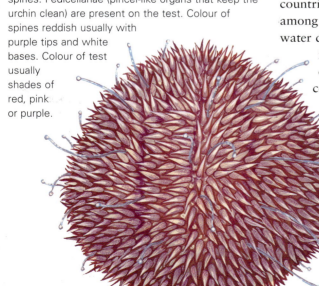

The sea urchins are members of the class Echinoidea, in which the body consists of chalky plates forming a shell called the test. From the test sprout bristling, mobile spines as well as long tube feet, which the animal uses when moving about. The black sea urchin has fairly short, sharp spines arising from an almost spherical test. Like other sea urchins, the mouth is on the underside of the body and from it protrude five white teeth – they are part of a chewing structure known as Aristotle's lantern, because of its resemblance to an old-fashioned oil lamp. The anus is on the top of the body. The black sea urchin crawls about among seaweeds and on rocks from the lower shore down to about 40m/130ft.

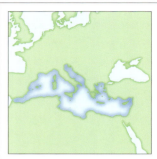

Distribution: Common in Mediterranean Sea.
Habitat: On seaweeds and rocks.
Food: Organic debris.
Size: Test 5cm/2in across; spines 3cm/1.2in long.
Breeding: Reproduces sexually; fertilization of eggs is external.
Status: Not listed by IUCN.

Edible sea urchin

Echinus esculentus

Identification: Test globular (may be flatter in those from shallow water) with close covering of robust spines. Pedicellariae (pincer-like organs that keep the urchin clean) are present on the test. Colour of spines reddish usually with purple tips and white bases. Colour of test usually shades of red, pink or purple.

This is a large, globular sea urchin often eaten as a seafood delicacy in many countries. It is found on rocks and crawling among seaweeds on the lower shore and in water down to about 40m/130ft, although it may also be encountered at greater depths than this. The animal's test is covered in short, solid spines; in some species of urchins the spines are clearly divided into primary and secondary types according to their sizes, but in the edible sea urchin this distinction is much less clear. The spines also provide a refuge for several other marine invertebrates: these include *Astacilla intermedia*, an amphipod related to sand hoppers, and the worm *Flabelligera affinis*.

Distribution: Associated with North Atlantic drift, from Norway to northern Portugal.
Habitat: On seaweeds and rocks from lower shore down to 40m/130ft or more.
Food: Organic debris.
Size: Test 10cm/4in across; spines 1.5cm/0.6in long; specimens sometimes bigger.
Breeding: Reproduces sexually; external fertilization.
Status: Not listed by IUCN.

Sea potato

Echinocardium cordatum

Distribution: North-eastern Atlantic including British Isles and North Sea; Mediterranean.
Habitat: In sand from lower shore down to about 200m/660ft.
Food: Organic debris.
Size: Test 9cm/3.5in across.
Breeding: Reproduces sexually; fertilization of eggs is external.
Status: Not listed by IUCN.

The sea potato is an echinoderm also known as a heart urchin. The test is heart-shaped with many short, and longer, backward-directed spines, giving the animal initially an almost furry appearance. Most of the heart urchin's tube feet – small, fluid-filled organs that enable the animal to move about – are on the upper surface, although some are below. It spends its life burrowing in clean sand to a depth of about 15cm/6in. Unlike the closely related sea urchins, the heart urchins do not have teeth and they feed on detritus passed to the mouth by the tube feet. The mouth is situated on the underside near the front, and the anus is also on the underside, at the back of the animal. The presence of a heart urchin can sometimes be detected by the small conical depression it makes near its head end; the depression is used to collect detritus prior to it being eaten.

Identification: Test heart-shaped, with an indentation at the front end; upper surface has a deep furrow; five rows of tube feet. Short and longer spines on test, mostly pointing backward. Colour yellowish-brown.

Savigny's sea urchin (*Diadema savignyi*): test 6m/2.4in long; spines 20cm/8in long
This Indo-Pacific species of sea urchin has a rounded test covered in long spines. Colour variable: often the test is black, but in some individuals the tests are a lighter colour. The spines, which are venomous and can cause severe pain if they puncture the skin, are often banded in a warning pattern of alternating light and dark colours. Savigny's sea urchin hides among rocks on sandy reefs by day.

Purple heart urchin (*Spatangus purpureus*): test 12cm/4.7in long
This somewhat flattened species is an attractive violet-red colour. It lives buried in sand and gravel in water that varies from about 5m/16ft to about 800m/2,600ft in the Atlantic Ocean and Mediterranean Sea; sometimes a few of the longer spines on its upper surface are visible at the surface.

Lyre urchin (*Brissopsis lyrifera*): test 7cm/2.8in long
This species gets its name from the lyre-shaped pattern on the upper surface of the test, which is visible when the spines are removed. The lyre urchin is red-brown in colour with dense, fur-like spines covering the test. It lives in sand in water down to about 300m/985ft in the Atlantic Ocean and Mediterranean Sea.

Sea cucumber

Holothuria forskali

The sea cucumber is a member of the class Holothuroidea. The holothuroids have sac- or cucumber-like bodies. They do not have arms or rays, and many have no obvious spines – although calcareous spicules are embedded in the skin. However, most have tube feet – sometimes arranged in rows down the sides of the animal or in a ring around the mouth, at the front of the body. The sea cucumber has a long, narrow body with three rows of suckered tube feet on the lower surface, which are used for movement, and some suckerless tube feet scattered on the animal's warty upper surface. There is a ring of about 20 modified tube feet around the mouth, which are used for feeding. As a means of defence, this species can eject a mass of sticky white threads from the hind end that entangle a would-be predator.

Distribution: North-eastern Atlantic including British Isles and North Sea; Mediterranean.
Habitat: Sand and rocks from extreme lower shore down to about 70m/230ft.
Food: Deposit feeder.
Size: 20cm/8in across.
Breeding: Reproduces sexually; fertilization of eggs is external.
Status: Not listed by IUCN.

Identification: Body cucumber-shaped. Upper surface warty with suckerless tube feet randomly arranged; lower surface bearing three rows of suckered tube feet. Ring of modified, feathery tube feet around mouth. Colour yellow-brown, darker on top.

GROUND SHARKS

*The seven families of sharks of the order Carcharhiniformes are collectively known as ground sharks,
and vary widely in size, shape and behaviour. All the sharks of this family have a nictitating membrane,
or third eyelid, capable of being drawn across the eyeball. These animals are found in temperate,
sub-tropical and tropical oceans, and the range of some species even includes fresh water.*

Bull shark

Carcharhinus leucas

Big, powerful and aggressive, the bull shark's tolerance of both sea and fresh water means it
is found in rivers as far apart as the Zambezi in Africa and the Mississippi in the US. It has
even been found 4,200km/2,600 miles up the River Amazon. Although implicated in a
number of marine attacks on humans, assaults in fresh water are comparatively rare. In
marine environments, bull sharks are found swimming close to the shore, where they feed
on almost anything they can catch. Inland, the shark's list of food items may include sizeable
mammals such as dogs and antelopes that stray into the water, and even hippos. In the
Ganges, corpses consigned to the river in funerals have also ended up on the menu. In the
Nile, bull sharks are themselves preyed upon by
crocodiles. Bull sharks frequently give birth
to their young in brackish water.

Distribution: All tropical
and subtropical regions; also
tropical rivers inland.
Habitat: Along coastlines
and estuaries; also found in
rivers and lakes.
Food: Almost anything
edible, such as fish,
turtles, birds, squid,
crustaceans, dolphins and
other mammals, including
land mammals when
populations range upriver.
Size: 3.5m/11.5ft.
Breeding: Ovoviviparous;
bears 1–13 young.
Status: Listed as Lower Risk
by IUCN.

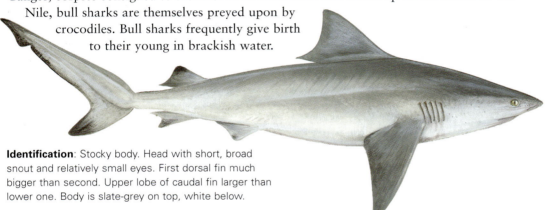

Identification: Stocky body. Head with short, broad
snout and relatively small eyes. First dorsal fin much
bigger than second. Upper lobe of caudal fin larger than
lower one. Body is slate-grey on top, white below.

Pyjama shark

Poroderma africanum

Identification: Body long and
slender. Head slightly flattened
with rounded snout. Large eyes.
Mouth bears small sensory
barbels. First dorsal fin bigger
than second dorsal fin. Pectoral
fins well developed. Body
brown-grey with seven black
stripes running length of animal
from from nose to tail; pattern
resembles pyjamas, hence
common name. Takes several
years for pyjama shark to
reach maturity.

Also known as the striped cat shark, the pyjama shark is a
small, attractively marked species that is often seen in public
aquariums. This slender-bodied shark feeds on a variety of
bottom-dwelling invertebrates, such as crabs and shrimps,
often using the sensory barbels around its mouth to locate
prey hidden from view. It also takes other fish, such as
gurnard and hake. The pyjama shark is found from the
intertidal zone downwards, where it prefers to hide by day
among seaweeds, rocks and crevices and in sea grass
meadows, using its cryptic body patterning to avoid the
attentions of other larger predatory fish. Female pyjama
sharks lay two leathery egg cases every three days or so
during the breeding season.

Distribution: South-eastern
Atlantic off coast of southern
Africa. Possibly also coasts of
Mauritius and Madagascar,
Indian Ocean, although
reports are not confirmed.
Habitat: Bottom-dwelling,
usually from the intertidal
zone down to about
250m/820ft.
Food: Fish, squid, octopuses,
crabs, shrimps.
Size: 1m/3.25ft.
Breeding: Oviparous; two
egg cases laid every three
days in the breeding season.
Status: Listed as Lower Risk
by IUCN.

Leopard shark (*Triakis semifasciata*): 2.1m/7ft
Slender shark that feeds on bottom-dwelling prey, such as crabs and fish. Found from eastern Pacific to Gulf of California, it frequents inshore sandy and muddy bays and estuaries near the bottom. Sometimes forms loose, nomadic schools with other shark species. Females give birth to between four and 33 live young.

Dogfish (*Scyliorhinus canicula*): 1m/3.25ft
Atlantic and Mediterranean shark with slender body, long tail, flattened head and rounded snout. Sandy-brown above with brown spots, creamy-white below. Rests among rocks by day, and at night hunts crabs, molluscs and small fish. Reproduction involves males entwining their bodies around females.

Grey smooth hound (*Mustelus californicus*): about 1.5m/5ft
Slender body and head with large, oval eyes. Body grey or brown above, lighter below. An eastern Pacific species often found in bays and rocky shallows, sometimes in company of other small sharks. Eats mainly worms, fish and crustaceans. Produces live young.

Blotchy swell shark

Cephaloscyllium umbratile

This is one of several species of sharks whose collective common name comes from their ability to swell, or inflate, their bodies as a defence mechanism against predators. When threatened, they can wedge themselves tightly into a crevice or hole by pumping up their bodies and so becoming almost impossible to dislodge. The rest of the blotchy swell shark's common name comes from its characteristic upper body markings – a series of blotches and bands that helps it to remain camouflaged on the bottom. The shark's fine, pointed teeth are perfectly adapted for dealing with prey items, such as octopuses, flatfish and skate, that it finds on the substrate. It is, however, a relatively sluggish species that soon gives up the chase if prey tries to escape.

Identification: Fairly slender body with longish tail. Head flattish. First dorsal fin set well back. Well-developed pectoral fins. Upper part of body and fins covered in dark blotches and saddles, underside pale.

Distribution: Western Pacific from Japan to South China Sea, possibly also New Guinea.
Habitat: Rocky bottoms and reefs from 20–200m/ 65–660ft.
Food: Bony fish, cartilaginous fish such as rays, squid, octopuses.
Size: 1.2m/4ft.
Breeding: Oviparous; pairs of egg cases laid throughout the long breeding season.
Status: Not listed by IUCN.

Tope

Galeorhinus galeus

Distribution: Temperate and subtropical oceans between latitudes 68°N and 55°S.
Habitat: Shallow bays and offshore waters.
Food: Mainly fish, such as herring, smelt, barracuda and hake; also squid, crabs, snails and sea urchins.
Size: 1.8m/6ft.
Breeding: Ovoviviparous; between 6 and 50 young born after year-long gestation.
Status: Listed by IUCN as Vulnerable globally and Near Threatened in New Zealand.

The tope is known by many common names, including soupfin shark – a sadly appropriate name for a shark whose fins are highly prized for making shark fin soup. It is caught throughout its range, both commercially and as a sport fish. The tope adapts well to life in large aquariums. A wide-ranging and abundant species, often occurring in small schools, the tope inhabits the surf zone and deep water, and is found both on the bottom and swimming in open water. In the higher latitudes of its range, it is highly migratory, occurring near the poles in summer and moving near the equator in winter. Tope can cover 50km/30 miles or more in a day. They have a lifespan of about 55 years, but like many sharks they mature slowly and have low breeding productivity; this, coupled with pressures of fishing, have caused numbers to decline.

Identification: Body slender. Head with long snout and large, almond-shaped eyes. Mouth with blade-like teeth bearing cusps. First dorsal fin much bigger than second dorsal fin. Second dorsal fin more or less aligned with anal fin and approximately same size. Terminal caudal lobe as long as rest of fin. Body colour grey to bluish above, becoming white on underside. Juveniles have black-tipped dorsal and caudal fins and white trailing edges on pectoral fins.

BULLHEAD SHARKS AND ANGEL SHARKS

Bullhead sharks are relatively small, bottom-dwelling sharks with a distinctive ridge over each eye, resembling a bull's horns, and a groove connecting the nostrils to the corners of the mouth. The 18 or so species of angel sharks have flattened bodies with wing-like fins. They swim gracefully but spend much time buried in the sand waiting for prey to come into range.

Port Jackson shark

Heterodontus portusjacksoni

The best-known of the nine species of horn, or bullhead, sharks, the Port Jackson shark has a large, blunt head and a prominent ridge over each eye. It is a bottom-dwelling species that often pumps jets of water over the substrate when feeding to expose hidden prey. Port Jackson sharks are highly migratory at breeding times, often travelling up to 800km/500 miles to the same winter spawning areas; sometimes individuals will even select the same caves and crevices used on previous occasions. Fertilization takes place internally, and although it is often stated that females use their mouths to place the eggs in a safe spot for hatching, this has never been observed.

Identification: Body tapers towards tail. Head big and blunt, with prominent ridge originating in front of each eye; eyes set high on head. Mouth has fine pointed teeth at front and flatter teeth at back. Stout spine in front of each dorsal fin. Large pectoral fins. Body colour greyish brown with dark banding.

Distribution: Pacific Ocean; mainly southern Queensland to Western Australia.
Habitat: Rocky, sandy and muddy bottoms from shallow water down to around 167m/550ft.
Food: Crabs and other crustaceans, molluscs, starfish, sea urchins, fish.
Size: 1.5m/5ft.
Breeding: Oviparous; bears 10–16 leathery eggs.
Status: Listed as Lower Risk by IUCN.

California horn shark

Heterodontus francisci

Identification: Tapering body. Large, blunt, pig-like head with prominent ridge originating in front of each eye; eyes set high on head. Mouth has fine pointed teeth at front and flatter teeth at back. Stout spine in front of each dorsal fin. Large pectoral fins. Body colour greyish brown with dark spots (although spots may be absent).

This small, solitary shark bears a resemblance to the Port Jackson shark, although it has a different form of body patterning. The California horn shark usually lies hidden in caves or under rocky ledges and other safe spots by day, emerging at night to hunt for food on the seabed and among kelp. Food consists of fish and invertebrates, such as crabs and squid. California horn sharks are found in water down to about 11m/36ft deep, and although they can swim freely, they are usually seen moving sluggishly along the bottom using their powerful pectoral fins. These sharks are egg layers, and the auger-shaped egg case – which is typical of *Heterodontus* species – has two filaments at one end. These are used to help anchor the egg case in place among rocks, where it hatches out about seven to nine months later.

Distribution: Eastern Pacific Ocean, mainly southern California; also Peru.
Habitat: Rocky, sandy and muddy bottoms and kelp beds down to around 11m/35ft.
Food: Crabs, squid, worms, sea urchins, anemones, fish.
Size: 1.2m/4ft.
Breeding: Oviparous; spiral egg cases laid.
Status: Listed as Lower Risk by IUCN.

Common angel shark

Squatina squatina

Distribution: Eastern North Atlantic coast (Norway to Spain); also Morocco, Mauretania and Senegal.
Habitat: Sandy and muddy seabeds.
Food: Other bottom-dwelling fish, crabs, molluscs.
Size: 2.4m/7.8ft.
Breeding: Ovoviviparous; bears 7–25 pups.
Status: Listed as Vulnerable by IUCN.

Lying motionless on the sandy bottom using its colouration and flattened shape to help it remain concealed from any potential prey, the common angel shark appears a placid creature. If prey comes within range, however, this ambush predator can strike with lightning speed to snatch the unsuspecting victim. It can also be highly aggressive if disturbed by divers, and when caught and landed in a boat it will snap dangerously at anything coming within range. Mostly active at night, the common angel shark frequents shallow water from about 2m/6.5ft down to 100m/330ft in summer, but it descends down to about 150m/500ft or so in the winter.
Also known as 'monkfish' (although not to be confused with *Lophius*), the common angel shark is popular for commercial fishing in many parts of the world.

Identification: Flattened body with large, wing-like pectoral and pelvic fins. Mouth bearing pointed teeth located near tip of snout. Eyes on top of head. Prominent spiracles behind eyes. Small spines on snout and above eyes. Body colour mottled greyish-brown to green above, underside lighter.

Japanese angel shark (*Squatina japonica*): 2m/6.5ft
Characteristic flattened body shape with broad, wing-like pectoral and pelvic fins. As in other angel sharks, it has fleshy appendages around its mouth. The body is blackish-brown with large, irregular dark blotches on upper side. Moderately large denticles on snout and above eyes, and on midline of back and tail from head to dorsal fins. One of the less well-known angels, this species is found in the subtropical western Pacific around Japan, Korea, northern China and the Philippines, on or near sandy bottoms. It produces live young.

Atlantic angel shark (*Squatina dumeril*): 1.8m/6ft
Its habit of rearing up out of the sand and biting anyone who disturbs it has earned the Atlantic angel shark the nickname of 'sand devil'. The term is sometimes also applied to other species in the genus, most of which are equally aggressive. Found along the Atlantic coast of North America from Massachusetts to the Florida Keys and the Gulf of Mexico; also parts of the Caribbean and northern South America. Possesses the flattened body and large pectoral fins characteristic of angel sharks. Body colouring is speckled grey-blue above, and whitish below. There are rows of denticles on the upper surface. A typical litter consists of about 16 pups.

Pacific angel shark

Squatina californica

Similar in shape and general habits to the common angel shark, the Pacific angel shark lives in the warm waters of the eastern Pacific Ocean, where it partly buries itself in sand or mud at the bottom. Like other bottom-dwelling angel sharks, instead of taking in water through the mouth when breathing as most other fish do, it pumps water in via the openings known as spiracles, which are located on top of the head behind the eyes. This evolutionary adaptation prevents sand and other debris from entering the respiratory system and clogging up the animal's delicate gill tissues. Sluggish when resting or waiting to ambush its prey, the Pacific angel shark attacks aggressively if provoked or even touched. Some specimens are reported to have lived for 35 years.

Distribution: Eastern Pacific from southern Alaska to Gulf of California; and from Costa Rica to southern Chile.
Habitat: Sandy and muddy seabeds, among rocks and in kelp forests down to about 200m/660ft.
Food: Other bottom-dwelling fish, crustaceans, molluscs.
Size: 1.5m/5ft.
Breeding: Ovoviviparous; bears 6–10 pups.
Status: Listed as Near Threatened by IUCN.

Identification: Flattened body with large, wing-like pectoral and pelvic fins. Mouth bearing numerous pointed teeth located near tip of snout. Eyes on top of head. Prominent spiracles behind eyes. Body greyish-brown with red, brown or grey speckles above, underside lighter.

EELS AND ELOPIFORMS

Eels are slender-bodied fish with long dorsal and anal fins but no pelvic fins. They occur worldwide, except in polar seas. The tarpon, ladyfish and bonefish are members of the order Elopiformes. They are related to eels and have slender bodies and forked tails. All produce eggs which hatch into thin, transparent planktonic larvae called leptocephali.

European conger eel

Conger conger

Lurking in caves and crevices, the powerful European conger eel is one of several species found worldwide. This species is usually a nocturnal predator, lying out of sight until likely prey comes near, at which time it launches itself from its hiding place to snatch its meal with large teeth. Congers, landed in boats and lashing about and snapping viciously, have been known to overturn small craft as well as well as biting their occupants. Once sexually mature, the conger migrates from its north Atlantic coastal waters to spawn in deep ocean of the continental slope. The young eels hatch into a stage known as leptocephali and are carried back across the Atlantic on ocean currents.

Identification: Muscular, snake-like body lacking scales. Head with large eyes and protruding upper jaw. Both jaws have powerful teeth. Prominent, pointed pectoral fins. Long dorsal fin originates well forward, near pectoral fins. Elongated anal fin. Colour black, grey or dull brown above, often depending on habitat; creamy below.

Distribution: Atlantic Ocean from Iceland and Scandinavia to Mediterranean and Senegal.
Habitat: Among shipwrecks and rocks in both shallow and deep water.
Food: Octopuses, crabs, fish.
Size: 3m/10ft.
Breeding: Oviparous; spawns in deep, subtropical Atlantic Ocean; eggs hatch into planktonic leptocephali.
Status: Not listed by IUCN.

California moray eel

Gymnothorax mordax

There are about 200 species of moray eels found in the world's tropical and warm-temperate oceans. Some have highly colourful body markings and prominent nasal appendages. All morays are predatory fish, with an often well-deserved reputation for aggressive behaviour if disturbed. Indeed, there are instances of moray eels chasing divers out of the water and then lunging at them from the surf. This species hunts at night, sometimes lurking in rocky crevices waiting to ambush prey, but also seeking it out

Identification: Muscular, snake-like body lacking scales. Head small with numerous sharp, pointed teeth. Body lacks pectoral fins. Dorsal and anal fins long, fused at tail with caudal fin. Colour light or dark brown or green, often mottled.

Distribution: Eastern Pacific Ocean from Baja California northward; also Galapagos Is.
Habitat: In crevices on rocky reefs from 1–20m/3–65ft.
Food: Octopuses, crabs, urchins, fish.
Size: 1.5m/5ft.
Breeding: Oviparous; external fertilization; eggs hatch into planktonic leptocephali.
Status: Not listed by IUCN.

using a well-developed sense of smell. The eel constantly opens and closes its mouth to ensure a constant supply of oxygenated water is forced over its gills. The red rock shrimp (*Lysmata californica*) is often found sharing the lair of the California moray eel. The shrimp keeps the eel free of parasites and dead skin, and in return the eel provides its 'cleaner' with protection and possibly scraps of food.

Tarpon

Megalops atlanticus

Distribution: Eastern Atlantic from Senegal to Angola; western Atlantic from North Carolina, US, to northern Brazil.
Habitat: Over reefs, in estuaries and in rivers.
Food: Fish, molluscs.
Size: 2.4m/7.8ft.
Breeding: Oviparous; spawns in shallow water; eggs hatch into planktonic leptocephali.
Status: Not listed by IUCN.

Although looking much more like a 'typical' fish, the huge Atlantic tarpon is, in fact, closely related to the eels. The tarpon has existed since the Cretaceous (about 130 million years ago), making it one of the longest-surviving living fish species. This species of tarpon is a common fish, often gathering in groups in its native Atlantic waters, frequently encountered around reefs, but also found in estuaries and rivers. This abundance, coupled with its large size, makes it a prime target for fishermen – both for food and sport. Luckily, the tarpon is also a prolific breeder – a female can produce 12 million eggs – and so it is not currently at risk. The fish has large, silvery scales, prized in some regions for making into jewellery. The tarpon often leaps high out of the water, especially when hooked by fishermen. True to its eel-related lineage, the eggs of the tarpon hatch into ribbon-like leptocephali.

Identification: Slightly elongated and compressed body. Large head with large eyes and large mouth with protruding lower jaw. The last ray of the dorsal fin is an elongated projection. Caudal fin deeply forked. Scales large and silvery, becoming darker and 'metallic' on back.

European eel (*Anguilla anguilla*): 1m/3.25ft
The European eel has a snake-like body with deeply embedded tiny scales. Adults have silvery bodies with blackish backs. The dorsal fin runs along much of the fish's back. There are no pelvic fins. Found in freshwater rivers and lakes, from which it travels, sometimes over land, to breed in the Sargasso Sea.

Ribbon eel (*Rhinomuraena quaesita*): 1.3m/4.3ft
With its bright blue body, orange-yellow jaws and fleshy nasal and jaw appendages, this Indo-Pacific eel is a striking-looking species. It usually lives in sand or rubble on reefs in water down to about 60m/200ft with just its head protruding, while it waits for small fish to grab as they pass.

Edward's spaghetti eel (*Moringua edwardsii*): female 50cm/20in
Spaghetti eels derive their common name from the fact that they resemble strands of spaghetti. Females of Edward's spaghetti eel are much larger than males, which grow to about 15cm/6in. Young and females are found in sand and among reefs in the Atlantic. Males live in deeper water.

Bonefish (*Albula vulpes*): 1m/3.25ft
A slender subtropical fish with silvery scales and dark streaks, a blunt, conical snout and a deeply forked tail. The fish appears blue-green above. The bonefish prefers shallow waters down to about 80m/260ft and feeds by rooting out crabs, worms and molluscs from the sea bed.

Ladyfish

Elops saurus

The slender-bodied, silvery blue ladyfish is a popular gamefish species, and has the habit of leaping clear of the water when hooked in an attempt to escape. It is often sold fresh, frozen or salted in markets, although its flesh is not considered to be a particular delicacy. The ladyfish often forms shoals near the shore, and sometimes swims several kilometres offshore, but it can tolerate a wide range of salinities and also frequently inhabits brackish waters, such as estuaries and mangroves, as well as rivers. The ladyfish is generally considered to be a warm-water species, but it can tolerate colder conditions for short periods. Spawning takes place offshore. The metamorphosing larvae – which at first have a transparent, ribbon-like appearance – and juveniles are usually encountered in inshore estuarine waters. When adult, the ladyfish's diet consists mainly of crustaceans and other fish; young larvae absorb nutrients in the water through their skin.

Distribution: Western Atlantic from Cape Cod, Massachusetts, to Gulf of Mexico and Caribbean and south to Brazil.
Habitat: Shallow inshore waters to about 50m/165ft.
Food: Fish, crustaceans.
Size: 1.2m/4ft.
Breeding: Oviparous: spawns offshore; leptocephalic larvae metamorphose inshore.
Status: Not listed by IUCN.

Identification: Slim-bodied but robust, streamlined fish; body covered with small scales. Head small and pointed with large mouth bearing small, sharp teeth. Caudal fin deeply forked. The dorsal surface is silvery blue or greenish. The sides and lower surface are silvery.

COD AND RELATIVES

The cod and their relatives comprise more than 1,200 species of fish, encompassing important commercial food species such as cod, haddock and whiting, as well as the rarely seen and highly modified anglers, goosefish and toadfish. Members of the group are found in a variety of environments, ranging from surface waters to the ocean depths.

Pearlfish

Echiodon drummondii

Identification: Thin, flattish, shallow, eel-like body – almost knife-like in shape; dorsal and ventral surfaces are fringed with a continuous fin. Its body is translucent, with silvery bands and patches of pale reddish pigment on the flanks, iris and operculum (gill cover). It has a silvery abdomen. Dark markings on head.

The 30 or so species of pearlfish, which are also known as cucumber fish, are inhabitants of tropical, subtropical and temperate seas. Many of them spend much of their lives inside other marine creatures, such as bivalve molluscs or sea cucumbers. Some species do this for protection only, while others also feed on the organs of the host. The pearlfish *Echiodon drummondii* has the typical thin, elongated shape of many pearlfish. This knife-like shape makes it easy to squeeze into the host's body through its anus. Most pearlfish have a fairly sedentary lifestyle, but their eggs hatch at the surface into glassy larvae that are dispersed widely on the ocean currents to exploit new habitats.

Distribution: North Sea and British Isles.
Habitat: Waters from about 50–400m/164–1,312ft.
Food: Probably small marine creatures.
Size: 30cm/12in.
Breeding: Oviparous; eggs hatch at surface and larvae are carried and distributed by ocean currents.
Status: Not listed by IUCN.

Shore rockling

Gaidropsarus mediterraneus

The shore rockling is one of several species of rockling that inhabit shallow Atlantic waters. The shore rockling has a preference for algae or sea grasses in which it can hide. Like the other rocklings, the shore rockling has a long, slender body with two dorsal fins. Rocklings have sensory barbels on the snout and chin; in the case of the shore rockling, there are two on the snout and one on the chin. The similar-looking five-bearded rockling (*Ciliata mustela*), with which it can be confused, has five barbels, however. The three-bearded rockling (*Gaidropsarus vulgaris*) also has three barbels around the mouth, but it is distinguished from the shore rockling by its colour, which is reddish brown with well-marked blotches.

Identification: Body is long and slender with smooth, scaleless skin. First dorsal fin is short, with a prominent first ray; second dorsal fin is long. Long anal fin. Caudal fin is rounded. Head bears two sensory barbels on the snout and one barbel on the chin. Colour is dark brown; the pigment on the dorsal area may be slightly mottled in appearance.

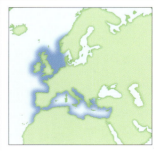

Distribution: North-eastern Atlantic, including North Sea, from British Isles to southern Morocco; also Mediterranean.
Habitat: Among rocks and in shallow water down to about 30m/98ft.
Food: Crustaceans, worms and fish.
Size: 50cm/19.7in.
Breeding: Oviparous; eggs hatch at the surface.
Status: Not listed by IUCN.

Spotted cusk eel (*Chilara taylori*): 36cm/14in
Despite their common name, cusk eels are not true eels at all, although they do have slender, eel-like bodies. The nocturnal spotted cusk eel usually rests on the bottom with its tail touching the substrate, and at the first sign of danger it corkscrews itself into the sand or mud or into a convenient crevice for safety. It is found in the eastern Pacific Ocean.

Atlantic cod (*Gadus morhua*): 1.2m/4ft
This is one of the world's most important food fish for humans, but it is now classed as Vulnerable due to long periods of overfishing. The omnivorous cod is found in north Atlantic coastal waters, usually in schools. The fish has a stout body with three dorsal fins, two anal fins and a large, triangular tail. The head bears a single chin barbel.

Whiting (*Merlangius merlangus*): 35cm/14in
Like many other species in the family Gadidae, the slender whiting has three dorsal fins and two anal fins; the first anal fin is much longer than the second anal fin. The whiting is an important commercial food fish and it is found in shallow Atlantic waters from Iceland in the north to Spain in the south, including the Mediterranean and Black Seas.

American oyster toadfish

Opsanus tau

Also known as the oyster-cracker, this sluggish species of toadfish lives in shallow water, usually hiding on the bottom until unwary prey comes close enough to be snapped up by its huge, wide mouth. Hard shells are crushed by the fish's powerful jaws. The American oyster toadfish makes grunting noises when threatened, and males also make a foghorn-like or whistling sound to attract females to spawn. After the female has laid her eggs, the male fertilizes them and guards them until they hatch. The toadfish has venomous dorsal spines, often erected when the animal is threatened.

Identification: Head is large with large, protruding eyes and a big, wide mouth; fleshy appendages around mouth and short snout. Skin is scaleless. First dorsal fin short; second dorsal fin long. Anal fin long. Large pectoral fins. Caudal fin rounded. Colour yellow-brown with brown markings extending on to the fins.

Distribution: Atlantic Ocean from Cape Cod to Miami.
Habitat: Among rocks and sand in shallow inshore waters.
Food: Crustaceans and other invertebrates, fish.
Size: 38cm/15in.
Breeding: Oviparous; eggs laid in a secluded nest, which the male guards.
Status: Not listed by IUCN.

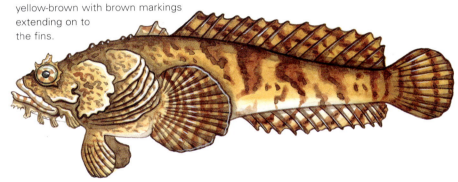

Angler

Lophius piscatorius

Distribution: North-eastern Atlantic from Scandinavia to Morocco; also North, Baltic and Mediterranean seas.
Habitat: Among rocks and sand in shallow, inshore waters.
Food: Crustaceans and other invertebrates, fish.
Size: 2m/6.6ft.
Breeding: Oviparous; eggs float at the surface in gelatinous masses.
Status: Not listed by IUCN.

Also known as the popular dish 'monkfish', the angler is a huge-headed creature with a range of unusual adaptations for capturing prey. Lurking on the bottom with its ragged-edged, flattened and mottled body helping it to blend with its surroundings, it waves and twitches an enticing lure (formed from its first dorsal fin spine) to attract victims. If a fish or crab comes close to the lure (presumably believing it to be a small food item), it is engulfed by the angler's mouth. Amazingly, even diving seabirds have ended up in the stomachs of anglers. Spawning takes place in deep water and the eggs float at the surface. Once hatched, the young spend their early lives feeding on plankton.

Identification: Head is massive and flattened, with large, upward-facing, gaping mouth and sharp, incurved teeth. Body flattened and tapering towards tail; body much narrower than head. Head and body bordered by a fringe of lobes. Dorsal surface has several elongated rays; first bears a fleshy lobe (the 'lure'). Pectoral fins broad and large. Pelvic fins small. Colour is variable.

GASTEROSTEIFORM FISH

Most of the fish in this group are characterized by having bodies covered in bony plates instead of scales. They range in shape from the familiar stickleback to the bizarre sea horses, pipefish and sea dragons. The snout of these fish is often elongated. Gasterosteiforms are found from temperate freshwater habitats and brackish waters to tropical seas.

Slender seamoth

Pegasus volitans

The common name of the slender seamoth comes from its habit of gliding over the sea bed using its broad, wing-like pectoral fins in a manner reminiscent of a flitting moth. With its hard, bony-plated body suffused with mottling and reticulated patterning, it is well camouflaged on the sea bed as it searches out the small invertebrates that form its diet, sucking them into a small mouth at the end of its elongated snout. Like other seamoths, the slender seamoth can use its stiff fins to walk about on the substrate. During mating, males and females swim up from the bottom, and the eggs are fertilized in the water. The eggs float at the surface and soon hatch. The larvae spend time among the plankton before sinking to the bottom to develop into adults.

Identification: Head narrow and tapering, with long snout. Mouth found at end of snout on the underside; eyes prominent. Body flattened and covered by bony plates. Pectoral fins large and wing-like. Dorsal and anal fins short. Tail squarish. Colour variable – brown or grey, with mottled or reticulated patterning.

Distribution: Indo-Pacific Ocean including Mozambique, Persian Gulf and Bay of Bengal; coast of Burma to Japan; tropical Australasia.
Habitat: Shallow muddy, sandy or silty substrates.
Food: Small invertebrates.
Size: 12cm/4.7in.
Breeding: Oviparous; external fertilization.
Status: Listed as Data Deficient by IUCN.

Three-spined stickleback

Gasterosteus aculeatus

Identification: Pointed head with small mouth and large eyes. Body slender and flattish, tapering to narrow caudal peduncle. Three dorsal spines in front of dorsal fin. Anal fin shorter than dorsal fin. Pectoral fins with rounded edges. Pelvic fins reduced to a single spine and ray. Colour outside breeding season: silvery on flanks and white below; male in breeding colours described on the right.

Found in many parts of the Northern Hemisphere from ponds and rivers to shallow seas, the three-spined stickleback is a lively little fish immediately recognizable by the three characteristic spines on its back. The body lacks scales, but is protected by bony plates, and carries pelvic spines as well as the dorsal spines. During breeding, the underside of the male becomes an intense red or orange colour, his back and sides turn blue-green, and his eyes become blue. When breeding, the male builds a nest and is highly territorial. The tunnel-shaped nest rests on the bottom and is made from plant material glued together with mucous secretions. Then he displays to attract several females who lay their eggs in the nest. Once the eggs are laid, he immediately fertilizes them. The male then fans and guards them until they hatch. He even protects the hatchlings for several days, until they disperse.

Distribution: Northern Pacific and Atlantic coasts; also Mediterranean and Black Seas; also inland in North American and European rivers.
Habitat: Shallow freshwater and marine habitats; preferably with gentle or no currents.
Food: Mainly invertebrates, fish eggs and larvae, small fish.
Size: Up to 10cm/4in.
Breeding: Oviparous; external fertilization.
Status: Not listed by IUCN.

Tubesnout (*Aulorhynchus flavidus*): 18cm/7in
Looking somewhat like an elongated stickleback, the tubesnout has bony plates on its body and about 26 spines on its back. It is found in shallow eel grass and kelp beds in the eastern Pacific. The male tubesnout builds a nest from plant material in which the female lays her eggs.

Fifteen-spined stickleback
(*Spinachia spinachia*): 23cm/9in
This slender species has a pointed head, a long caudal peduncle and 14–17 spines on its back. It is the largest member of the stickleback family. It is found usually among seaweed in coastal areas near the shore in the eastern Atlantic.

Shortsnouted seahorse
(*Hippocampus ramulosus*): 15cm/6in
Like other seahorses, this species has a horse-like head and swims with its body held vertical or nearly so. The pectoral fins are situated just behind the eyes. The body is covered with bony plates. Favours habitats among the seaweeds and grasses in Atlantic and Mediterranean waters.

Chinese trumpetfish (*Aulostomus chinensis*): 80cm/31in
The Chinese trumpetfish has an elongated body and a long head with the mouth at the tip. It lives on Indo-Pacific coral reefs, where it often floats towards unsuspecting prey before darting forward and sucking it into its tube-like mouth.

Longsnouted seahorse

Hippocampus guttulatus

Among the most instantly recognizable of all marine creatures, seahorses get their common name from the shape of the head, which is essentially like that of a horse. With their strange appearance, unusual fins and habit of floating upright in the water or resting with their tails entwined around vegetation, it is not surprising that many people do not realize that seahorses are, in fact, fish. However, the mating behaviour of seahorses is even more atypical of fish. During mating, as with other seahorse species, male and female longsnouted seahorses perform an elaborate display by linking their tails and undertaking a courtship 'dance'. Then they bring their bellies together and the female transfers some of her eggs into the male's abdominal pouch. He then fertilizes the eggs. The young develop in the male's pouch for several weeks before he 'gives birth' to live young that resemble miniature versions of their parents.

Distribution: Eastern Atlantic from Great Britain to Morocco; also Mediterranean.
Habitat: Shallow waters, especially among algae and sea grasses, down to 20m/66ft; in water down to about 80m/260ft during winter.
Food: Mainly invertebrates.
Size: Up to 15cm/6in.
Breeding: Male broods fertilized eggs in abdominal pouch until they hatch.
Status: Listed as Data Deficient by IUCN.

Identification: Long snout; fleshy appendages on back of neck resemble a 'mane'. Head and body bony, angular and ridged. Body elongated, especially from region of dorsal fin to end of tail. Pectoral fins and anal fin small. Pelvic fins and caudal fin lacking. Colour yellowish-green to reddish-brown, marked with blue patches and spots.

Leafy sea dragon

Phycodurus eques

Distribution: Indo-Pacific.
Habitat: On reefs among kelp beds down to about 50m/165ft.
Food: Mainly fish and crustacean larvae.
Size: 45cm/18in.
Breeding: Male broods fertilized eggs in abdominal pouch until they hatch.
Status: Listed as Data Deficient by IUCN.

Drifting among the reefs of Indo-Pacific waters, the leafy sea dragon resembles a clump of seaweed. This bizarre-looking fish is a master of disguise – avoiding the attentions of predators while at the same time floating horizontally unnoticed towards its own prey, using imperceptible movements of its body and tiny fins. Beneath the 'leafy' outgrowths that sprout from its body, the fish has a body not unlike that of a seahorse, to which it and the other sea dragon species are closely related. Also like seahorses, the male receives eggs from the female which he fertilizes and then broods in a special part of his body between the belly and the lower part of the tail.

Identification: Head with long, trumpet-like snout. Body elongated and angled. Pelvic and caudal fins lacking. Head and body angular, bony and ridged, with elaborate plant-like appendages resembling seaweed. Yellowish-orange with white ridges and olive-green appendages.

MAIL-CHEEKED FISH

The mail-cheeked fish in the order Scorpaeniformes include some of the most dangerous fish known and all have venom glands and spines. Species such as the stonefish are masters of disguise and spend much of their lives lying partly concealed waiting for prey, while others, like more flamboyant lionfish, actively hunt their food.

Estuarine stonefish

Synanceia horrida

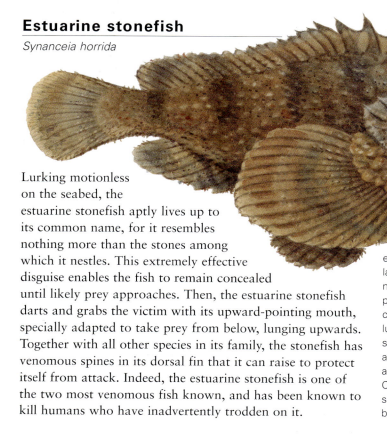

Lurking motionless on the seabed, the estuarine stonefish aptly lives up to its common name, for it resembles nothing more than the stones among which it nestles. This extremely effective disguise enables the fish to remain concealed until likely prey approaches. Then, the estuarine stonefish darts and grabs the victim with its upward-pointing mouth, specially adapted to take prey from below, lunging upwards. Together with all other species in its family, the stonefish has venomous spines in its dorsal fin that it can raise to protect itself from attack. Indeed, the estuarine stonefish is one of the two most venomous fish known, and has been known to kill humans who have inadvertently trodden on it.

Identification: Body elongated and tapering. Head large with big, upward-facing mouth and upward-looking, protuberant eyes. Body surface covered in rough warts and lumps, resembling rocks and stones; may also be covered with algae. Venomous spines on back and on anal and pelvic fins. Colour variable to match surroundings; often shades of brown-yellow or reddish-grey.

Distribution: Indo-West Pacific Ocean: India to China, Philippines, Papua New Guinea and Australia.
Habitat: In shallow water, partly buried among rocks and sand.
Food: Fish and crustaceans.
Size: 60cm/24in.
Breeding: Oviparous; external fertilization.
Status: Not listed by IUCN.

Longspine waspfish

Paracentropogon longispinis

Identification: Body laterally compressed. Large head with relatively small mouth. Dorsal fin tall and running from top of head, above the eyes; 12–15 prominent spiny rays in dorsal fin. Body colour mottled reddish-brown with white patches.

The longspine waspfish is a highly venomous member of the family Scorpaenidae – a family containing some of the most poisonous fish in the world. This species is found in inshore waters among reefs and other hard-bottomed substrates, where it conceals itself partly by its mottled body markings and partly by its body texture, which resembles the coral on which it hides. The poison from the venomous spines can prove fatal if not treated. Seek emergency medical attention immediately if affected. If this is not possible, steeping the wounded area in very hot water as quickly as you can may render the poison harmless. Despite its reputation, this species is one of several venomous fish that are popular with aquarists.

Distribution: Indo-Pacific Ocean.
Habitat: Among silt, rocks and coral down to about 70m/230ft.
Food: Fish and crustaceans.
Size: 15cm/6in.
Breeding: Oviparous; external fertilization.
Status: Not listed by IUCN.

Northern sea robin

Prionotus carolinus

Distribution: Western Atlantic Ocean from Nova Scotia to Gulf of Mexico.
Habitat: On sandy bottoms in water down to about 180m/590ft.
Food: Fish, crustaceans, molluscs, worms.
Size: 30cm/12in.
Breeding: Oviparous; external fertilization.
Status: Not listed by IUCN.

This species spends much of its life on the bottom, where it feels for food on the seabed using three elongated rays on its large, wing-like pectoral fins. The sea robin can also support itself above the substrate with its fins, giving the impression of walking. At the first sign of danger, the fish will quickly bury itself in the sand, leaving just the top of its head and eyes exposed. Unlike most bottom fish, it is a very strong swimmer. By using special muscles attached to the swim bladder, the sea robin can also make loud noises, especially during the breeding season. A popular commercial fish, its flesh is used for pet food and fish bait, the tissues as fertilizer and the eggs are sold as gurnard 'caviar'.

Identification: Body tapering. Head large, encased in bony plates, with big eyes situated at the top of the head. Front of dorsal fin bears prominent spines. Broad caudal fin. Long anal fin. Large pelvic fins. Large pectoral fins, with lowest three rays free and elongated. Body colour mottled reddish-brown above with saddle-shaped blotches, whitish below.

Red gurnard (*Aspitrigla cuculus*): 30 cm/12in
This reddish-coloured fish has a large, distinctly sloping head and prominent eyes. First dorsal fin tall and spiny; second dorsal fin lower and longer. Anal fin about same length and size as second dorsal fin. First three rays of pectoral fins separate and used for sensing the substrate for food and for resting on bottom. Found in eastern Atlantic, Mediterranean and Baltic waters.

Kelp greenling (*Hexagrammos decagrammus*): 50cm/19.7in
One of several species of greenlings found in the North Pacific, the kelp greenling has large fins, including a dorsal fin with a deep undulation about halfway along its length. The males have blue spots on their heads and bodies; the females reddish-brown spots. The kelp greenling has five lateral lines along each side of its body.

Cabezon (*Scorpaenichthys marmoratus*): 76cm/30in
This species lives in the North Pacific at depths ranging from surface waters down to about 200m/656ft. A bulky fish with smooth, grey-brown mottled skin, it has a broad head, wide mouth and large fins. It eats mainly crabs, crustaceans and small fish.

Lumpsucker (*Cyclopterus lumpus*): 55cm/22in
The lumpsucker has a deep, rounded, scaleless body with four rows of bony plates embedded in it. Although the fish has two dorsal fins, in older specimens the first dorsal fin becomes incorporated into the body. The pelvic fins are modified into a ventral sucker, with which the fish attaches itself to rocks. Males in breeding condition develop a reddish belly.

Pogge

Agonus cataphractus

With its large, heavily armoured head and upturned snout, barbel-fringed mouth and narrow, tapering body, the pogge is a highly distinctive fish. It usually lives on the bottom, preferring sandy or muddy seabeds, although it is also encountered in estuaries. An underslung mouth restricts its food to bottom-living animals, and it uses the sensory barbels around its mouth to probe the substrate for small hidden crustaceans, worms, brittlestars and molluscs on which to feed. The pogge often burrows in the mud or sand, where its body colouration makes it difficult to see.

Identification: Head and body covered in hard, bony plates. Head large and longish, with eyes set on top of head; snout upturned and bearing a pair of hooked spines; mouth fringed with numerous barbels. Spine on each gill cover. Two dorsal fins. Body colour mottled grey-brown with four or five dark saddles across back; underside whitish.

Distribution: North-eastern Atlantic, including Shetland and Faroe Is., southwestern Iceland and southern Baltic.
Habitat: On sandy and muddy bottoms from 5–500m/16–1,650ft.
Food: Echinoderms, crustaceans, molluscs, worms.
Size: 15cm/6in.
Breeding: Oviparous; external fertilization.
Status: Not listed by IUCN.

PERCHLIKE FISH

Perciforms, commonly known as perchlike fish, account for just over 40 per cent of all fish, with over 7,000 species. It is the largest order of vertebrates on Earth. Fin spines are prominent in the physical make-up of this group: in many species, the dorsal section is divided into spiny and soft-rayed portions. Although a small percentage of perciforms have adapted to freshwater habitats, the majority are marine.

Potato cod

Epinephelus tukula

One of the largest of the groupers is the potato cod. It is also one of the biggest bony fish to be found on Indo-Pacific coral reefs, growing to weights of 100kg/220lb or more. It tends to lurk in deep channels and around seamounts, in places where the current is quite strong. It is highly territorial, and can be aggressive towards intruders, both of its own species and others, including human divers. However, it usually confines itself to an intimidating close approach and, paradoxically, this makes it a favourite with reef divers who enjoy close encounters with big fish. It is hand fed at some sites on the northern Great Barrier Reef, Australia. However, this behaviour also makes it vulnerable to spear fishers where it is not protected, and since it is a slow breeder this can have a serious impact.

Identification: A bulky fish with large, pointed head, thick-lipped mouth and relatively small eyes. Spiny first dorsal fin, continuous with taller, soft-rayed second dorsal fin. Generally creamy white or pale grey-brown with black or dark brown blotches. These are usually widely spaced, but large adults may be nearly black. The head has linear blotches radiating outwards from the eyes, and there are dark spots on the fins.

Distribution: Indo-West Pacific: Red Sea and East Africa to southern Japan and Queensland, Australia. Also Paracel Is., South China Sea.
Habitat: Coral reefs at depths of 10–150m/35–500ft.
Food: Smaller fish and crustaceans, such as crabs and spiny lobsters.
Size: 1.8m/6ft.
Breeding: Adults are initially female, maturing at a length of about 1m (3ft), but become males as they grow larger. Oviparous; eggs fertilized externally.
Status: Not listed by IUCN.

Rainbow wrasse

Thalassoma pavo

Identification: A sleek, streamlined fish with a rounded head, large eyes, and a long, low dorsal fin extending to the tail. Young adults are female, with golden-yellow bodies barred with pale blue-green, darker above, and with a rust-red head marbled with a pattern of turquoise lines. Older adults become male, with bright turquoise dorsal and anal fins, a brighter head pattern and fewer bars on the body.

This colourful, streamlined subtropical fish is one of many wrasses that is a protogynous hermaphrodite – that is, a species that is first female, and then changes to become male. This remarkable transformation is emphasized by a change in colour pattern, although unlike some wrasses the basic range of colours remains the same. It is commonly found in warm, shallow waters, where it preys on animals such as prawns, small crabs and marine snails. Recent research indicates that it is extending its range northwards in the Mediterranean in response to rising water temperatures.

Distribution: Eastern Atlantic, from Portugal to south of Cape Lopez, Gabon including Azores, Madeira and Canaries. Also Mediterranean.
Habitat: Rocky reefs and seagrass beds, at depths of 1–150m/3–500ft.
Food: Small molluscs and crustaceans.
Size: 25cm/10in.
Breeding: Adults are initially female, becoming male and changing colour with age. Oviparous; eggs fertilized externally.
Status: Not listed by IUCN.

Red mullet (*Mullus surmuletus*): 40cm/16in
Most common in warm, shallow Mediterranean and eastern Atlantic waters, the red mullet occasionally occurs in Scandinavia. Reddish-brown above with yellow stripes on its flanks, it is a slender fish with a steeply arched head profile and large eyes. It has two long sensory barbels beneath the jaw, enabling it to feel for prey such as shrimps and molluscs on sandy or muddy seabeds.

Ballan wrasse (*Labrus bergylta*): 60cm/24in
The bulky ballan wrasse occurs in the North Atlantic. It has large conical teeth for crushing the shells of molluscs and crabs. It usually forages among rocks about 20m/65ft down, although the young often occur in large intertidal rockpools. Young fish are often emerald green. Adults are mottled greenish-brown females, but change sex to become reddish males.

Stargazer (*Uranoscopus scaber*): 30cm/12in
Lying half-buried in soft sediments on the seabed, the stargazer has a robust, flattened head with eyes set on top, pointing upwards. Usually dark brown or blackish with grey-brown flanks, it is well camouflaged and attracts prey with a mobile lure on the lower lip of its large mouth. It has a venomous spine behind each gill cover, and an electric organ behind each eye. Occurs in Mediterranean and eastern Atlantic.

Greater weever

Trachinus draco

The weevers have venom glands associated with grooved spines on their gill covers and in the first dorsal fin. The venom provides defence against bottom-feeding rays and large flatfish, since during the day the fish typically lie buried in the sand with just their eyes and the tip of the first dorsal fin exposed. If not disturbed, the fish stay buried all day, emerging at night to swim about in search of prey. The greater weever favours deeper water than the very similar lesser weever, which frequently occurs in the shallows off sandy beaches and is regularly trodden on by bathers. The resulting wounds are extremely painful, often causing swelling and bruising.

Distribution: Eastern Atlantic from southern Norway to Morocco, Madeira and Canaries; also Mediterranean and Black Seas.
Habitat: On sandy, muddy or gravelly seabeds, at depths of 1–150m/3–500ft.
Food: Small invertebrates and fish.
Size: 40cm/16in.
Breeding: Oviparous; eggs fertilized externally.
Status: Not listed by IUCN.

Identification: An elongated fish with a small, compressed head, an upward-slanting mouth and large eyes. The first dorsal fin is short, black, spiny and fan-like, while the second dorsal fin and anal fin are long and low, extending to the tail. It has a small tail fin, but large pectorals. There are two or three small spines above each eye, and a large spine on each gill cover. Greenish above with yellowish-white oblique stripes; paler below.

Large-scale (seven-spot) archerfish

Toxotes chatareus

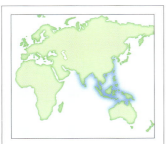

Distribution: India and South-east Asia to New Guinea and northern Australia.
Habitat: Brackish, tidal mangrove swamps and river estuaries.
Food: Mainly insects dislodged from vegetation by well-aimed jets of water.
Size: 30cm/12in.
Breeding: Oviparous; eggs fertilized externally.
Status: Not listed by IUCN.

This is one of several species of archerfish that live and hunt primarily among the tidal mangrove swamps of tropical Asia and Australasia. It specializes in targeting insects that perch on the arching roots and foliage of the mangroves, bombarding them with jets of water shot from its mouth. Its object is to knock the insects into the water, where it can seize and eat them. A ridge along the top of its tongue fits into a deep groove in the roof of its mouth, forming a tube like a rifle barrel. By rapidly contracting its gill covers, the fish forces water along the tube, which gives good accuracy up to a range of about 1.5m/5ft. The profile of its upper body allows it to approach a potential victim just below the surface, so it can see its target well without creating ripples that might distort its view or alert its prey.

Identification: A deep-bodied, small-headed fish with a virtually straight profile from the tip of its sharp snout to the top of its dorsal fin. It has large eyes and an upward slant to its mouth. It is silvery, darker above, with six or seven black spots of varying size on each upper flank.

Tompot blenny

Blennius gattorugine

A common fish of rocky shores, the tompot blenny is usually found from just below the low-tide mark to depths down to about 12m/40ft, where it conceals itself in crevices or under rocky ledges. It is most active at dusk and dawn, but its cryptic colouration and pattern make it hard to be seen by the small crustaceans that largely make up its diet. Young fish sometimes occur in large tidal pools on the lower shore among thick seaweed. The blennies use the same areas for spawning, with each male selecting a suitable crevice and encouraging one or more females to attach their adhesive eggs to the rock. The male then fertilizes the eggs and guards them until they hatch. The presence of tentacles above each eye makes identification of this species definitive.

Distribution: North-eastern Atlantic from Ireland to Morocco; also Mediterranean Sea. Found inland throughout mainland Portugal.
Habitat: Shallow coastal waters off rocky shores, from 3–30m/10–100ft.
Food: Mainly small crustaceans.
Size: 20cm/8in.
Breeding: Oviparous; sticky eggs are laid in a submerged rock crevice.
Status: Not listed by IUCN.

Identification: A stoutly built blenny with a long, high dorsal fin that is stiff and spiny at the front. It has a long anal fin and large pectoral fins, and a flattened, branched tentacle above each eye. It is typically yellowish brown with seven or more dark brown bars on each flank; spawning males are chocolate-brown. Guards fertilized eggs for a month until hatching.

Barred mudskipper

Periophthalmus argentilineatus

This is the most widespread and familiar of all the mudskippers – specialized gobies that live part of their life out of the water on the mudflats of brackish mangrove swamps. It uses its strong pectoral fins to jump, or skip, over the mud, often very rapidly, and may even climb on to the exposed roots and trunks of the mangroves, clinging to them with its pectoral sucker. Like all fish, it absorbs oxygen through its gills, but it also carries a supply of oxygenated water in its gill cavity for use when it is not submerged. It can also absorb oxygen through its skin, like a frog, provided it stays moist. Mudskippers are territorial fish, warning off rivals by displaying their colourful dorsal fins. The males also display to females in this fashion, before spawning in flooded, crater-like burrows in the mud.

Identification: An elongated fish with a large head and protruding, high-set eyes. It has powerful, limb-like pectoral fins. The pectoral fins are fused to form a sucker. Colour is generally brownish-grey with darker blotches or bands along the flanks. The dorsal fin has a conspicuous black band and may be edged in bright red.

Distribution: Southern Red Sea to South Africa: east to the Marianas and Samoa; north to Ryukyu Islands; south to western Australia and Oceania.
Habitat: Intertidal, brackish mudflats among estuarine mangroves, mainly when exposed at low tide.
Food: Marine worms, crustaceans and insects such as mosquito larvae.
Size: 15cm/6in.
Breeding: Oviparous; eggs laid and fertilized in specially excavated pools. Eggs and larvae guarded for about 50 days until the young are able leave the water.
Status: Not listed by IUCN.

Distribution: Eastern North Atlantic from Norway to Spain; parts of Mediterranean and Black Seas.
Habitat: Sandy and muddy shallows close to the shore, and estuaries, mainly from mid-tide level to about 20m/66ft.
Food: Small crustaceans and marine worms.
Size: 6cm/2.4in.
Breeding: Oviparous; female attaches eggs to the inside of an empty clam shell where they are fertilized by the male, who guards the eggs.
Status: Not listed by IUCN.

Sand goby

Pomatoschistus minutus

A very common fish of inshore sandy and muddy areas, the sand goby has a sleeker profile than most of its relatives and sometimes swims in small schools. Active by day, it feeds mainly on tiny crustaceans, such as copepods, amphipods and young shrimps, as well as marine worms. In turn, it is eaten by a wide variety of marine predators, including various species of cod and bass, as well as seabirds such as terns. It spawns in shallow waters in summer, the male luring the female into the empty shell of a bivalve mollusc to lay her eggs, but retreats to deeper waters in winter. Juvenile fish may enter the lower reaches of estuaries, but adults avoid brackish water.

Identification: A slender goby with high-set, prominent eyes. The two dorsal fins are well separated, the first with six rays. Rounded pectoral fins. Pelvic fins are fused into an oval sucker. Colour generally light sandy brown with dark dots and faint bars on the back. The male has a white-rimmed dark-blue or black spot on the first dorsal fin.

Butterfish (*Pholis gunnellus*): 25cm/10in
The skin of the almost eel-like butterfish is coated in slippery mucus, making it difficult to grip and accounting for its common name. Usually brown or greenish with blurred vertical bars on its flanks and about 12 white-ringed black spots on each side at the base of the dorsal fin. On rocky coasts on both sides of the North Atlantic, and Baltic, from intertidal pools to depths of about 100m/330ft. It is often found beneath stones or among seaweeds, where it feeds on small crustaceans and marine worms.

Black-rayed shrimp goby (*Stonogobiops nematodes*): 5cm/2in
One of several tropical coral reef gobies that live in association with a pistol shrimp or snapping prawn. The fish has an elongated, pale body with dark oblique bars, a bright yellow head and eye, and a long, black first dorsal fin ray. It lives in mated pairs, in a burrow excavated by the shrimp. The pair hover around the burrow entrance, and dive into the burrow at the first sign of danger.

Shanny (*Lipophrys pholis*): 18cm/7in
Common on rocky shores in the eastern North Atlantic and Mediterranean, the shanny is found in rockpools where it eats barnacles, small crabs, molluscs and seaweed. It can survive out of the water for some time, and uses its paired fins to move between rockpools. Its elongated body is usually a dull brown or greenish, with darker blotches, but its colour is variable.

Northern (shore) clingfish

Lepadogaster lepadogaster

This is the most common of the five genera of clingfish, with a total of eight species occurring in the north-east Atlantic. The powerful sucker beneath its body enables it to attach itself to rocks to resist the waves and tidal streams of rocky shores, although it is more frequently found in partly sheltered sites. It is always discovered clinging upside down beneath boulders and ledges, often among kelp growing low down on the shore. It uses the same habitats as breeding sites, attaching its eggs to the rocks. The adult fish guard the eggs, but despite this they are often eaten by sea slugs and other animals.

Identification: Rather flattened, tapered, scaleless body. Head long and triangular with a 'duck-billed' snout. It has a fringed flap in front of its large eyes. Long dorsal and anal fins set well back on the body. A sucker on the underside is formed partly from the pelvic fins. Body colour varies from pink to red, with two yellow-rimmed, deep blue spots on top of the head.

Distribution: Eastern North Atlantic from Britain to Morocco; also eastern and central Mediterranean Sea.
Habitat: Intertidal pools on rocky shores.
Food: Small crustaceans and other planktonic animals.
Size: 6cm/2.4in.
Breeding: Oviparous; eggs attached to the underside of boulders, where they are fertilized. They are guarded by a parent until they hatch.
Status: Not listed by IUCN.

DOLPHINS AND PORPOISES

These widely distributed, powerful marine mammals are social animals, highly adapted for an aquatic life. The body is streamlined and is totally lacking hair, the limbs are modified to form flippers and a broad tail is used for swimming. They are found all over the world in rivers, inshore waters and the open ocean. The young are born at sea.

Common dolphin

Delphinus delphis

With its markings, long beak and pointed flippers, the common dolphin has been the inspiration of artists and sculptors. It is an intelligent animal with a well-developed, hierarchical social structure, often occurring in schools several hundred strong. It is frequently encountered cavorting around boats. The common dolphin's behaviour includes many instances of individuals coming to the aid of injured companions. Dolphins are air-breathing mammals, but can dive for five minutes or more at depths down to several hundred metres as they search for fish and squid, which they often find using a sophisticated system of echo location.

Identification: Body slender and torpedo shaped. Slender, sickle-shaped dorsal fin. Long, slender beak and distinct forehead. Body colour variable: brownish-black or black upper parts; chest and belly cream-white; tan or yellowish hourglass pattern on flanks; black stripe from lower jaw to front of flipper and from beak to eye; flippers black, grey or white.

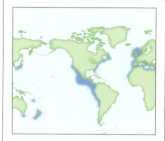

Distribution: Warm and temperate waters of Atlantic, Pacific and probably Indian oceans.
Habitat: Coastal and offshore waters.
Food: Fish, squid.
Size: 2.2m/7.2ft.
Breeding: One calf; calving period once every 2 years.
Status: Not listed by IUCN.

Killer whale

Orcinus orca

This is the largest member of the dolphin family Delphinidae, a robust animal with a rounded head and no beak. The huge, triangular dorsal fin of an adult male is 2m/6.5ft high, but is smaller and more curved in female and juveniles. The killer whale can travel at speeds of up to 65km/h/40mph – the fastest of all sea mammals – and can track prey by echo location. Its body markings help it to remain concealed in the shallow, turbid waters in which it often stalks. Killer whales sometimes cooperate when hunting. This species is known to live for up to 100 years.

Identification: Body robust but streamlined. Rounded head with no beak. Mouth with about 50 teeth. Large, paddle-shaped flippers. Dorsal fin tall and erect in males; smaller and sickle-shaped in females and juveniles. Body colour black on sides and back; white under head and chest extending up to flanks; white patch above and behind the eye.

Distribution: All oceans.
Habitat: Coastal and offshore waters.
Food: Fish, squid, marine mammals, such as seals, porpoises, walruses.
Size: Male 7m/23ft or more; female slightly smaller.
Breeding: One calf; calving period every 3–5 years.
Status: Listed as Lower Risk; Conservation Dependent by IUCN.

Common porpoise

Phocoena phocoena

Distribution: Panglobal in temperate regions of North Atlantic and North Pacific Oceans; occasionally also ventures into adjoining seas, especially Baltic and Black seas.
Habitat: Coastal waters.
Food: Fish, crustaceans.
Size: 1.8m/6ft.
Breeding: One calf; calving period once every 2 years.
Status: Listed as Vulnerable; Conservation Dependent.

The common or harbour porpoise is also known as the sea pig, due to the snorting noises it makes when it breathes. The smallest of all the cetaceans, the common porpoise also has a relatively short lifespan – rarely living for more than about 12 years. It is a gregarious species, usually found in groups, and although it lives close to land, it spends much of its time submerged, diving for up to six minutes at a time, and so is not frequently seen. Numbers of the common porpoise have been reduced by habitat loss and prey reduction as well as by pollution and fatal encounters with fishing nets, in which they become entangled.

Identification: Body small and robust with rounded head sloping to mouth. Small, slightly rounded flippers. Triangular, blunt-tipped dorsal fin. Body colour dark greyish on back; white or light grey on belly. Black lips; black invariably extends to cover part of the chin. Has a slightly upcurved mouth that gives impression of smiling.

Bottlenose dolphin (*Tursiops truncatus*): 3.9m/12.8ft
This familiar dolphin of zoos and films has a broad, high dorsal fin and a short, wide beak. Intelligent and sociable, bottlenose dolphins live in groups. It has an echo-location system that emits a range of sounds at different frequencies for analysing objects precisely. Found worldwide in temperate and tropical waters.

Irrawaddy dolphin (*Orcaella brevirostris*): 2.5m/8.2ft
This species has a rounded head, no beak, and a small, triangular dorsal fin with a rounded tip. It varies in colour from light and dark blue-grey to pale blue. Found in coastal waters, estuaries and some rivers from the Bay of Bengal to northern Australia, where it feeds on crustaceans, fish and squid. Although generally listed Data Deficient, it is Critically Endangered in some places.

Spectacled porpoise (*Phocoena dioptrica*): 2.3m/7.5ft
An inhabitant of the temperate and subarctic waters of the Southern Ocean, the species gets its common name from the black rims around its eyes. Sharply marked with black dorsal and lateral regions contrasting with a white abdomen. Little is known about its habits, although anchovies and crustaceans were found in the stomach contents of a dead individual.

Finless porpoise

Neophocaena phocaenoides

Easily distinguished from other porpoises by its prominent, humped forehead, beak-like mouth and lack of a dorsal fin, the finless porpoise is a quick and agile mammal, diving for short periods to catch fish and other marine creatures using its system of echo location. Although found all year throughout its range, in some areas the finless porpoise undertakes seasonal movements that are reflected by changes in abundance. Usually sighted near coasts, the species feeds on a variety of prey, including fish, shrimps and squid. Unfortunately, the finless porpoise is often found drowned, ensnared in fishing nets. In the Yangtze River in China, finless porpoises sometimes become caught on baited hooks that are intended for fish.

Identification: Body lacks dorsal fin. Humped forehead and mouth with beak-like appearance. Body colour light grey with paler abdomen; newborn calf mainly black.

Distribution: Indo-Pacific from Persian Gulf to Indonesia and Japan.
Habitat: Coastal and estuarine waters; also rivers.
Food: Fish, crustaceans, molluscs.
Size: 1.8m/6ft.
Breeding: One calf; calving period once every 1–2 years.
Status: Listed by IUCN as Data Deficient throughout range, except China where listed as Endangered.

TRUE SEALS

Seals are marine mammals that are adapted to live in the sea, although they all spend some part of their life ashore, moving about clumsily on their flippers when on land. True seals are distinguished from the similar-looking sea lions because they lack external ear pinnae, or structure, and their hind flippers cannot be brought forward in front of the body.

Leopard seal

Hydrurga leptonyx

Sleek, powerful and streamlined, the leopard seal is built for hunting a range of marine animals from penguins to krill – although it will also take carrion. It usually waits to take penguins under water as they move off the ice. It is one of the largest species of seal, with an almost reptilian-like head armed with massive jaws and large teeth. The leopard seal is known to be aggressive towards small boats and their occupants when approached too closely. Females give birth to young on the pack ice, but the males are not present at the time. The coats of young leopard seals are similar to those of adults. This species is known to live for 26 years or more.

Identification: Sleek and elongate seal. Neck well defined. Wide-gaping mouth with large canines and large post-canine teeth. Long foreflippers. Coat colour silver to grey above, lighter below, with a mixture of light and dark spots.

Distribution: Polar and subpolar waters of Southern Hemisphere.
Habitat: At the edge of the pack ice, on Antarctica and around some islands.
Food: Penguins, krill, seals, carrion.
Size: Females 3.3m/10.8ft; males slightly smaller.
Breeding: Little known of behaviour; pups born September–January.
Status: Not listed by IUCN.

Common/harbour seal

Phoca vitulina

The common seal is a non-migratory, usually solitary species with a wide distribution. There are five subspecies known, ranging from one found in the north-east Atlantic Ocean to one that lives in the north-west Pacific Ocean. The common seal frequently hauls out to sleep and bask on sheltered tidal rocky and sandy sites, and sometimes travels up rivers and is seen in lakes. It feeds mostly during the day, and can dive for up to 30 minutes in search of squid and other food, although dives are usually only of durations of five minutes or so. Pre-mating behaviour includes males and females blowing bubbles and biting each other's necks.

Identification: Body rounded and relatively short, with large head proportionately. The face somewhat dog-like in appearance. The flippers are short. The coat colour is highly variable, ranging from grey-white, brown or black overlaid with rings, blotches or spots in adults.

Distribution: Northern Atlantic and Pacific Oceans.
Habitat: Temperate and subarctic coastal waters.
Food: Crustaceans, squid, fish.
Size: Males 1.8m/6ft; females slightly smaller.
Breeding: Mating takes place in the water; typically one pup born per year.
Status: Not listed by IUCN.

Crabeater seal (*Lobodon carcinophagus*): 2.4m/8ft

These sleek seals with long muzzles are among the most abundant of all pinnipeds, with numbers estimated at about 12 million. Fast-moving and agile, the crabeater seal feeds on krill mainly at night, using its cusped, interlocking teeth to sieve the prey from the water. It occurs around pack ice in Antarctic seas. The coat is silver grey or brown.

Grey seal (*Halichoerus grypus*): 2.4m/8ft
This is a large seal found on both sides of the North Atlantic Ocean, usually around coasts or near ice floes. It has a long head and snout, resulting in its nickname of 'horsehead'. Males usually have a grey, dark brown or black coat with lighter blotches. Females are usually light tan or grey with dark patches and spots. Squid, fish and crustaceans form the bulk of the diet.

Weddell seal (*Leptonychotes weddellii*): 2.9m/9.5ft
This most southerly breeding seal has a circumpolar distribution in the Antarctic. Usually solitary, large numbers may gather around breathing holes in the ice outside the breeding season. A diver capable of spending over an hour under water searching for fish and other food. The Weddell seal has a small head and short muzzle; coat blue-grey above, whitish grey below.

Harp seal

Phoca groenlandica

The harp-shaped markings on the back, together with the dark head, make this species one of the more easy to recognize. The harp seal lives much of its life in the open sea on the edge of the pack ice, maintaining holes through which it dives for fish and crustaceans, sometimes descending to 274m/900ft. At mating time, in autumn, thousands of harp seals may congregate together. Males fight each other with their flippers and teeth to gain access to females.

Identification: Body plump. Head small and flattened. Large eyes set close together. Foreflippers small and pointed. Coat colour: background silvery white; two black bands joined over shoulders and extending over rear flanks forming harp-shaped pattern; head black. Pups camouflaged with white fur.

Distribution: Northern Atlantic and southern Arctic Oceans.
Habitat: Arctic and subarctic waters.
Food: Crabs and other invertebrates, fish.
Size: Males 1.9m (6.2ft); females slightly smaller.
Breeding: Usually one pup born per year; pups weaned at about 12 days.
Status: Not listed by IUCN.

Northern elephant seal

Mirounga angustirostris

Distribution: Mainly Pacific coast of North America.
Habitat: Coastal waters and shores.
Food: Molluscs such as squid, fish.
Size: Males 5m/16.4ft; females 3m/10ft.
Breeding: Gestation period about 1 year. Usually one pup born per year.
Status: Not listed by IUCN.

The largest pinniped in the Northern Hemisphere. Females usually weigh up to about 900kg/1,984lb, but the males can reach 2,300kg/5,070lb. Much of this weight is accounted for by a thick layer of blubber under the skin. Such a large source of blubber and meat became a ready target for commercial seal hunters, and numbers dwindled almost to extinction by the end of the 19th century, although they recovered after the animal was protected. The northern elephant seal makes regular long dives (an hour or more has been recorded) when hunting for food. Mating takes place on land, with each dominant male controlling access to a group of females, and threatening rival males by rearing up and displaying his proboscis. After the pup is weaned, it is left to fend for itself as the mother returns to sea.

Identification: Males, especially, are massive and often scarred from battles with rivals. Male has a large, trunk-like snout, or proboscis, at the front of the face. Foreflippers relatively small. Hind flippers lobed. Coat colour tan, brown, or greyish on top, lighter underneath.

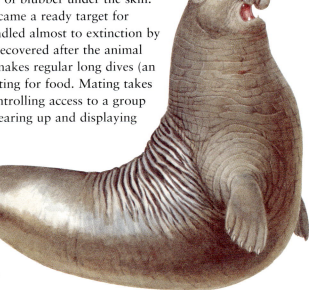

SEA LIONS, WALRUS AND SEA COWS

Sea lions are distinguished from true seals by having external ear pinnae, and because they can bring their hind flippers underneath the body. The walrus, the only member of its family, is a huge, tusked mammal found in the Arctic. The sea cows are slow-moving, plant-eating aquatic mammals such as dugongs and manatees that exist entirely in the water.

California sea lion

Zalophus californianus

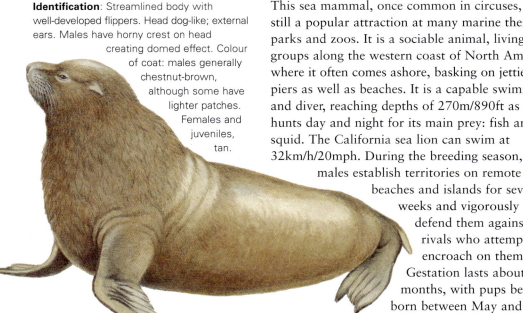

Identification: Streamlined body with well-developed flippers. Head dog-like; external ears. Males have horny crest on head creating domed effect. Colour of coat: males generally chestnut-brown, although some have lighter patches. Females and juveniles, tan.

This sea mammal, once common in circuses, is still a popular attraction at many marine theme parks and zoos. It is a sociable animal, living in groups along the western coast of North America, where it often comes ashore, basking on jetties and piers as well as beaches. It is a capable swimmer and diver, reaching depths of 270m/890ft as it hunts day and night for its main prey: fish and squid. The California sea lion can swim at 32km/h/20mph. During the breeding season, males establish territories on remote beaches and islands for several weeks and vigorously defend them against any rivals who attempt to encroach on them. Gestation lasts about 11 months, with pups being born between May and June.

Distribution: Pacific Ocean, from Baja California to Alaska; also Galapagos Islands.
Habitat: Breeds on coasts and islands.
Food: Fish, squid.
Size: Males 2.4m/8ft; females 1.8m/6ft.
Breeding: One pup, nursed for 5 or 6 months or up to 1 year. Pups and their mothers communicate in rookeries through vocalizations.
Status: Not listed by IUCN.

Northern fur seal

Callorhinus ursinus

The northern fur seal spends most of its life at sea, usually feeding at night, and rarely comes ashore except to breed. A northern fur seal pup may spend up to 22 months at sea before returning to land. At breeding time, nearly three-quarters of the species' total population (about 1 million individuals) congregate on the Pribilof Islands of St George and St Paul in the Bering Sea. After the pup is born, it is left for days at a time while the mother goes back to sea to hunt. On her return, she is able to locate her offspring by its unique call. Although no longer hunted in huge numbers, the northern fur seal is still caught in some places. It also becomes ensnared in trawl nets that have been set for fish.

Identification: Moderately built seal; males have stockier neck, shoulders and chest than females. Muzzle short and downcurved. Flippers long, wide and tapering. Fur on foreflippers extends only to 'wrist'. Coat colour: males grey, black, reddish or brown with yellow or grey frosting on mane; females silver-grey with cream or tan chest; pups born blackish with lighter chin and muzzle.

Distribution: North Pacific Ocean: Bering Sea to waters of northern Japan and southern California.
Habitat: Breeds on islands in range.
Food: Mainly squid, fish.
Size: Males 2.1m/7ft; females 1.5m/5ft.
Breeding: One small, black pup produced in June.
Status: Listed as Vulnerable by IUCN.

Walrus

Odobenus rosmarus

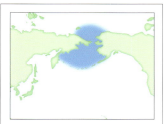

Distribution: Bering and Chukchi Seas in Arctic Ocean.
Habitat: Pack ice, rocky islands, open water.
Food: Molluscs, worms, fish, crustaceans; occasionally seals.
Size: Males 3.2m/10.5ft; females 2.7m/8.9ft. Tusks up to 55cm/21.6in in males.
Breeding: Females give birth to young every other year; one well-developed pup produced.
Status: Listed as lower risk by IUCN.

The gregarious walrus is an impressive creature, immediately recognizable by the pair of prominent tusks – larger in males – that extend downward from the mouth. The tusks have many uses. They are employed in defence, as tools to smash holes in the ice, as icepicks to help haul the animal out of the water, but primarily they are used to signal social position in the hierarchy. Those with the biggest tusks are the most dominant animals and can secure the most advantageous sites for mating. If challenged by another individual, however, a walrus' tusks can become fearsome stabbing weapons. Cumbersome on land, the walrus is an agile and strong swimmer. It feeds on a variety of mainly bottom-dwelling bivalve molluscs, which it senses with the 'moustache' of bristles around its mouth, and then digs out with its horny lips.

Identification: Massively built with short neck and squarish head. Flat, wide snout bears stiff, sensory bristles. Upper canines modified to form two tusks. Colour of skin brown to tawny, darker on chest and abdomen. Skin becomes pinker when exposed to sun.

Steller sea lion (*Eumetopias jubatus*): 2.8m/9ft
This species, the largest of the family Otariidae, or eared seals, overlaps its range with the California sea lion, but its larger size and lighter body colour help distinguish it. The Steller sea lion inhabits the North Pacific Ocean. After breeding, individuals disperse far and wide, sometimes travelling thousands of kilometres. The species is an opportunist feeder, hunting near the shore and over the continental shelf for fish and molluscs and, occasionally, seals.

Australian sea lion (*Neophoca cinerea*): 2.4m/8ft
This sea lion has a large head, tapering muzzle and small external ears. It breeds on sandy beaches on islands off the coast of western and southern Australia. A non-migratory species, it lives close to its breeding site in fairly large colonies, feeding on fish, squid and penguins. It is much less awkward out of water than many sea lion species, and may occur inland when rough weather forces it from the sea.

Dugong (*Dugong dugon*): 4m/13ft
Also known as the sea cow, the dugong bears a close resemblance to the manatees, although it can be told apart by its crescent-shaped tail fluke. The dugong can be found in the southwest Pacific Ocean, Indian Ocean and Red Sea – also in coastal shallows, where it grazes on sea grasses. It is classed as Vulnerable.

West Indian manatee

Trichechus manatus

This large, docile aquatic mammal is found in coastal areas and rivers. Together with three other species, including the dugong, it comprises the order Sirenia. Early mariners thought these creatures were mermaids – hence the name sirenians (sirens of the sea). Among mammals that never leave the water, sirenians are the only ones that exploit plants as their chief food source. The West Indian manatee only has foreflippers, the rear part of the body terminating in a broad, rounded tail fluke. It feeds by foraging for plants. The animal's eyesight is poor, but both its hearing the sense of touch are good. The manatee is a sociable animal, living in small groups. When not feeding it usually lies on the seabed, coming to the surface to take in air through its large nostrils. Newborn calves stay with their mothers for up to 18 months. In captivity, the species has been known to live for about 30 years.

Distribution: US coasts: mainly Florida, also west to Texas and north to Virginia. From coastal Central America to Brazil, South America.
Habitat: Shallow coastal waters, estuaries, rivers.
Food: Water hyacinths, sea grasses.
Size: Up to 4.3m/14ft.
Breeding: One calf produced every 2–5 years.
Status: Listed as Vulnerable by IUCN.

Identification: Heavy bodied with short neck and blunt, oblong head. Broad snout bears sensory bristles (vibrissae) on upper lip and nostrils are set far back. Foreflippers long with rudimentary nails. Tail fluke broad and rounded. Body colour grey-brown; hairless.

SHALLOW SEAS AND CORAL REEFS

The sunlit waters of the world's shallow seas can be phenomenally productive, and their proximity to shore means they are also among the best studied marine waters. Sadly, they are also the most polluted and exploited and all are susceptible to the effects of global climate change.

Temperate shallow seas teem with life, much of it microscopic – such as the algae and other plankton that give such waters their characteristic greenish tint. In contrast, the clear blue water of the tropics contain relatively little nutriment and can be relatively devoid of life. But if such waters are the marine equivalent of deserts, at their margins are great forests and swathes of pasture in the form of kelp and sea grass beds. These provide shelter and grazing for a diverse host of fish, mammals and invertebrates. In the tropics coral reefs may develop, and these rival tropical rainforests as the world's most biodiverse ecosystems. Each of these habitats supports its own characteristic assemblages of animals, and there are many species that cruise from one environment to another, turning each to different advantage – feeding, spawning, rearing young or seeking shelter from predators.

Above, left to right: Giant clam (Tridacna maxima)*; spotted eagle ray* (Aetobatus narinari)*; clown triggerfish* (Balistoides conspicillum).

Right: This shallow reef in Indonesia is clearly visible above the surface of the water.

JELLYFISH

These cnidarians consist of a bell-shaped, jelly-like structure enclosing internal organs. Suspended from the bell are the animal's tentacles, covered in stinging cells. Most jellyfish undergo a life cycle involving a free-swimming medusa stage and a sessile polyp stage. In scyphozoan jellies, often referred to as 'true jellyfish', the former is the dominant stage – and the state in which they are most likely to be seen.

Moon jelly
Aurelia aurita

Among the world's most common true jellyfish species, the moon jelly (or common jellyfish) often occurs in large numbers, drifting together on currents and tides. Each animal is a disc of jelly with a central mouth on the underside surrounded by four short arms. Inside the body is a branching system of channels – the jellyfish version of a digestive and vascular system – which distributes nutrients and oxygen around the body. There is no brain or central nervous system, just a loose network of nerves that coordinates responses to stimuli, such as light and the 'scent' of chemicals in the water. The moon jelly feeds mainly on particles that accumulate around the edges of the bell among the short tentacles. Moon jellies have only a very mild sting.

Identification: Saucer-shaped bell fringed with short, fine tentacles. Four frilly edged arms hanging down from bell. Four pinkish or purple, horseshoe-shaped reproductive organs visible inside the body among radiating channels of branched gut.

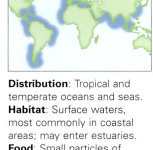

Distribution: Tropical and temperate oceans and seas.
Habitat: Surface waters, most commonly in coastal areas; may enter estuaries.
Food: Small particles of organic debris and plankton.
Size: Up to 50cm/20in across.
Breeding: Alternating sexual and asexual generations: medusae produce eggs and sperm. Fertilized egg develops into a larva, then a sessile polyp, which buds off more sexually reproducing medusae.
Status: Not listed by IUCN.

Sea wasp
Chironex fleckeri

Also known as the box jellyfish, this member of the class Cubozoa is probably the world's most venomous marine animal. Drifting in shallow coastal waters, and relatively inconspicuous due to its pale coloration, bathers unfortunate enough to bump into the sticky, stinging tentacles of this species may be injected with cardiotoxic and neurotoxic venom of enormous potency, often resulting in death. It is thought that the stinging cells are stimulated to 'fire' by sensing chemicals present on the skin. Such lethal and fast-acting venom is designed to immobilize quickly the jellyfish's natural prey of shrimps and other small creatures, thus avoiding damage to the sea wasp's delicate tissues caused by struggling food animals. Food is transferred to the mouth to be digested. Adult sea wasps spawn in shallow water near river mouths, and the fertilized eggs develop into polyps, which attach themselves to rocks. Later, small jellyfish develop from the polyps and migrate to the sea to grow.

Identification: The bell is cube- or box-shaped. In each corner there are between 10 and 60 stinging tentacles hanging down. Apart from a blue tinge, bell and tentacles are almost transparent.

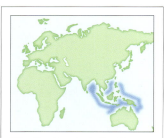

Distribution: Indo-Pacific Ocean, including northern Australian waters.
Habitat: Shallow waters at the edges of beaches.
Food: Small fish and crustaceans.
Size: Bell 20cm/8in across; tentacles up to 3m/10ft long.
Breeding: Alternating sexual and asexual generations: medusae produce eggs and sperm. Fertilized egg develops into a larva, then a sessile polyp, which buds off more sexually reproducing medusae.
Status: Not listed by IUCN.

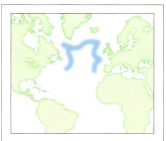

Distribution: North Atlantic.
Habitat: Floating in
surface waters.
Food: Small marine animals.
Size: Umbrella about
15cm/6in across.
Breeding: Alternating sexual
and asexual generations:
medusae produce eggs and
sperm. Fertilized egg
develops into a larva, then
a sessile polyp, which buds
off more sexually
reproducing medusae.
Status: Not listed by IUCN.

Blue jellyfish

Cyanea lamarckii

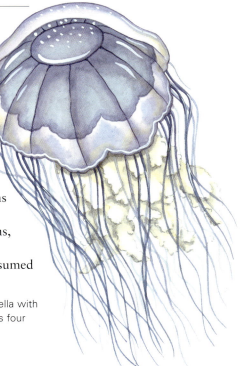

Floating majestically in the waters of the
North Atlantic Ocean, the medusa stage of the
blue jellyfish (*cyaneus* means 'dark blue' in
Latin) is an attractive species, but do not be
deceived as it can deliver powerful stings from its
numerous dangling tentacles. The animal's
umbrella is saucer-shaped, and a characteristic of
the species at this stage of its life cycle is that all
around the edge it is drawn out into about 32 lobes.
The tentacles, armed with nematocysts (stinging organs
found in jellyfish), hang down from the umbrella in
clusters. Inside the tentacles are four shorter, frilly arms,
which are used to transfer prey immobilized by the
nematocysts to the central mouth, where they are consumed
before being digested.

Identification: A blue-white jellyfish with a saucer-shaped umbrella with
32 peripheral lobes. Tentacles hang down in eight clusters. It has four
frilly arms, shorter than tentacles.

Upside-down jellyfish (*Cassiopea andromeda*):
30cm/12in across
This jellyfish is often mistaken for a large sea
anemone, which it resembles as it lies on the
bottom, mouth upward, with its frilly tentacles on
outstretched arms waving in the current created
by its pulsating bell. It is brown-yellow with
white streaks and spots. Found in lagoons and
intertidal shallows in the Indo-Pacific Ocean, the
upside-down jellyfish
feeds on plankton as
well as food produced
by the symbiotic algae in
its tissues. Can deliver a
painful sting.

Compass jellyfish (*Chrysaora hysoscella*):
30cm/12in across
The compass jellyfish has a large, saucer-shaped
umbrella with a pattern of radiating lines. The
edge of the lobed umbrella bears 24 trailing
tentacles armed with stinging cells and a series
of sense organs. The four mouth arms of this
species are shorter than the tentacles. Drifting
with the tides and currents, the compass
jellyfish is found in the Atlantic Ocean.

Sea wasp (*Carybdea alata*):
Up to 23cm/9in high
This Indo-Pacific species carries a powerful
venom in its stinging cells. It may come close to
shore in regular monthly swarms, when it can
pose a real hazard to bathers. The bell is rounded
in cross-section but flattened at the top, and is
typically taller than it is wide. Hanging from the
transparent bell are four pink or yellow-pink
tentacles, often marked with brown rings.

Stalked jellyfish

Haliclystus auricula

Unlike most jellyfish, in which the
medusa stage is a graceful, free-swimming
organism floating in the ocean currents, a
few species spend this part of their life
cycle firmly anchored in one place. One
such jellyfish is the stalked, or sessile,
jellyfish. It attaches itself to seagrasses,
seaweeds such as *Fucus* species or firmer
supports, such as rocks, by means of an
adhesive stalk. The
trumpet-shaped bell is
drawn out into
eight lobes,
each one
bearing a
cluster of
small, club-
like tentacles
that the
creature uses to catch
plankton and other small
marine animals. There are
also kidney-shaped anchors
found between the tentacles.
Although the stalked jellyfish
is fairly common throughout
its range, it is not a large
creature and so is often
overlooked, particularly when it
is not fully extended.

Distribution: North Pacific to
California; North Atlantic;
Baltic Sea.
Habitat: Attached to
seaweeds or rocks in
rockpools and
shallow water.
Food: Small
marine animals.
Size: Bell about
2.5cm/1in across; stalk
about 1.5cm/0.6in high.
Breeding: Alternating sexual
and asexual generations:
medusae produce eggs
and sperm.
Status: Not listed by IUCN.

Identification: Bell is a trumpet-
or flower-like cup extended into
eight lobes, each one bearing
club-like tentacles. Attaches to
substrate by an adhesive stalk.
Colour variable: mainly
translucent shades of green,
brown, orange or red.

GASTROPOD MOLLUSCS

Although well represented in terrestrial habitats by snails and slugs, more than two-thirds of all gastropod species are marine, and indeed the group's geological origins were exclusively marine. As demonstrated by many nudibranchs, not all gastropods have shells, but the species included here have some of the most distinctive and beautiful shells seen in this class of molluscs.

Purple topshell

Gibbula umbilicalis

Many of the marine gastropod molluscs known as topshells have attractively marked shells, and the purple topshell is no exception. As its common name suggests, the shell is characterized by purple stripes radiating down from the apex. On the underside is a large, round umbilicus (the point around which the whorls of the shell are coiled) – although a form without the umbilicus has also been recorded. The inner part of the shell is lined with a layer of mother-of-pearl. The purple topshell is a relatively small species that frequently occurs on sheltered rocky shores, where it grazes on seaweeds. This species is tolerant of brackish water conditions and it is also found in estuarine areas.

Identification: The shell has flattish whorls; overall, the shell is wider than it is high. Large umbilicus present on the underside of the shell. Colour dull grey-green with reddish-purple stripes radiating from the apex. It is not unusual for areas at the top of the shell to become abraded, revealing attractive mother-of-pearl surfaces.

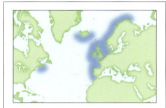

Distribution: North-eastern Atlantic; also from Nova Scotia to Maine.
Habitat: On seaweeds and rocks on the middle and lower shore; also estuaries.
Food: Seaweeds, mainly of the *Fucus* species.
Size: 1.5cm/0.6in high; 2.2cm/0.9in across.
Breeding: Reproduces sexually; eggs are shed and fertilized externally; larval phase follows.
Status: Not listed by IUCN.

Giant triton

Charonia tritonis

Identification: Elegant shell with rounded whorls, a tall spire and a large, flared lip. Colour of outer shell creamy with dark brown swirls and crescent-shaped blotches; shell aperture is orange-brown, alternating with cream around the lip.

The tritons are a group of gastropod molluscs that are widely distributed in warm, tropical oceans – mainly because their larvae have a long free-swimming period and may, therefore, travel great distances before settling. The giant triton is the largest member of the family, and is characterized by its tall, elegant spire, wide, flared lip and the beautiful markings on both the outside and the aperture of the shell. Because of its size and its appearance, this shell is very popular with collectors. The giant triton is also famous for being one of several species of gastropod shell that is used as a trumpet (once the apex has been cut off). In fact, it is also known as the trumpet triton. It is a carnivorous species found on coral reefs, where it will hunt other invertebrates.

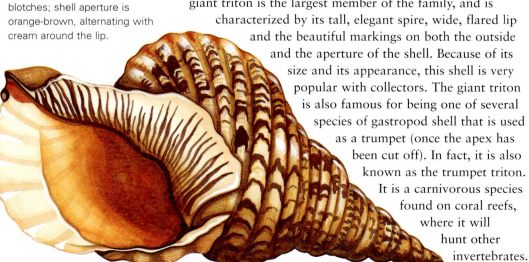

Distribution: Western part of Indo-Pacific Ocean.
Habitat: On reefs in water down to about 25m/82ft.
Food: Other molluscs and sea urchins.
Size: 40cm/15.75in high.
Breeding: Reproduces sexually; eggs are shed and fertilized externally; larval phase follows.
Status: Not listed by IUCN.

Eyed cowrie

Cypraea argus

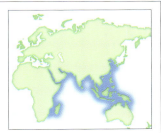

Distribution: Red Sea and East Africa, including Madagascar; widespread in shallow waters of Indo-Pacific.
Habitat: On reefs in water down to about 25m/82ft.
Food: Algae.
Size: 7.5cm/3in high.
Breeding: Reproduces sexually; eggs are shed and fertilized externally; larval phase follows.
Status: Not listed by IUCN.

Smooth, lustrous and beautifully and variously marked, the 200 or so species of cowrie – a member of the gastropod family Cypraeidae – have long been popular with shell collectors. In some cultures, cowrie shells have been used as money. Many have evocative common names that describe the type of markings seen on the shell. The eyed cowrie is a widespread species, with a heavy, somewhat elongated, cylindrical shell. Like other cowries, the underside of the shell has a long, narrow aperture, the edges of which are marked by prominent tooth-like projections. It is from this aperture that the animal extends its muscular foot, which it uses to move around the substrate. By day, the eyed cowrie hides among rocks and crevices on reefs, but at night it leaves its refuge to feed on algae.

Identification: Shell roughly cylindrical, the apex a flattened coil of about three whorls. The aperture is wider at the front than at the rear. Light brown or beige above with several darker, broad encircling bands; brown circles over upper surface and sides. Underside light brown with dark-brown bands either side of aperture.

Common topshell (*Calliostoma zizyphinum*): 2.5cm/1in high
Topshells come by their common name because of their resemblance to spinning tops – an old-fashioned children's toy. Also known as the painted topshell, this species has a straight-sided, conical shell that is approximately as wide at the base as it is high. It is either cream or brown in colour with pink or brown markings. It is found in Atlantic waters on rocks from the lower shore down to about 100m/330ft.

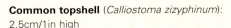

Geographer cone shell (*Conus geographicus*): 10cm/4in
All species of cone shell are predatory, injecting venom into their prey from an extensible proboscis or 'harpoon'. The geographer cone shell is one of the most venomous of all. The shell of this Indo-Pacific species has a low spire and a very large aperture. The colour of the shell is cream to light brown or blue-white with thin reticulation, and there are two or three encircling brown bands.

Rough star shell (*Astraea rugosa*): 5cm/2in
The thick, conical shell of this species is about as wide at the base as it is high. It is reddish-brown in colour and has about seven whorls with thorny ridges. In life, the aperture can be sealed by a spiral calcareous operculum, or cover. It is found on rocks from the lower shore downwards in the Mediterranean Sea and Atlantic Ocean.

Common whelk

Buccinum undatum

A common and widespread mollusc, the common whelk has long been a popular seafood snack, often sold cooked and ready to eat at seaside 'whelk stalls'. In life, the common whelk is a scavenger, feeding on virtually anything edible, including the remains of fish. The shell is thick, with a tall spire and a bulging body whorl. The shell does not have any distinctive colour patterning, but is clearly marked with growth ridges. Because of their size and durability, empty common whelk shells are a common sight on beaches. The shape and size of the common whelk's shell is ideally suited to soft-bodied hermit crabs, which frequently choose empty whelk shells as a 'home'. Another feature of the common whelk is sometimes seen on the seashore – the spongy, spherical mass of egg cases from which the embryos hatch.

Distribution: North-eastern Atlantic; also from Nova Scotia to Maine.
Habitat: On muddy and sandy bottoms in water down to about 100m/330ft.
Food: Virtually anything that is edible.
Size: 8cm/3in high.
Breeding: Reproduces sexually; eggs are shed and fertilized externally; larval phase follows.
Status: Not listed by IUCN.

Identification: Shell heavy and durable with a tall spire and an inflated body whorl. Shell is marked with growth lines and ribs. Short siphonal canal. Large, smooth aperture. Colour is pale brown, cream or grey with some darker-coloured bands.

BIVALVE MOLLUSCS

The members of the class Bivalvia described here include the heaviest of all molluscs, which can grow to a prodigious weight, as well as some smaller-growing species that swim by clapping the two valves of their shell together to expel water. In some species, particularly the giant clams, the shell's interior, known as the mantle, is very brightly coloured, and can dwarf the outer edges entirely when on display.

Giant clam

Tridacna maxima

Identification: Valves are massive and thick; elongated oval in shape with about five undulating ribs. Edges of valves are scalloped and interlocking. Interior of shell is white; exterior is usually encrusted with marine growths, such as barnacles, sponges and bryozoans.

Giant clams are the heaviest-known mollusc and specimens can reach a weight of 230kg/507lb, although this particular species is smaller than some of its relatives. Giant clams lie, hinge downwards, among coralline and rocky bottoms in shallow water. The gaping valves normally remain open to allow light to reach the symbiotic algae embedded in the clam's mantle tissues. The algae manufacture sugars and other nutrients on which the clam feeds, in addition to the food particles it obtains by filter feeding. The size and permanence of the clams mean that it is also an attractive site for other organisms to colonize, and the shells are often encrusted with marine growths. Giant clams are an important food source to humans in some regions, which has led to overfishing.

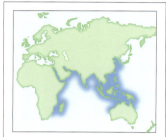

Distribution: Red Sea and East Africa, including Madagascar; widespread in shallow waters of Indo-Pacific.
Habitat: On coral reefs in shallow water, down to about 20m/65ft.
Food: Filter feeds on minute particles; also absorbs nutrients manufactured by symbiotic algae.
Size: Up to 1m/3.25ft across.
Breeding: Reproduces sexually; eggs are shed and fertilized externally; larval phase follows.
Status: Listed as Lower Risk by IUCN.

Fan mussel

Pinna fragilis

This species of mussel is a member of the group of bivalves known as pen shells. These are large, thin, paddle- or fan-shaped molluscs that live in the calm waters of warm and temperate oceans. They remain in an upright position with the narrow end of their shells attached to rocks by strands of tough byssus threads or by embedding themselves partly in supportive muddy sand or gravelly substrates. The fan mussel is a gregarious species, and once anchored by its byssus threads *en masse*, individual specimens are very difficult to dislodge. The gold-coloured byssus threads are very durable and fine in texture, and they were once used for weaving into fine garments for royalty – the 'Field of the Cloth of Gold' mentioned in the time of English king Henry VIII is believed to be a reference to him wearing a garment made of fan mussel byssus threads and byssus fabric is also mentioned in the Book of Genesis.

Identification: Valves are fan-shaped, equal in size and shape and smooth-edged. The outer surface bears concentric ribs and lines and the colour is brown.

Distribution: North-east Atlantic and northern Pacific from Nova Scotia to Maine; western Mediterranean.
Habitat: In sand or gravelly sea floors or on rocks, lower intertidal or subtidal regions.
Food: Minute food particles filtered from the water.
Size: 30cm/12in long.
Breeding: Sexes are separate; little else known.
Status: Not listed by IUCN.

Great scallop

Pecten maximus

Distribution: Patchy; north-eastern Atlantic and parts of the Mediterranean.
Habitat: Sand or gravelly ocean and sea floors at depths of 5–150m/16–490ft.
Food: Minute food particles filtered from the water, including algae, bacteria and other microscopic organic matter.
Size: 15cm/6in long.
Breeding: Hermaphrodite.
Status: Not listed by IUCN.

The shell of the great scallop is one of the best-known mollusc shells. As well as the food value of the animal living inside, the fluted shell is used for purposes ranging from ashtrays to dishes. The shell also features in the painting *The Birth of Venus* by Sandro Botticelli. Like other scallops, it has a fan-shaped shell characterized by two large 'ears', one on each side of the umbones, the often tapering, first part of the shell to be formed. When the great scallop gapes its shell, a fringe of sensory tentacles dotted with numerous small eyes can be seen. The scallop rests with the flatter of its two valves uppermost. When threatened, it claps the valves together, expelling water in a jet propulsion action, and swimming to safety.

Identification: Broad, fan-shaped valves; upper (left) valve flatter than lower (right) valve; 'ears' prominent; valves each bear about 16 conspicuous ribs; the edges of the valves are broadly serrated. Upper valve brownish-red; lower valve brownish-white.

Common saddle oyster (*Anomia ephippium*): 6cm/2.4in long
The brown-white upper (left) valve of this bivalve mollusc is thick, domed and scaly; often encrusted with marine organisms. The lower (right) valve is thin, flat and saddle-shaped.

Attaches to shells and rocks from the middle shore downwards in the Atlantic Ocean and Mediterranean Sea.

File shell (*Lima lima*): 2.5cm/1in long
This species has the characteristically asymmetrical shape of other file shells, although each valve is similar. It swims by clapping its valves together to expel water. Found in crevices in shallow Mediterranean waters.

Warty venus (*Venus verrucosa*): 5cm/2in
The thick-walled, robust shell is rounded and its exterior has concentric ridges bearing tubercles towards the anterior and posterior margins. Exterior is grey, white or yellow; interior is white. Found in sand or gravel from the lower shore to about 100m/328ft in the Atlantic Ocean and Mediterranean Sea.

Sand gaper (*Mya arenicola*): 15cm/6in
The sand gaper is one of a group of molluscs that typically burrow in soft, muddy substrates in cool waters. The off-white shell is elongate, with rough growth lines covering the exterior surface. Found from the lower shore and in estuaries down to 70m/230ft in Atlantic Ocean waters.

White hammer oyster

Malleus albus

The small family of hammer oysters gets its common name from the shape of the shells, which is reminiscent of a hammer or mallet. Indeed, when first encountered, the shell has sometimes been mistaken for a small, abandoned, growth-encrusted hammer. The narrow shell of the white hammer oyster is very elongated, with slightly wavy or undulating edges. The long 'hammerhead' part of the shell is formed by the very extended hinge lines. Like most other hammer oysters, this species lies partly buried in mud or sand in tropical intertidal reef areas. Its unusual shape means that the shell is popular with collectors.

Distribution: Red Sea and East Africa, including Madagascar; widespread in shallow waters of Indo-Pacific.
Habitat: In sand or mud in intertidal reef areas.
Food: Minute food particles filtered from the water.
Size: 15cm/6in long.
Breeding: Reproduces sexually by eggs and sperm.
Status: Not listed by IUCN.

Identification: Valves elongated and narrow with long, narrower wings at right angles, formed by extended hinge lines. Edges of shell undulating. Exterior of shell consists of overlapping lamellae. Colour of shell creamy-beige or dirty white with a blue-black muscle scar on the inner, nacreous surface.

CEPHALOPOD MOLLUSCS

Cephalopods are mainly active creatures with well-developed senses. They have cylindrical or sac-like bodies, and most species have no external shell – although some have a small internal shell. The foot is modified to form a ring of suckered tentacles surrounding the mouth, which itself has a parrot-like beak. Octopuses can swim by jet propulsion, forcing water rapidly from a siphon.

Greater blue-ringed octopus

Hapalochlaena lunulata

Identification: Slightly pointed, sac-like body covered with papillae. Mouth a horny beak surrounded by eight relatively short arms, each bearing two rows of suckers. Colour usually beige, dark brown or yellow; turns vivid yellow with electric blue rings if threatened.

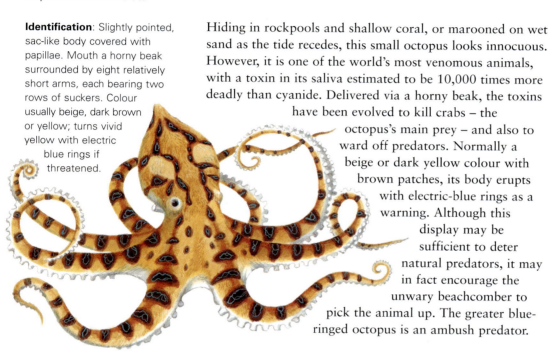

Hiding in rockpools and shallow coral, or marooned on wet sand as the tide recedes, this small octopus looks innocuous. However, it is one of the world's most venomous animals, with a toxin in its saliva estimated to be 10,000 times more deadly than cyanide. Delivered via a horny beak, the toxins have been evolved to kill crabs – the octopus's main prey – and also to ward off predators. Normally a beige or dark yellow colour with brown patches, its body erupts with electric-blue rings as a warning. Although this display may be sufficient to deter natural predators, it may in fact encourage the unwary beachcomber to pick the animal up. The greater blue-ringed octopus is an ambush predator.

Distribution: Western part of Indo-Pacific, particularly Japan to Australia.
Habitat: Hiding in crevices in tidal pools and among coral in shallow water down to about 20m/65ft.
Food: Mainly crabs; also shrimps and molluscs.
Size: 20cm/8in across arms.
Breeding: 50–100 eggs guarded by female until they hatch.
Status: Not listed by IUCN.

Common octopus

Octopus vulgaris

Identification: Sac-like body lacking a shell; warty upper surface. Eight arms, each bearing two rows of muscular suckers; arms relatively long. Colour variable: greenish or grey-brown, according to mood.

This eight-legged cephalopod is one of the most widespread of all marine animals. Highly territorial, it lurks in holes and under ledges waiting for its prey, which is captured at night with long, suckered arms. New research suggests that it 'stockpiles' supplies of bivalves and other sedentary food items near its lair, and sometimes it camouflages its lair with stones and shells. The octopus can change shape to squeeze into tiny gaps, and change colour according to its mood and surroundings. The common octopus has highly developed sense organs. In laboratories, it has been shown to have the ability to learn simple tasks and undertake problem solving.

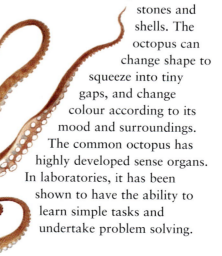

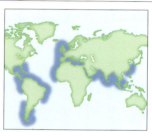

Distribution: Found worldwide in most temperate and tropical oceans and adjoining seas.
Habitat: In crevices of rocks close to the shore and in shallow water down to 200m/650ft.
Food: Crustaceans, molluscs and other marine animals.
Size: Up to 1m/3.25ft long.
Breeding: Internal fertilization; up to 500,000 eggs laid on substrate in shallow water and protected by female.
Status: Not listed by IUCN.

Paper nautilus

Argonauta argo

Distribution: Worldwide in tropical and subtropical oceans.
Habitat: Swimming in surface water as well as creeping on the bottom. Rarely found near shores.
Food: Plankton and other small organisms.
Size: Female up to 20cm/8in; male 1cm/0.4in. Shell up to 30cm/12in.
Breeding: Internal fertilization; eggs carried by the female, protected within her shell until they hatch.
Status: Not listed by IUCN.

Despite its common name, *Argonauta* is not a nautiloid, but is a member of the order Octopoda. The female is about 20 times larger than the male. Her body is partly encased in a thin, coiled shell, which she holds tightly using two modified arms with flattened ends. During reproduction, the male inserts his sperm into the female's pouch with a modified arm called a hectocotylus. The fertilized eggs are protected inside the shell as they develop. Due to its fairly small size and pelagic habits, the paper nautilus is rarely seen by seashore visitors, although it is not especially rare. The shell, sometimes washed ashore – usually without its attendant female – is prized by collectors.

Identification: Female has sac-like body bearing eight arms, two of which are modified and have spatulate ends for gripping shell. Shell is coiled, laterally compressed, and has a narrow keel and numerous sharp nodules. Male is much smaller and lacks shell. Colour and pattern of animal variable: from silver-white to grey, red or blue. Shell white.

Long-finned squid (*Loligo vulgaris*): 50cm/20in
The pink or whitish body of this squid has brown mottling on the upper surface. Wide, conspicuous fins running halfway along the body and joined at the end form a spearhead shape. The head bears eight short arms, and two long, retractable, suckered tentacles for capturing prey. Found in shallow and deeper water in the Atlantic Ocean.

Lesser octopus (*Eledone cirrhosa*): 50cm/20in
This octopus is normally red-brown above and paler below, but it can rapidly change colour to match its surroundings. The lesser octopus has only one row of suckers on each of its eight, slender arms. The body is warty in appearance. Found among rocks and in crevices in the Atlantic Ocean from the lower shore downwards, where it lies in wait for prey.

Caribbean reef octopus (*Octopus briareus*): 60cm/24in
This species is blue-green, with mottled brown markings. It is solitary and, like other octopuses, it can rapidly change colour to match its surroundings. It feeds at night on crustaceans, other molluscs and small fish, which it hunts on reefs and seagrass beds. Found in warm, shallow waters of the western Atlantic Ocean.

Common cuttlefish

Sepia officinalis

The cuttlefish are active, swimming molluscs with a reduced, internal shell (the 'cuttlebone' often offered to cagebirds). The common cuttlefish has a head bearing eight short, suckered arms and two long tentacles; these surround a mouth armed with a horny beak. Food is grabbed in the tentacles and transferred by the arms to the mouth. Large eyes help it detect prey and navigate with speed and precision. Swimming is achieved by the rippling action of lateral fins that run along each side of the body. On the underside of the body is a large funnel through which water is expelled to help the cuttlefish shoot rapidly backwards to escape predators. It can also quickly change colour to help it blend in with its surroundings.

Identification: Flattened, oval, cylindrical body bearing lateral fins. Large head bears eight short arms and two long, suckered tentacles with spatulate pads that can be extended and retracted; eyes large and well developed. Colour variable: often brown or black lateral stripes or mottled pattern over cream or off-white ground colour, but colour and pattern may be rapidly changed at will.

Distribution: North-eastern Atlantic including North Sea down to equatorial Africa; Mediterranean Sea.
Habitat: Swimming or lying on bottom, often near shore.
Food: Molluscs, fish, crabs and other crustaceans.
Size: 30cm/12in.
Breeding: Internal fertilization; egg masses protected by female.
Status: Not listed by IUCN.

SHRIMPS, PRAWNS AND LOBSTERS

The protective exoskeleton, which is common to all animals in the phylum Crustacea, must be shed and replaced to allow for growth. Their abundance and good-tasting flesh means that several of the species described here – particularly those of temperate, muddy waters – are important commercial species.

Spiny lobster

Palinurus elephas

Identification: Typical elongated lobster shape with carapace covered in tiny, hair-like spines, and segmented, flexible abdomen terminating in broad telson (tail). The species is notable for its long, stout antennae. Lacks large, crushing pincers. Predominantly red-brown in colour.

This heavily armoured, bottom-dwelling crustacean is distinguished by its extremely long, flexible antennae, which it uses to locate food by touch and scent. Its pincers are very small and not obvious, although the limbs that carry them are slightly stouter than its walking legs. The pincers are not strong enough to crush hard-shelled prey, so the spiny lobster feeds on soft-bodied animals, such as starfish and marine worms. It frequently hunts on the open seabed, but retreats to crevices if threatened. These lobsters are heavily fished in some areas, and this has made them increasingly scarce.

Distribution: North-eastern Atlantic Ocean and Mediterranean Sea.
Habitat: Rocky seabeds below the intertidal zone, mostly below 20m/66ft.
Food: Worms, small crabs, starfish, soft-bodied molluscs and dead animals.
Size: 50cm/20in.
Breeding: Females carry eggs for 5–9 months until they hatch. The larvae drift in the plankton for many weeks before settling on the seabed.
Status: Not listed by IUCN.

Scampi

Nephrops norvegicus

The well-armed scampi, Dublin Bay prawn or Norway lobster is an opportunist predator that spends much of the day in a burrow on a soft, muddy seabed, particularly in shallow, sunlit water. At night it emerges to hunt for prey, especially other crustaceans, such as prawns and small crabs. Having a relatively heavy, calcified skeleton, it lives mainly on the bottom, but it can swim if necessary. It can also use its broad tail-fan to propel itself rapidly through the water to escape from enemies. It is heavily fished to be peeled and prepared as scampi, or served whole as langoustine.

Identification: A slender, elegant, bright orange and white lobster with large black eyes, two pairs of antennae – one pair being longer than its body – and slim, though quite powerful, spiny pincers. It also has small claws or pincers on the second and third pairs of legs. It is reasonably heavily armoured and has a broad tail-fan (or telson).

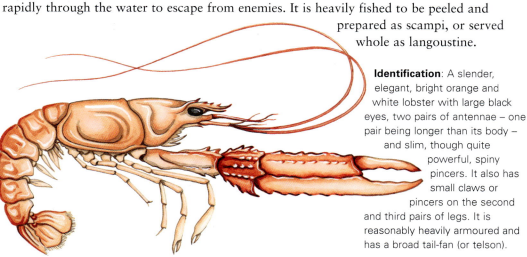

Distribution: North-eastern Atlantic Ocean, from Iceland to Morocco, and in the Mediterranean Sea
Habitat: Soft seabeds down to 20–800m/66–2,625ft.
Food: Other crustaceans, molluscs, marine worms, starfish, sea urchins.
Size: Up to 25cm/10in.
Breeding: Fertilized eggs are carried under the female's abdomen for 8–9 months, during which time females tend to stay in their burrows. They emerge to allow their planktonic larvae to hatch and disperse in the currents.
Status: Not listed by IUCN.

Broad-clawed porcelain crab

Porcellana platycheles

Although this species looks like a very hairy crab in its basic shape, it is, like all porcelain crabs, more closely related to the squat lobsters. Like the latter, it has a pair of long antennae and only three functioning pairs of walking legs. It does have a fourth pair of legs, but they are small and usually tucked out of sight. It walks sideways, however, like the true crabs – an adaptation that allows it to move quite fast when necessary. Its flattened body is perfect for hiding beneath rocks, which it grips with the claws on its legs. It uses the hairs on its claws to filter edible debris from the the water, wiping them through its mouthparts to feed.

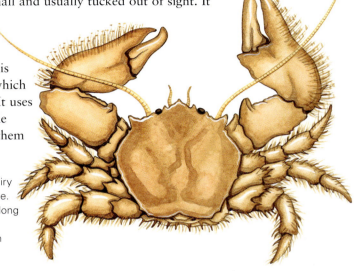

Distribution: North-eastern Atlantic from Shetland to the Canaries; Mediterranean Sea.
Habitat: Sheltered muddy, stony shores down to a few metres.
Food: Edible detritus filtered from the water.
Size: Carapace up to 1.5cm/0.6in long.
Breeding: Females carry eggs beneath their bodies until they hatch into planktonic larvae, which then disperse in the currents before settling to metamorphose into adult form.
Status: Not listed by IUCN.

Identification: A small, conspicuously hairy looking crab with an almost round carapace. Large, flattened, hairy claws, one pair of long antennae and only three visible pairs of walking legs. Usually greyish-brown on top, and a dirty yellowish-white below.

Slipper lobster (*Parribacus antarcticus*): up to 25cm/10in
This species lives on Indo-Pacific coral reefs. Its legs are hidden beneath a broad, flattened carapace with shovel-like extensions that are actually modified antennae. Its eyes are mounted on top of its carapace. During the day, it hides in crevices, but at night it emerges to forage over the reef for prey, such as shellfish, worms and fish. It also scavenges dead animals.

Painted dancing shrimp (*Hymenocera picta*): 6cm/2.4in
This beautiful coral reef shrimp from the Pacific Ocean is white with pale red-brown blotches that resemble patches of wet watercolour paint. Its body cuticle and claws are extended into flared plates that the shrimp uses in a dancing display. It lives in pairs, hiding in crevices by day and slipping out at night to hunt. It preys on starfish, flipping them on to their backs and eating them alive.

Camel (candy) shrimp (*Rhynchocinetes durbanensis*): 4cm/1.6in
Often found living inside large sponges, this Indo-Pacific shrimp is transparent with a dazzling pattern of red and white lines and dots, and a long, toothed, moveable rostrum that is usually held up at an angle. It prefers to congregate in coral crevices or under overhangs, and feeds on invertebrates such as sea anemones.

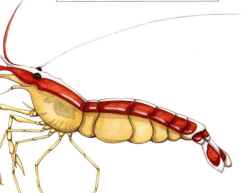

Scarlet skunk cleaner shrimp

Lysmata amboinensis

This fragile-looking tropical shrimp feeds mainly on parasites and dead skin tissue and scales picked from the bodies of reef fish. The fish recognize that this is a useful service, and make deliberate visits to the 'cleaning stations' where the shrimps live and ply their trade. Several shrimps often work together, for unlike some species – such as the banded coral shrimp – they are not aggressively territorial. They will remove parasites from fish that would normally pose a threat to small crustaceans, but sometimes fall victim to fish that are more concerned with finding a meal than maintaining skin hygiene.

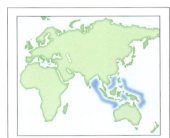

Distribution: Indo-Pacific.
Habitat: Coral reefs.
Food: Parasites and dead skin picked from other fish, plus detritus and planktonic organisms from the water.
Size: Up to 8cm/3.2in.
Breeding: Females carry green eggs beneath their bodies; these hatch into tiny transparent larvae that disperse over the reef.
Status: Not listed by IUCN.

Identification: A delicate shrimp with slender white pincers, six long, white antennae and black eyes. Very colourful: yellow flanks and legs and a scarlet back, with a white 'skunk stripe' running from between the eyes to the base of the tail. The tail fan is scarlet with white patches.

CRABS

Most of us tend to be more familiar with the types of crabs we seeing scuttling around our seashores and swimming in rockpools at low tide. Many of these same crustaceans, however, are also found in sub-littoral habitats, including several of the species shown here. Some of these shallow-water crabs tend to hunt for food, or seek shelter from predators, by digging deep into the sand and gravel of the sea bed.

Shame-faced crab

Calappa granulata

Identification: Rounded crab with ridged carapace, short legs and broad, flattened pincers, each with a crest like a cock's comb. Very light brown in colour with reddish spots.

One of the most common crabs in the Mediterranean, this burrowing species is named for the way it holds its very broad, crested pincers over its 'facial' region, with just its eyes peeping over. One of the pincers is specialized for breaking into the shells of the clams and cockles that form much of its food, with a blunt projection on the mobile part of the pincer that acts against the basal part of the pincer like a nutcracker. It finds its prey by digging through the sand or mud, and spends much of its time wholly or partly buried in the seabed. If alarmed, it retracts both its pincers and legs to form a tight, armoured ball.

Distribution: Eastern Atlantic from Bay of Biscay to Western Sahara including Azores, Madeira, Canaries, Cape Verde Is.; also Mediterranean Sea.
Habitat: Soft seabeds from 10–400m/33–1,300ft.
Food: Small burrowing animals, such as clams, and other molluscs; also scavenges.
Size: Carapace about 11cm/4.3in wide.
Breeding: Females carry eggs beneath their bodies; these hatch into planktonic larvae, which are dispersed by tides and currents to new habitats.
Status: Not listed by IUCN.

Decorator crab

Camposcia retusa

Identification: Long-legged, short-clawed crab with a narrow, pointed carapace and twin horns projecting between its black, teardrop-shaped eyes. Often found in coral rubble area. Very variable camouflage of sponges, algae, seaweed and other organisms and debris attached to its carapace and legs by a dense covering of hooked hairs.

Almost impossible to detect until it moves, this small spider crab conceals its identity by 'decorating' itself with encrusting animals, algae and debris. It uses its pincers to nip off bits of living sponges and seaweed, or selects suitable shell fragments, and then sticks them firmly on to the fine, hooked hairs that cover its body and legs. The attached sponges and algae often continue to grow, and tiny animals frequently settle among them to create a whole mobile community. Only the black eyes and tips of the pincers remain undecorated, enabling the crab to find and then deal with its food.

Distribution: Coral seas of the western Pacific and Indian Oceans.
Habitat: Sandy places on coral reefs, such as lagoons and among coral rubble.
Food: Small animals as well as carrion.
Size: About 5cm/2in wide.
Breeding: Females carry eggs that hatch into planktonic larvae; these are dispersed over the reefs by water currents before settling.
Status: Not listed by IUCN.

Marbled rock crab

Pachygrapsus marmoratus

Distribution: North-eastern Atlantic Ocean from Brittany to the Canaries; Mediterranean and Black Seas.
Habitat: Rocky shores and adjacent shallow, rocky seabeds. Also under stones on sandy mud in estuaries and lagoons.
Food: Omnivorous.
Size: About 8cm/3in wide; carapace about 3.8cm/1.5in wide.
Breeding: Female carries eggs beneath her body; these hatch into swimming larvae that drift with the plankton.
Status: Listed by IUCN as Vulnerable in certain regions.

This species is the most common shore crab found in southern Europe. It is also known as the running crab because of its ability to run rapidly over rocks and then slip quickly into tight cracks to escape from predators. It is able to survive for long periods out of the water by carrying a supply of oxygenated water in its gill cavity, and takes the opportunity to scavenge over the shoreline at low tide looking for dead and damaged molluscs and other edible material stranded on the shore. These crabs are often caught and eaten by land predators, such as introduced American mink.

Identification: A usually dark, violet-brown or green crab, often with a marbled pattern. Fairly small pincers – larger on the male – flattened legs and an almost square, convex carapace. The front edge between the eyes is virtually straight, but there are three pointed teeth on each side.

Edible crab (*Cancer pagurus*): 14cm/5.5in
Carapace reddish-brown in colour and broadly oval and with approximately nine indentations on the edge at each side giving a 'pie-crust' appearance. Primarily a scavenger, but it will also prey on molluscs that are crushed by the crab's massive, black-tipped claws. Found from the shore down to 90m/300ft in the Atlantic Ocean.

Red-and-white painted crab (*Lophozozymus pictor*): up to 20cm/8in
Deep red or orange with white spots, this thick-bodied crab is common on coral reefs, where it shelters in crevices between the coral heads or beneath broken slabs of coral rock. It feeds on marine algae and small planktonic organisms, as well as scavenging for debris. Its flesh can be extremely poisonous, causing paralytic shellfish poisoning (PSP), because the crab feeds on molluscs that accumulate toxins produced by certain planktonic organisms.

Pea crab (*Pinnotheres pisum*): up to 2cm/0.8in
Female pea crabs live in the mantle cavities of bivalve molluscs, such as clams, as well as starfishes and sea squirts. The variable Atlantic and Mediterranean species favours mussels and oysters, where it feeds on material trapped by the shellfish. Several may live in one mussel. The smaller males are free-swimming, but enter the molluscs to mate.

Lissa chiragra

Found in shallow waters of the Mediterranean Sea, this small spider crab is frequently disguised from predators by the encrusting organisms that cover its carapace. The carapace itself is pear shaped and sculpted with nodular growths and has two central humps on the dorsal surface. The nodular pattern is continued on to the legs. This species frequently hides from view among other organisms on the seabed.

Distribution: Mediterranean Sea and eastern Atlantic Ocean off Portugal.
Habitat: Mainly coral beds at depths of 14–90m/46–295ft; also muddy sea floors.
Food: Various small marine creatures.
Size: Carapace about 4.5cm/1.75in long.
Breeding: Females carry eggs beneath their bodies, which hatch into planktonic larvae that are dispersed by tides and currents.
Status: Not listed by IUCN.

Identification: A small spider crab with a roughly triangular carapace (less wide than it is long), ornamented with a complex pattern of nodules and spines. The legs are similarly ornate. Two rostral spines appear fused together at the top to form a 'T' shape. The colour is rich orange-red.

STARFISH

The members of this major group of echinoderms do not have a central processing centre, or brain. Instead, a series of nerves running down the rays, or arms, coordinates the animal's movements and actions. Despite their attractive, often delicate appearance, many are extremely capable hunters, and may engulf prey almost as large as themselves. Some species even cannibalize other starfish.

Purple starfish

Henricia oculata

Also known as the bloody Henry starfish, this colourful species has a very stiff body with blunt, skin-covered spines on its upper surface. It often lives in kelp forests below the low-tide mark, but it also thrives in very exposed rocky sites, such as tide races, where the currents are powerful enough to sweep many animals away. The fast water flow carries a large amount of food material with it, and the starfish exploits this by using its sticky tube feet to gather edible items from the water. It also attacks and eats encrusting animals such as sponges.

Identification: A rigid, five-armed starfish with a rough skin, like sandpaper. The colour is very variable: from purple to red, brown or yellow. The outer portions of the arms are sometimes paler than the inner parts and the central disc.

Distribution: North-eastern and north-west Atlantic Ocean.
Habitat: Rocky or sandy seabeds on open coasts with plenty of water movement, at depths down to 100m/330ft.
Food: Encrusting animals, including sponges and hydroids, as well as edible particles suspended in the water.
Size: Up to 20cm/8in.
Breeding: Females produce up to 1,000 eggs that develop into miniature starfish without going through a larval stage.
Status: Not listed by IUCN.

Sand-burrowing starfish

Astropecten irregularis

As its common name indicates, this starfish spends much of its time partly hidden in the sediment, burrowing into the sand with its pointed, suckerless tube feet. It rarely buries itself completely, but uses the tips of its arms to maintain contact with the surface. It often emerges to feed at dawn or dusk, digging into the sand to find small molluscs and crustaceans. It does not feed by turning its stomach inside out over its victims as many starfish do; instead it swallows them whole. It is easily dislodged by heavy wave action and is sometimes stranded on beaches after storms.

Identification: A flattened species with five short, tapering arms and a grainy upper surface. There is a double series of large marginal plates at the edge of each arm, with long spines extending from the upper plates. The colour is variable, from sandy to yellowish-orange, pink or brown. It often has a purple spot at the centre of the disc, and purple tips to each arm.

Distribution: North-eastern Atlantic: Norway to Cape Verde Islands, Mediterranean Sea. Also north-west Atlantic.
Habitat: Soft seabeds of sand or muddy sand, from low water to depths of about 1,000m/3,280ft.
Food: Small burrowing molluscs and crustaceans.
Size: Up to 20cm/8in.
Breeding: Eggs and sperm are released into the water where fertilization takes place. Fertilized eggs develop into planktonic larvae that are dispersed by ocean currents.
Status: Not listed by IUCN.

Crown-of-thorns starfish

Acanthaster planci

Distribution: Indo-Pacific Ocean, including Red Sea.
Habitat: Coral reefs.
Food: Coral polyps.
Size: Up to 50cm/ 20in across.
Breeding: Female produces up to 20 million eggs each summer, which are fertilized in the water. They hatch into planktonic larvae that drift in the ocean for several weeks before settling and changing into their adult form.
Status: Not listed by IUCN.

Notorious for its destructive impact on coral reefs – particularly the Great Barrier Reef along the east coast of Australia – the crown-of-thorns starfish is a voracious predator that feeds exclusively on live corals, usually by night. Settling on the reef, it everts its stomach over a coral head so its digestive juices can break down the soft tissues, allowing the starfish to ingest them. Meanwhile, the scent of semi-digested coral disperses through the water, attracting other starfish. Each individual eats about its own diameter of coral each night, leaving bare, white coral rock, but they can multiply to plague numbers and denude huge areas of coral. After a few years these plagues subside, and the reef usually recovers.

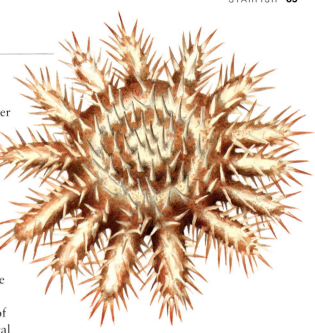

Identification: Very large, orange to purple-brown, with 12–23 arms and a broad, central disc covered in stout, dark spines. The spines are coated in toxic mucus that causes intense pain and inflammation, followed by itching that can last for a week.

Seven-armed starfish (*Luidia ciliaris*): 40cm/16in
Distinguished by its seven long arms that taper only at the ends, and its conspicuous fringe of stiff white spines, this large orange-brown or reddish starfish preys mainly on other starfish and brittlestars. It often lies partly buried in gravel, but can move quickly on its long, tapering tube feet in pursuit of its prey. It lives on sandy sediments or rocks from the lower shore to depths of about 400m/1,300ft in the Atlantic Ocean and Mediterranean Sea.

Six-armed Luzon sea star

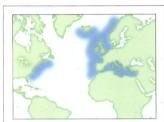

(*Echinaster luzonicus*): 15cm/6in
A tropical reef species of the western Pacific Ocean, this long-armed starfish may be orange, red, brown, pink or even yellow, often with darker tips. Like many starfish, it can regenerate lost limbs, but it may multiply by voluntarily shedding a limb, which then grows into a new individual. It also reproduces sexually, shedding eggs and sperm into the water.

Purple sun star (*Solaster endeca*): 40cm/16in
Although often purple, the colour of this rough-skinned starfish is more variable than the name suggests and ranges from pale yellow to bright red. It usually has nine triangular arms, but may have from 7 to 13. It occurs in the north Atlantic, on gravelly or rocky bottoms. It is a voracious predator, eating other starfish as well as bivalve molluscs, which it pulls apart with its tube feet before everting its stomach over the animal.

Cushion star

Asterina gibbosa

This stumpy coastal starfish usually lives beneath stones and boulders by day. It emerges at dusk to feed on organic debris in the sand or gravel. It also scavenges from the carcasses of dead animals – including those of its own kind. Like many other starfish, it digests large food items externally, by everting its stomach lining to smother the food with digestive juices. Unusually, it places its well-developed eggs in a sheltered site rather than shedding them into open water, and the eggs hatch as miniature starfish instead of planktonic larvae.

Distribution: North-eastern and north-west Atlantic Ocean and Mediterranean Sea.
Habitat: In rockpools and under rocks and stones on the lower shore, on sheltered and semi-exposed rocky coasts, to depths of 100m/330ft.
Food: Microorganisms, decaying seaweeds and dead invertebrates.
Size: Up to 5cm/2in.
Breeding: Individuals are male when young, but turn into females with age. These lay up to 1,000 orange eggs beneath stones. The eggs hatch into tiny starfish, without passing through a larval stage.
Status: Not listed by IUCN.

Identification: Short, broad arms with rounded tips. Upper surface with short, stiff, often orange, spines. Colour variable: most are blue-grey, green or orange, but some mottled. Specimens from deeper water paler.

MACKEREL SHARKS

Mackerel sharks comprise about 16 species of varied appearance and lifestyle. Among the seven families in the order are some of the best-known of all sharks, including the great white and the mako. However, there are also some rarely seen species, such as the goblin shark and the megamouth. As a group, mackerel sharks are found in most of the world's oceans at depths ranging from shallow water to deep water.

Great white shark

Carcharodon carcharias

The great white, the largest predatory shark, has a reputation as a ruthless killer. Attacks on humans may occur because the shark mistakes swimmers for its natural food of seals or turtles. When a great white attacks, it usually lunges up from below, delivering a lightning-fast bite before pulling back. Once the prey has been rendered helpless, it returns to shear off chunks with its triangular, serrated teeth. Smaller prey may be taken whole. After a large meal, the shark may not feed again for several weeks. Wide-ranging and usually solitary, the great white breeds at about 10 to 12 years, producing live young after a gestation of about 12 months.

Identification: Torpedo-like body with pointed, conical snout. Mouth bears large (7.5cm/3in), serrated teeth in both jaws. Well-developed lateral keels on caudal peduncle. Upper part of body blue-grey or brownish, lower part white. Large caudal (tail), dorsal and pectoral fins; pectoral fins with blackish tips on underside.

Distribution: Temperate and tropical oceans worldwide.
Habitat: One of the more coastal mackerel sharks, but also found in open water to depths of 1,300m/4,260ft.
Food: Fish, turtles, seabirds, seals, sealions, dolphins.
Size: Up to 6m/20ft, but occasionally larger.
Breeding: Two to ten young; livebearer.
Status: Listed as Vulnerable by IUCN.

Basking shark

Cetorhinus maximus

This giant, the second-largest species of shark, gets its common name from its habit of cruising leisurely at the surface of the water in summer as if sunbathing, although it may also swim at depths of about 200m/650ft. Basking sharks may be found alone, in pairs or in groups. Despite its size, the basking shark feeds solely on tiny plankton, which it filters from the water using comb-like structures on its gill arches. To help it obtain sufficient food, the basking shark swims along at about 5km/h/3mph with its huge mouth wide open, taking in thousands of litres of water per hour.

Identification: Huge, with pointed snout and cavernous mouth. Gill slits very large and prominent. Large caudal fin with longer upper lobe. Has small teeth, but these used for mating, not feeding. Body variably coloured blackish, brown or blue on back, becoming pale towards belly. Fins prized for making shark-fin soup.

Distribution: Temperate oceans worldwide. Common along Pacific coasts of US during winter months.
Habitat: Highly migratory species. Found inshore in surface waters, but possibly also deeper water.
Food: Plankton.
Size: 10m/33ft, but occasionally up to 15m/50ft.
Breeding: Little known about breeding behaviour; it may produce up to six young in a litter; livebearer.
Status: Listed by IUCN as Vulnerable to Endangered.

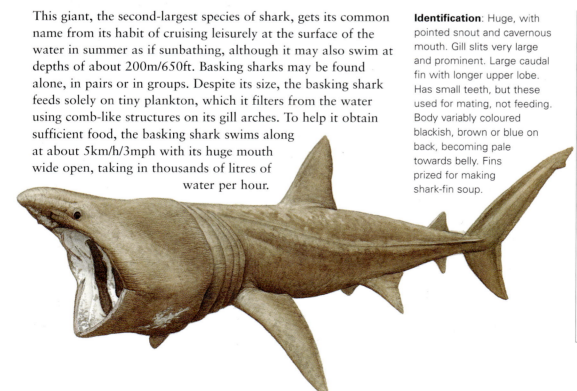

Common thresher shark

Alopias vulpinus

Distribution: Widely distributed continental shelf species. Especially prominent along eastern and south-western coasts of Australia.
Habitat: Deep coastal waters to open surface waters.
Food: Fish, squid, crustaceans.
Size: 6m/20ft.
Breeding: Two to seven young; livebearer.
Status: Probably declining in numbers.

The common thresher is the largest of the three species of thresher sharks. All three are recognizable by the upper lobe of the tail fin, which is almost as long as the body itself. It is thought that the shark may use its tail to lash out and stun prey before devouring it. Threshers may even join together to herd prey together with their tails before feeding on them. The common thresher is wide-ranging, swimming in deep water close to the shore as well as in open water near the surface. The thresher's breeding habits are only partly known, but like other mackerel sharks the young feed on the yolk of unfertilized eggs as they develop, which helps ensure they are well formed at birth. Threshers are hunted for their meat and fins, and their numbers have dropped as a result.

Identification: Muscular body. First dorsal fin much bigger than second dorsal fin. Upper lobe of tail fin almost as long as rest of body. Large, scythe-shaped caudal and pectoral fins. Body variably purple-grey to black on top, creamy white below.

Grey nurse shark
(*Carcharias taurus*): 4.3m/14ft
Stout-bodied with jaws lined with forward-projecting, needle-sharp teeth. It has two large dorsal fins and a tail fin with an elongated upper lobe. It feeds on fish – including small sharks – and invertebrates that it usually hunts near the seabed in sandy coastal waters of the Atlantic, Pacific and Indian Oceans.

Porbeagle (*Lamna nasus*): 3.7m/12ft
A fast-swimming, stout-bodied shark of mainly cool coastal and inshore waters of the North Atlantic, Pacific and Indian Oceans, the porbeagle's distinguishing features include a white patch on the trailing edge of the first dorsal fin and relatively large eyes. A popular gamefish, the porbeagle is also caught for its oil and for making into fishmeal.

Small-tooth sand tiger shark (*Odontaspis ferox*): about 1.8m/6ft, but 3.7m/12ft also recorded
The small-tooth sand tiger can be distinguished from the similar grey nurse shark (*Carcharias taurus*) by the fact that its first dorsal fin is significantly larger than the second; in the grey nurse they are the same size. The small-tooth sand tiger is sometimes encountered by divers on coral reefs near the drop-off zone of continental shelves, but is also known to live in waters 530m/1,750ft deep. This shark is most active at night, feeding on fish, shrimps and squid.

Shortfin mako shark

Isurus oxyrinchus

A sleek, spindle-shaped, metallic blue shark, the mako bears a resemblance to the porbeagle (see panel left), but is distinguished from it by its longer body and lack of a secondary keel on the caudal fin. The mako also lacks lateral cusps on its dagger-like teeth. One of the fastest of all the sharks, the highly predatory mako can accelerate to speeds of up to 35km/h/22mph – sometimes even faster – for short distances, and it can also maintain a higher body temperature than that of the surrounding water. An opportunist hunter, its food includes schooling fish, such as tuna and herring, but it is also known to take porpoises. The mako is a popular sport fish and is often caught on rod and line from boats; at such times, it often leaps spectacularly from the water, and jumps up to a height of 6m/20ft are sometimes recorded. The mako may even try to attack the boat. These sharks may live up to 20 years or more.

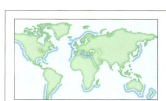

Distribution: Worldwide distribution in temperate waters; also found tropical oceans.
Habitat: From surface waters down to 150m/490ft or more.
Food: Fish such as mackerel and tuna; also porpoises and turtles.
Size: 4m/13ft, perhaps exceptionally to 6m/20ft
Breeding: Usually about 10–12 young; livebearer.
Status: Listed as Lower risk by IUCN.

Identification: Streamlined body. Head has long, conical snout. Curved teeth lack lateral cusps. First dorsal fin much bigger than second dorsal fin. Crescent-shaped caudal fin with no secondary keel. Body colour metallic blue above, white below.

REQUIEM SHARKS

All of these sharks belong to the family Carcharinidae, often known as Requiem sharks, which is one of the seven families of ground sharks that, altogether, amass more than 200 members. Taxonomists sometimes group hammerheads in a separate family, Sphyrinidae. The species shown here include some of the best-known and most voracious sharks to be found anywhere in the world's oceans.

Great hammerhead shark

Sphyrna mokarran

The largest of the eight or nine species of hammerheads (family Sphyrinidae), this shark, like all hammerheads, has extended lateral lobes on either side of the head forming the so-called 'hammer'. However, in other species the lobes may be more scalloped, wing-like or shovel shaped. Ranging from inshore reefs to depths of about 300m/980ft, the great hammerhead hunts a variety of animals including rays and sea snakes, feeding mainly at dusk. It migrates to cooler waters at the poles during the summer months. Unlike most other sharks, mating often takes place near the surface. After about an 11-month gestation, young are born in the Northern Hemisphere.

Identification: Muscular body with prominent first dorsal fin; pectoral and pelvic fins relatively small; caudal fin with long upper lobe bearing notch. Head with conspicuous lateral lobes; eyes and nostrils on lobes. In all species, eyes and nostrils located at the ends of hammer; this may give them a wider sensory field for locating prey. Hammer also acts as a bow-plane, improving manoeuvrability. Body brown, grey or olive above, fading to white below.

Distribution: Circumtropical, coastal warm temperate and tropical waters between latitudes 40°N and 37°S.
Habitat: From shallow coastal areas to far offshore at depths of 300m/985ft, but usually less than 80m/260ft.
Food: Wide variety of marine creatures from invertebrates to bony fish, sharks and rays.
Size: 6m/20ft.
Breeding: From 6 to 42 young; livebearer.
Status: Listed as Data Deficient by IUCN.

Bonnethead shark

Sphyrna tiburo

The bonnethead is the smallest of the hammerhead species. Like other hammerheads, the head has conspicuous lateral lobes bearing the eyes and nostrils, but in this species the profile resembles a flattened shovel or bonnet. The shape may have evolved to improve prey-finding capabilities and to make swimming more efficient by increasing lift. The bonnethead usually feeds by day. Darting swiftly forward, it grabs prey with its pointed front teeth, and then uses the flattened molars at the back of the mouth to crush hard shells. Often occurring in schools of up to 15 individuals, during migration this number may be hundreds. It is thought that bonnetheads may communicate with each other using chemical scents. It travels great distances daily, staying in warm waters. In winter it is found near the equator.
Gestation is between four and five months – a short time for sharks.

Identification: Compact body shape with tall first dorsal fin. Short pectoral fins. Caudal fin has long upper lobe. Head flattened; shovel- or bonnet-shaped, with eyes and nostrils located at ends of rounded lobes. Front teeth pointed. Body colour greyish-brown, occasionally with dark spots, fading to white below.

Distribution: Temperate Atlantic Ocean from New England to Gulf of Mexico and Brazil. Common in Caribbean Sea. Also found warm-temperate and subtropical Pacific Ocean from southern California to Ecuador.
Habitat: Over reefs, in estuaries and shallow bays down to about 80m/262ft.
Food: Crabs, prawns, molluscs, small fish.
Size: 1.5m/5ft.
Breeding: 4–14 young; livebearer.
Status: Listed as Low Risk by IUCN.

Smooth hammerhead shark

(*Sphyrna zygaena*): 5m/16.5ft
Head bearing an elongated 'hammer' produced by lateral projections, but lacks the notches of other species of hammerheads. Body colour olive or brownish-grey with a whitish underside. Found worldwide in temperate oceans, it prefers depths of less than 20m/65ft deep, but it may be found deeper, and is frequently seen around bays and estuaries, where it feeds primarily on bony fish, small sharks and rays.

Scalloped hammerhead shark (*Sphyrna lewini*): 4.3m/14ft

This species has a centrally located indentation on the front margin of the laterally expanded head. Either side of it are two further indentations, producing a scalloped appearance. Eyes and nostrils are located at the ends of the lateral head projections. Colouration brown-grey to bronze or olive with lighter underside. Females grow larger than males. Found worldwide in coastal temperate and tropical oceans, where it feeds on rays, bony fish and invertebrates, mostly at night. On occasions, several hundred individuals, mainly females, congregate in groups called 'shivers', during which time they perform headshaking, corkscrewing and other movements; this activity is probably linked to mating.

Whitetip reef shark

Triaenodon obesus

As night approaches, schools of whitetip reef sharks leave their daytime resting places among caves and overhangs to fan out over reefs and atolls in search of prey. One of the most common species of shark on reefs, whitetips often appear to hunt and attack as a pack, although this is less of a coordinated activity and more a case of them all going for the same prey and ending up in a feeding frenzy. As with some other sharks, mating involves the male biting the female and grasping her pectoral fins so he can ensure the correct position for sperm transfer. The whitetip reef shark is a curious species and often approaches divers.

Identification: Tapering body. Head with large, blunt nose. Broad pectoral fins. Caudal fin with long upper lobe. First dorsal fin and upper lobe of caudal fin have distinct white tips. Body colour grey-brown, fading to white on underside.

Distribution: Indo-Pacific range from Red Sea and East Africa to Micronesia and south to New South Wales; also eastern Pacific Ocean.
Habitat: Over reefs and in shallow water down to 40m/130ft.
Food: Crabs, lobsters, squid, bony fish.
Size: 2m/6.6ft.
Breeding: 1–5 young; livebearer.
Status: Listed as Near Threatened by IUCN.

Tiger shark

Galeocerdo cuvier

Distribution: Circumglobal in temperate and tropical oceans and seas. Common around Australian coasts.
Habitat: Coastal waters, including estuaries, and over continental shelf down to about 140m/460ft, but sometimes deeper.
Food: Very varied: scavenger as well as predator of range of creatures including fish, marine reptiles, seabirds, mammals (such as dolphins and sea lions), crustaceans and molluscs.
Size: Up to 6m/20ft.
Breeding: 11–82 young; livebearer.
Status: Listed as Near Threatened by IUCN.

This species gets its common name from the tiger-like body markings. One of the largest and most aggressive of all sharks, the tiger shark is renowned for its varied tastes in food. A powerful and fast swimmer when attacking its prey, it will swallow almost anything that will fit into its mouth, including sea lions, sea snakes, turtles, other sharks and seabirds. It has also been known to swallow items of more dubious nutritional value, such as car licence plates and tyres. It has also been implicated in attacks on human bathers. Tolerant of both marine and brackish conditions, the tiger shark sometimes enters river estuaries and is known to attack land mammals that come to the water to drink.

Identification: Fast-swimming aggressive shark. Body tapers towards tail. First dorsal fin much longer than second dorsal fin. Upper lobe of caudal fin long with subterminal notch. Head with large eyes and a broad, blunt snout. Wide mouth bears rows of large, serrated teeth. Body colour greyish with black spots and vertical bars (reminiscent of a tiger), more prominent in young individuals, pale below.

OTHER SHALLOW-WATER SHARKS

The species featured here originate from a number of different shark families. Bottom-dwelling carpet sharks include the giant whale shark – the largest fish in the world – and the well-camouflaged wobbegongs. Saw sharks have long snouts with rows of lateral teeth, while frilled and cow sharks are distinctive for retaining six or seven pairs of gills, whereas most sharks have five.

Nurse shark

Ginglymostoma cirratum

Identification: Body with relatively large fins. Upper lobe of caudal fin held almost level with body. Head with blunt snout (or rostrum) and small eyes. Tiny spiracles (breathing orifices). Mouth bears two distinct sensory barbels. Body colour tan to brown, paler below. Juveniles have spotted markings on their dorsal surface.

This generally docile shark may get its name from the suckling noise it makes when feeding, which is thought by some to be similar to the sounds of a suckling baby. One of just two recorded nurse shark species, the shark rests for much of the day on the sea bottom, sometimes in groups, but at night it hunts for bottom-dwelling invertebrates and fish. It has only a small mouth, but its powerful, bellows-like pharynx (the passage from mouth to stomach) allows it to suck in food with great speed. In summer, nurse sharks migrate to gather in shallow waters in large numbers for several weeks in a frenzy of courtship and mating. Sometimes a single female will be chased by several males before one succeeds in mating with her. The nurse shark is an approachable species that can be touched and hand fed, and it is sometimes even ridden on by young children; however, this practice can be dangerous, for as docile as it is, this shark can deliver a painful, vice-like bite without warning.

Distribution: American range extends from Rhode Island, US, to Brazil, including Gulf of Mexico and Caribbean. Also south-eastern US Pacific seaboard to Baja California. Eastern Atlantic range extends from Cape Verde to Gabon.
Habitat: Waters from about 1m/3.25ft down to 50m/160ft.
Food: Crabs, octopuses and other invertebrates, fish.
Size: Up to 2.7m/8.8ft.
Breeding: 20–30 young; livebearer.
Status: Not listed by IUCN.

Tasselled wobbegong

Eucrossorhinus dasypogon

Identification: Body flattened. Large pectoral and pelvic fins. Head flattened and bearing many appendages around mouth, thought to act as lures for small prey. Body yellowish-brown in colour and marked with a mosaic of numerous dark spots and lines evolved for camouflage when lying motionless on the sea bed.

With its broad, flat head, its mouth fringed with a mass of outgrowths and flaps and its superb camouflage markings, the tasselled wobbegong, like other wobbegongs, is hard to spot on the seabed. Lying motionless on the bottom for long periods, it has evolved a system of pumping in water through its gill cavity when breathing instead of taking in water through the mouth. Despite its sedentary nature, the wobbegong can react extremely quickly when prey comes within range, snatching it with sharp teeth and gulping it down. The waving appendages around its mouth may even attract small creatures to approach. There are six other species of wobbegongs in the family Orectolobidae, all found in the western Pacific region.

Distribution: South-western Pacific, including eastern Indonesia, Papua New Guinea and northern Australia.
Habitat: Bottom dwelling, on sand and reefs down to about 40m/130ft.
Food: Fish, squid, octopuses, crabs, shrimps.
Size: 1.2m/4ft; sometimes larger.
Breeding: Not known.
Status: Listed as Near Threatened by IUCN.

Longnose saw shark

Pristiophorus cirratus

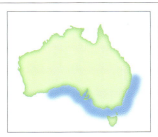

Distribution: Southern Australia to New South Wales.
Habitat: Sandy and muddy seabeds down to 300m/1,000ft. Sometimes also brackish waters.
Food: Squid, prawns, crabs, small fish.
Size: 1.4m/4.6ft.
Breeding: 6–20 young; livebearer.
Status: Listed as Least Concern by IUCN.

The nine species of saw sharks are identified by their long, blade-like snout, or rostrum, bearing on each side a row of pointed, lateral teeth. In some species, the rostrum can be as long as the rest of the body. The longnose saw shark is a sedentary species, probing the seafloor for invertebrates and bottom-dwelling fish with its sensitive rostrum, aided by long, sensory barbels that extend on either side of the rostrum. When prey is detected, it may be dug out and dispatched by being slashed with the shark's sharp-toothed saw. Saw sharks are not equipped to bite and swallow large prey in the way that many other sharks do, and so their food consists of items such as small fish and invertebrates. Females give birth to live young after a gestation period of about a year. To avoid damaging the mother with their saw teeth, the baby saw sharks are born with the teeth lying flat against the rostrum in a protective sac. Age span is about 15 years.

Identification: Body long and slender. No anal fin. Head with particularly long rostrum bearing conspicuous lateral teeth and two sensory barbels. Large eyes. Body colour generally grey-brown with dark banded markings above, greyish-white on underside.

Northern wobbegong (*Orectolobus wardi*): 60cm/24in

The northern wobbegong has a much less-elaborate colour pattern and less-developed mouth appendages compared with the tasselled wobbegong (*Eucrossorhinus dasypogon*). There are several dark saddles on the head and lightish body, as well as brown blotches. Around the mouth are sensory barbels and flap-like nasal lobes, and there are also lobes on the head. Like other wobbegongs, the northern wobbegong inhabits shallow reefs, where it can lie concealed among overhangs and crevices becoming active at night when it hunts for prey. It is found in waters around northern Australia.

Brown-banded bamboo shark (*Chiloscyllium punctatum*): 1m/3.25ft
These carpet sharks get their common name from the markings seen on juveniles. The alternating dark and light bands resemble the patterning on bamboo stems. However, as the fish becomes adult the body colouring usually assumes a more uniform drab grey or brown. The shark has a long, slender body with well-developed dorsal, pectoral and pelvic fins and a long tail. The head bears short nasal barbels, which help it to locate food hidden on the bottom and among coral reefs. This egg-laying species is found in the Indo-Pacific Ocean. Due to its relatively small size and attractive juvenile markings, the shark is a popular aquarium fish.

Zebra shark

Stegostoma fasciatum

The beautifully patterned zebra shark, also called the leopard shark, is the only member of its family, the Stegostomatidae. It has a body that is scalloped longitudinally, with two ridges running from behind the blunt head to the caudal fin (or tail). Both dorsal fins are low and long, the pectoral fins are broad and well developed, and the caudal fin is long. This shark is often encountered near reefs both inshore and offshore, where it feeds at night on molluscs, crustaceans and fish. With its long, narrow body it can wriggle into caves and crevices using the fleshy sensory barbels to search for prey. It is not known whether the female lays more than one egg at a time. This species is harmless to humans and is regularly taken in inshore fisheries.

Distribution: Indo-West Pacific: Red Sea and East Africa to New Caledonia, north to southern Japan and south to New South Wales.
Habitat: Sandy bottoms of coastal waters to about 60m/200ft.
Food: Molluscs, crabs, shrimps, small fish.
Size: 3.5m/11.5ft.
Breeding: Oviparous; number of eggs unknown.
Status: Listed as Vulnerable by IUCN.

Identification: Body cylindrical with prominent ridges running down, giving a scalloped effect. Head broad with small barbels and a wide, transverse mouth. The spiracles (breathing orifices), situated behind the eyes, are large. The first (anterior) dorsal fin is longer than the second (posterior) dorsal fin. The tail has no ventral lobe and is as long as the body. The body is creamy or yellow with leopard-like dark brown to black spots. Juveniles have zebra-like alternating dark brown and creamy stripes.

SAWFISH AND ELECTRIC RAYS

Sawfish and rays are grouped, along with sharks and chimaeras, in the class Chondrichthyes. The sawfish have elongated rostrums bearing rows of lateral teeth, and resemble the saw sharks described previously in this section. The electric rays have flattened bodies and broad, wing-like pectoral fins. They can produce pulses of electricity to stun prey and ward off predators.

Great-tooth sawfish

Pristis microdon

Identification: Body long and robust; flattish below. Two large dorsal fins. Flattened head with long rostrum bearing 14–22 large teeth on each side. Eyes large. Large spiracle behind each eye. Body colour greenish-grey or brown above with darker fin edges; underside dirty cream.

With its elongated rostrum, or snout, bearing horizontal teeth, and its shark-like fins, this species looks similar to a saw shark. However, the sawfish's gill slits are on the underside of the body. Sawfish also lack sensory barbels. A solitary species, it feeds on bottom-dwelling fish and other creatures. This species often frequents rivers and lakes. Human demand for the sawfish's meat, liver oil and skin, as well as for its rostrum – which is sold as a curio – have all led to a reduction in numbers. This problem is exacerbated by the fact that the fish is a slow breeder and may not breed until it is 20 years old.

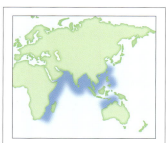

Distribution: Indo-Pacific, including East Africa, India, South-east Asia, Philippines and northern Australia.
Habitat: Near to coasts; also estuaries and in rivers and lakes.
Food: Small bottom-dwelling fish, invertebrates.
Size: 6m/20ft.
Breeding: About 20 young; livebearer.
Status: Listed as Endangered by IUCN.

Small-tooth sawfish

Pristis pectinata

The largest of the six or so species of sawfish, the small-tooth sawfish is found around reefs at depths down to about 10m/33ft, although it often occurs in brackish or even freshwater conditions. It may sometimes venture into deeper water to reach offshore islands. Like other sawfish, the snout is extended to form a long rostrum bearing sharp, horizontal teeth, which it uses to rake up the sea bed, searching for hidden prey, or to ward off predators. Once prey – such as open-water or bottom-living fish – has been found, the sawfish disables it with sideways swipes of its rostrum. Valued not only as a food fish, it is also prized for other parts of its body, such as its oil (used in medicine) and its rostrum. Overfishing and habitat destruction have seen the species eradicated from much of its range.

Identification: Body long and flattened with wing-like pectoral fins. Two large dorsal fins. Flattened head with long rostrum bearing 24–32 teeth on each side. Eyes large. Large spiracle behind each eye. Body colour brownish-grey above, underside white.

Distribution: Western Atlantic: North Carolina, USA, to Brazil; Eastern Atlantic: Gibraltar to Namibia; Indo-Pacific: Red Sea and East Africa to Indonesia, parts of South-east Asia and northern Australia.
Habitat: Near to coasts; enters estuaries and rivers.
Food: Small fish, invertebrates.
Size: 5.5m/18ft; sometimes up to 7.6m/25ft.
Breeding: About 15–20 young; livebearer.
Status: Listed as Threatened by IUCN.

Atlantic torpedo ray

Torpedo nobiliana

Distribution: Subtropical and temperate waters of the Atlantic Ocean.
Habitat: Pelagic but also on sandy seabeds and reefs from 2–800m/6.5–2,600ft.
Food: Mainly small fish.
Size: 1.8m/6ft.
Breeding: About 60 young; livebearer.
Status: Not listed by IUCN.

One of the largest members of the family Torpedinidae, the Atlantic torpedo ray is one of 50 or more species of rays that can produce an electric current using specially modified muscle cells. In some species, including the Atlantic torpedo, the strength of the shock delivered can be up to 220 volts. Electric rays use the electricity both as a form of defence and to capture prey. Fish are the main food of Atlantic torpedos, and prey is usually caught as the ray delivers a stunning shock while wrapping its pectoral fins around it. The ray then manoeuvres the victim into the mouth. Using this method, the ray can catch even fast-moving fish. Juveniles are usually found on the bottom, but adults often swim in open water.

Identification: Most of body flattened and disk-like. Two dorsal fins. Paddle-shaped caudal fin. Snout short. Large spiracle behind each eye. Body colour blackish to chocolate-brown above, white below.

Knife-tooth sawfish (*Anoxypristis cuspidata*): 4.7m/15.5ft
Shark-like in appearance but with slender, elongated snout with lateral teeth. Body greyish above, pale below. Found in marine, brackish and possibly also in freshwater conditions in Indo-Pacific Ocean. Ranges from very shallow water down to about 40m/130ft. Sharp teeth of babies embedded in a protective sheath to avoid damaging the mother during birth. Endangered.

Tasmanian numbfish (*Narcine tasmaniensis*): 47cm/18.5in
Occurring on sandy and muddy bottoms, and sometimes on rocky reefs, the Tasmanian numbfish lives in waters from about 5m/16.4ft down to 640m/2,100ft. It is found in the Pacific including south and southeast Australia. This ray is a fairly uniform chocolate-brown to yellow-brown above, white below. It feeds on worms and crustaceans such as shrimps.

Cortez electric ray (*Narcine entemedor*): 76cm/30in
Found in shallow, sandy places, sometimes close to reefs, along the eastern Pacific from California, USA, to Peru. It has two equally sized dorsal fins and a paddle-shaped caudal fin. It is nocturnal, resting on the bottom by day, often buried in the substrate, before moving into bays to feed on worms and sea squirts. Body greyish-tan.

Spotted torpedo ray

Torpedo marmorata

This ray's common name comes from the mottled appearance of its dorsal surface. Like other members of its family, it has the ability to emit an electric shock that will deter most predators (although large sharks are often not put off) or stun prey, rendering it helpless before being eaten. By day, the spotted torpedo usually lies buried on the seabed with just its eyes visible, but at night it hunts for crustaceans and small fish, which it first overpowers with an electric discharge. The electricity produced by these rays was used from ancient times up until around the 1600s as a form of therapy intended to cure diseases from gout to headaches.

Distribution: Eastern Atlantic Ocean from Britain to southern Africa. Also the Mediterranean Sea.
Habitat: Soft sea bottom around reefs and seagrass meadows.
Food: Small fish and crustaceans.
Size: 1m/3.25ft.
Breeding: About 5–30 young; livebearer.
Status: Not listed by IUCN.

Identification: Most of body flattened and disc-like. Two dorsal fins. Paddle-shaped caudal fin. Snout short. Slightly stalked eyes on top of head. Large spiracle behind each eye. Body colour mottled brown above, underside creamy white.

SKATES, GUITARFISH AND STINGRAYS

There are more than 120 species of skates – flattened cartilaginous fish found in most oceans of the world. In these fish the pectoral fin is fused to the head to give a more or less disc-shaped body. The guitarfish are so called because their body shape resembles the musical instrument. Stingrays have venomous spines at the base of the tail, which are used primarily for defence.

Common skate

Dipturus (Raja) batis

Identification: Body flattened and diamond-shaped. Elongated snout. Eyes on top of head. Conspicuous spiracles behind eyes. Tiny dorsal fins. Thin tail with spiny thorns on upper surface. Body colour grey to brown with white spots on upper surface, white below.

A sought-after and now heavily overfished commercial species, the common or blue skate can grow to 2.9m/9.5ft or more. The snout is elongated and the pectoral fins form broad 'wings', giving the flattened body a more or less diamond shape when viewed from above. Swimming with a typical undulating action of its pectoral fins, the impression of having wings is further enhanced, since the fish seems to be flying through the water. Along the dorsal surface is a series of spiny thorns that may help give some protection from predators. It can also emit a small electric discharge, like the electric rays, but this is insufficient to deter predators and is probably used in courtship. Fertilization is internal, and the leathery eggs are laid in summer. The cases have tendrils to help them attach to weeds and other objects.

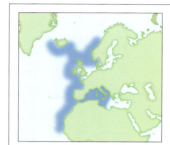

Distribution: Eastern Atlantic Ocean, from Iceland to Senegal, and western Mediterranean.
Habitat: Near seabed, usually down to 100–1,000m/ 330–3,300ft.
Food: Fish, crabs, lobsters.
Size: 2.9m/9.5ft.
Breeding: One or two eggs.
Status: Listed as Endangered by IUCN.

Atlantic guitarfish

Rhinobatos lentiginosus

Somewhat between a ray and a shark in overall shape, the 40 or so species of guitarfish get their common name from their distinctive body shape. The body is long, like that of a typical shark, with well-developed dorsal fins, but it is rounded at the front with broad pectoral fins, and the gill slits are on the underside, like those of a ray. Guitarfish swim by moving their caudal fins from side to side, in the same fashion as sharks. The Atlantic guitarfish is one of the smaller species in the family Rhinobatidae. It often buries itself in the sand or mud and is sometimes found in brackish or even fresh water. The Atlantic guitarfish feeds on bottom-dwelling fish, molluscs and crustaceans. It often uses its snout, or rostrum, to hold the prey down before eating it. Fertilization is internal, with live young being born. This species is of little commercial fishing interest.

Identification: Body flattened and guitar shaped. Two well-developed dorsal fins. Pectoral fins fused to head. Elongated snout. Eyes on top of head. Conspicuous spiracles behind eyes. Paddle-like tail. Body colour brown, grey or olive above, usually with white speckles, yellowish-white below.

Distribution: Western Atlantic range extends from North Carolina, USA, to Yucatan, Mexico.
Habitat: Mainly tropical coastal areas near seabed down to about 30m/100ft; also in estuaries and fresh water.
Food: Fish, molluscs, shrimps, other invertebrates.
Size: 76cm/30in.
Breeding: About six young; livebearer.
Status: Not listed by IUCN.

Spotted eagle ray

Aetobatus narinari

Distribution: Wide-ranging in tropical and temperate Atlantic, Pacific, Indian Oceans and Red Sea.
Habitat: Sandy coastal regions and reefs but also found in estuaries and open water.
Food: Clams, oysters, shrimps, octopus, squid, sea urchins, fish.
Size: 2.5m/8.2ft excluding tail; may reach 5m/16ft in total with tail.
Breeding: Up to four pups; livebearer.
Status: Listed as Data Deficient by IUCN.

The spotted eagle ray's common name is due to its large size and also because of its swimming movements, which resemble those of a flying eagle. Beautifully marked with white spots on a black, grey or brown background above, and with contrasting white below, the diamond-shaped spotted eagle ray is an active swimmer, often forming into large schools as it migrates across the oceans. This large ray is also found close to the bottom in shallow water, where it digs into the substrate for food such as clams and other molluscs using its curious flat, duck-billed snout. At the base of the long, whip-like tail the eagle ray has a battery of highly potent stinging spines. These are used in defence to deter or injure would-be predators. The spotted eagle ray can also leap out of the water when pursued. This species is no less dangerous if caught and hauled aboard a boat; the lashing fish can deliver painful, occasionally fatal, stings to humans.

Identification: Body disc flattened and diamond-shaped. Eyes on side of head. Large spiracles. Broad, bill-shaped snout.

Thornback ray (*Raja clavata*): 1.2m/4ft
This species gets its common name from the dense covering of protective spines that cover the body. The thornback ray is an attractive fish with the typical diamond-shaped body seen in many rays produced by the wide pectoral fins and pointed snout. The tail is narrow and spiny. The upper surface is brown with variously shaded blotches and, sometimes, marbling. Found near coastal seabeds in the eastern Atlantic from Iceland to southwest Africa, it also lives in the Mediterranean and Black seas, and possibly also off South Africa.

Southern ray (*Dasyatis americana*): 1.5m/5ft
Often seen gliding over sandy areas near reefs, the southern ray is common in tropical and subtropical waters in the southern Atlantic Ocean from New Jersey, USA, to Brazil, as well as the Caribbean. It may occur alone, in pairs or in large groups. The southern ray eats a variety of fish, molluscs and crustaceans, which are detected in the substrate by smell, touch and electro-sensitive receptors. Other opportunist fish species often hover nearby to glean morsels disturbed by the feeding ray. The ray's tail can be flicked up to deliver venom from spines to deter potential predators, such as sharks. The broad, diamond-shaped body is grey above and white below. Three to five young are born alive.

Manta ray

Manta birostris

This impressive fish is the largest of all rays. Despite its size, it eats mainly plankton. The horn-like cephalic fins in front of the head can be rolled up to form a funnel that helps channel water and food into the mouth when feeding. The word 'manta' originates from the resemblance of this ray's wide, flapping fins to a cloak or mantle. The manta ray is a solitary species, but individuals are often accompanied by other fish species, such as cleaner fish, remoras and pilot fish. The lifespan of the manta ray is approximately 20 years.

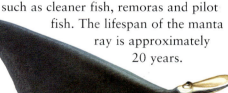

Distribution: Worldwide tropical coastal regions of Atlantic, Pacific and Indian Oceans. Also sometimes in temperate regions.
Habitat: Usually inshore surface waters down to 120m/390ft; occasionally further from shore.
Food: Planktonic crustaceans and small schooling fish.
Size: 5.2m/17ft long; width is approximately 2.2 times greater than length.
Breeding: One young; livebearer.
Status: Listed by IUCN as Data Deficient globally, but Vulnerable in some areas.

Identification: Body flattened. Large, wing-like pectoral fins. Front lobes (cephalic fins) extend on both sides of rectangular mouth. No dorsal or caudal fins. Small teeth, in lower jaw only. Gills on underside of body. Whip-like tail. Body colour variable, but usually brown, grey-blue or black above, white below.

SALMON, TROUT AND ALLIES

The Salmoniformes are characterized by having a fatty adipose fin on the back between the dorsal fin and tail. Many species in this group make long-distance migrations between the sea and their breeding grounds in rivers. The related smelts are sardine-like fish, many of which are important commercially. Galaxiids are relatives of the salmon and trout that inhabit the Southern Hemisphere.

Arctic charr

Salvelinus alpinus

Identification: Form typically trout-like, with rounded, streamlined body. Slightly pointed snout and large mouth with teeth in both jaws. Adipose fin present. Caudal fin slightly forked. Colour highly variable according to habitat, size and time of year: often brown or greenish on back, flanks silvery with pinkish or red spots; underside paler. Spawning adults usually have bright orange-red ventral surface and pelvic, pectoral and anal fins.

The arctic charr is found mainly in cold, northern waters. There are both landlocked, freshwater varieties and others that migrate between freshwater habitats – where they spawn – and the sea. The species is an opportunist feeder, taking food from small crustaceans to members of its own species. Spawning takes place between September and October, with the preferred site being shallow, gravelly bottoms. The female builds a nest by turning on her side and using her caudal fin to clear away an area, known as a redd, in which to lay her eggs. After a period of courtship, eggs are laid in the redd and fertilized by the male. Where charr are migratory, the young first venture to the sea after a period of between two and six years.

Distribution: North Atlantic including northern Norway, southern Greenland and Iceland. Also north-western Canada and USA; Beaufort Sea.
Habitat: Deep runs of rivers and lakes, and – in migratory individuals – brackish waters and shallow seas.
Food: Small crustaceans and fish, including other charr.
Size: Usually about 45cm/17.7in, but may be bigger.
Breeding: Nest builder; eggs shed in gravel beds of rivers, and fertilized externally.
Status: Listed as Least Concern by IUCN.

Trout

Salmo trutta

Few fish are more variable than the trout. This is partly because many populations are resident in different types of waters, and isolated from each other, but also because some populations migrate downstream to the sea when adult, where they live on a diet of marine fish and invertebrates. The two types are usually known as brown trout (resident form) and sea trout (migratory form). Both are found only in well-oxygenated, clean water. They spawn in winter in gravelly shallows, the sea trout migrating back from the ocean to reach favoured sites. When mature, sea trout then migrate to the ocean, where they feed for one to five years before returning to breed. Brown trout, however, remain in fresh water. Both are prized food and sports fish.

Identification: Streamlined fish with small scales, an adipose fin and a square-cut tail fin. The area of the body in front of the tail fin is relatively deep and flattened. Colour very variable, ranging from brownish with black spots on the back, plus red spots on the sides, often with pale rings, to silvery with fewer spots (especially in migratory fish returning from the sea). The belly is pale coloured, and the fins are dark and only sparsely spotted.

Distribution: Native range mainly Atlantic: Europe and Scandinavia, and east to the Urals. Migratory group introduced to other regions.
Habitat: Cool, clear rivers and lakes, and – in migratory sea trout – mainly shallow seas.
Food: Small crustaceans and insect larvae in fresh water, plus fish; fish and larger crustaceans in the sea.
Size: River trout 40cm/16in; sea trout 1m/3.25ft.
Breeding: Nest builder; eggs shed in gravel beds of rivers, and fertilized externally.
Status: Listed by IUCN as Least Concern. Some decline in migratory groups.

Atlantic salmon

Salmo salar

This is one of the most famous of all fish, partly because it is a valuable food species – so much so that it is now raised in fish farms – but also because of its spectacular spawning migrations. After some years feeding in rich ocean waters, adult wild salmon navigate their way back to the rivers where they spent their early lives, and swim upstream to reach spawning sites in shallow, gravelly streams. This involves adapting from salt to fresh water, and up rapids and waterfalls against the current. They use so much energy in the process that many die after spawning, but some migrate back to sea and return to spawn again.

Identification: Large, streamlined fish with a relatively small head, an adipose fin and a shallowly forked tail. Breeding males develop a hooked lower jaw (kype). Adults fresh from the sea are silver-sided with greenish-blue backs, heads and fins; white below. They become darker and browner as spawning nears, with black and red spots. Young salmon in fresh water are dark, with a line of dark blotches and red spots on flanks.

Distribution: North Atlantic from Canada and Greenland to Iceland, northern Europe and Scandinavia, and Barents Sea. Also adjoining rivers.
Habitat: Rivers when young and when spawning; mainly coastal waters at sea.
Food: Crustaceans, insect larvae when young in fresh water; small fish and shrimps when at sea. Spawning salmon do not feed.
Size: 1.2m/4ft.
Breeding: Nest builder; eggs shed in gravel beds of rivers, and fertilized externally.
Status: Listed as Least Concern by IUCN.

Atlantic rainbow smelt (*Osmerus mordax*): 30cm/12in
This small-sized relation of the salmon has a pale green back and silvery flanks with a purple, blue and pink iridescent sheen. It feeds in North Atlantic coastal waters or in large lakes when it is adult, consuming small planktonic crustaceans and insect larvae, but in spring it migrates up to about 1,000km/620 miles against the current to spawn in rivers draining into the Arctic Ocean.

Jollytail (*Galaxias maculatus*): 15cm/6in
Widespread in the Southern Hemisphere from the southern tip of South America to Australia, including Tasmania, and New Zealand, this slim, scaleless, silvery green fish is one of several related species known as galaxiids. It is found in coastal rivers and lakes and estuaries, and feeds principally on insects, aquatic insect larvae, and on crustaceans.

Rainbow trout (*Oncorhynchus mykiss*): 50cm/20in
Familiar as a farmed food fish, the rainbow trout has been introduced to many freshwater environments worldwide, where it is also valued as a game fish. It can now be found in 45 countries on all continents, apart from Antarctica. The rainbow trout is a native of the eastern Pacific Ocean and rivers from Alaska to northwest Mexico. It resembles a European trout with an iridescent rainbow stripe along each flank, but a large, silvery migratory form, called the steelhead, lacks this characteristic stripe.

Sockeye salmon

Oncorhynchus nerka

The sockeye is one of six species of *Oncorhynchus*, collectively known as Pacific salmon. Like Atlantic salmon, they feed at sea before returning to their home rivers to spawn, running upstream to reach shallow headstreams with gravel beds. Spawning males turn a vivid red, and many are taken by predators such as bald eagles and bears. Those that do spawn die within a few weeks. After hatching, the young fish feed in rivers and lakes for one or two years before migrating out to sea. In some places they remain in fresh water to form landlocked populations. These fish, known as kokanee salmon, are genetically identical to sockeyes but much smaller, owing to a poorer diet.

Identification: A streamlined, laterally compressed fish. A spawning male develops hooked jaws, long teeth and a dorsal hump. Colouration is normally dark steely to greenish-blue on the head and back, with silvery sides and a white to silvery belly; at spawning time the males turn bright red, with greenish heads, paired fins and tails.

Distribution: North Pacific and adjoining coastal rivers, from northern Japan to Alaska and California. Also landlocked populations (kokanee) in North America, from Alaska to Oregon (US).
Habitat: Fresh water when young, then they migrate to coastal ocean waters. Kokanee are permanently resident in lakes and streams.
Food: Planktonic crustaceans and insect larvae in fresh water; marine crustaceans and fish at sea.
Size: 60cm/24in. Landlocked populations (kokanee) smaller.
Breeding: Nest builder; eggs shed in gravel beds of rivers and streams, and fertilized externally.
Status: Not listed by IUCN.

COD AND RELATIVES

The fish described here are some of the best-known relatives of the Gadiformes, or common codfish. Both the haddock and coalfish are heavily exploited by commercial fishing fleets, causing concern among conservationists. Also fished commercially are hake, which tend to be bottom-dwelling during the day, moving up the water column to feed at night.

Haddock

Melanogrammus aeglefinus

Identification: A large-eyed fish with three dorsal fins – the first triangular with long anterior rays – and two anal fins. It has a very short barbel beneath its short lower jaw. Dark greenish brown on the back, greyish silver on the sides and white below, it has a conspicuous, thumb-print-like black blotch between the pectoral fin and the arched lateral line.

One of the most heavily exploited of food fish, becoming scarce as a result, the haddock is a close relative of the cod (*Gadus morhua*) that feeds on the bottom in the relatively shallow waters of the continental shelves. In the north of its range it feeds inshore in summer, migrating to deeper water in winter, but further south it does the opposite. Although adult fish feed on the bottom, their eggs are buoyant, floating near the surface. The young then feed in the plankton, often swimming with large, drifting jellyfish whose trailing tentacles provide some protection from predators. When they reach about 5cm/2in in length, the young haddock move down to the sea bed in order to feed on worms, crabs, molluscs, brittlestars and small fish.

Distribution: North Atlantic from eastern Canada and New England to southern Greenland, Iceland, northern Europe, Scandinavia and the Barents Sea.
Habitat: Close to the seabed on continental shelf, mainly at depths of 40–300m/ 130–980ft.
Food: Bottom-dwelling invertebrates and small fish such as sandeels.
Size: 75cm/30in.
Breeding: Eggs shed are fertilized externally and hatch into planktonic larvae.
Status: Listed as Vulnerable by IUCN.

Coalfish

Pollachius virens

Also known as the saithe or pollock, and not to be confused with the similar pollack (*Pollachius pollachius*), the coalfish lives in large schools in continental shelf seas. These waters are richer in food resources than the deep oceans, owing to the nutrients scoured up from the relatively shallow sea bed, so even surface-dwelling fish favour them. Mature coalfish feed mainly on smaller schooling fish, frequenting coastal waters in spring and summer, and returning to deeper waters in winter. They spawn from January to April, and their eggs and larvae drift into the coastal shallows where the young fish feed on planktonic crustaceans and small fish for two years before moving into deeper water.

Identification: A typical cod, deep in the belly but tapering towards the tail, with large eyes, a small chin barbel when young that disappears with age, three dorsal fins and two anal fins. Brownish-green back, with silvery sides and belly and a cream-coloured or lighter grey lateral line.

Distribution: North Atlantic from eastern Canada and New England to southern Greenland, Iceland, northern Europe, Scandinavia and the Barents Sea.
Habitat: Schools near the surface and in mid-water to depths of 200m/656ft.
Food: Marine crustaceans and fish.
Size: 1.3m/4.25ft.
Breeding: Eggs shed are fertilized externally; the larvae drift in plankton.
Status: Not listed by IUCN.

Southern hake

Urophycis floridana

Distribution: Western central Atlantic Ocean and Gulf of Mexico.
Habitat: Near seabed in continental shelf seas, to depths of 400m/1,300ft.
Food: Crustaceans, marine worms, fish and squid.
Size: 30cm/12in.
Breeding: Eggs shed into the water are fertilized externally; they are buoyant, and hatched larvae are planktonic.
Status: Not listed by IUCN.

The hakes are closely related to cods and are similar in form, but the second and third dorsal fins present in cod are fused to form a single fin extending all the way down the back to the tail. The single anal fin is similar. This subtropical species occurs in the warm waters of the Gulf of Mexico, and in the western Atlantic as far north as the Carolinas. It is an active predator that travels in schools, generally at depths of less than 300m/980ft, feeding on fish and squid – although younger fish in shallow water also eat a lot of marine worms and small crustaceans. The schools move into shallower coastal waters in cold weather. The southern hake has been the subject of so much overfishing that there are concerns that some populations may not be able to replenish themselves.

Identification: Basically cod-like in form, with a deep belly and tapering tail, it has two dorsal fins instead of three, with the second being very elongated, and one elongated anal fin. It has long barbels beneath the head. Generally brown above and white below, it has dark spots above and behind the eyes and round, white spots at regular intervals along the black lateral line.

Pouting (*Trisopterus luscus*): 45cm/17.7in
This member of the cod family is a rich copper-brown above, and has yellowish-grey flanks with four or five dark bars. It has a single chin barbel and a black spot at the base of each pectoral fin. It occurs in the eastern Atlantic Ocean and the western Mediterranean Sea, and is a common sight on rocky reefs and wrecks. Young pouting often occur in large schools swimming close to the shore.

Poor cod (*Trisopterus minutus*): 40cm/15.75in
Resembling its close relative the pouting (*Trisopterus luscus*) described above, but smaller, the poor cod is a common species in the coastal waters of the eastern Atlantic Ocean and the western Mediterranean Sea. It lives in schools close to sandy or muddy sea beds, and in mid-water, and feeds on crustaceans, marine worms and small fish. In turn, it is preyed on by larger fish and dolphins.

White hake (*Urophycis tenuis*): 1.3m/4.25ft
Ranging from Labrador and Newfoundland to North Carolina, the white hake is a western North Atlantic species that favours soft, muddy areas of the continental shelf, and feeds on small crustaceans, fish and squid.

Atlantic hake

Merluccius merluccius

This moderately deep-water species, also called the European hake, lives near the bottom by day, but makes feeding forays into mid-water at night to find its prey. It feeds mainly on squid and fish, such as anchovies, sardines and herrings, as well as small hake. After spawning in spring and summer, the buoyant eggs and larvae drift into shallower inshore waters where the young hake are less vulnerable to cannibalistic predation, which is a common breeding strategy among fish, and there they feed mainly on planktonic crustaceans. It is an important food species, especially in southern Europe, but has suffered from over-exploitation and is now scarce in many sea areas.

Identification: A slender, large-headed fish with a protruding lower jaw and large, curved teeth, a triangular first dorsal fin and second dorsal and anal fins with elongated bases. Blue-green on the back and silvery on the sides and belly, with a straight, dark lateral line.

Distribution: Eastern Atlantic Ocean from Norway and Iceland to Mauritania; also Mediterranean Sea and southern Black Sea.
Habitat: Near the bottom on the middle and lower continental shelf, usually at depths of 70–370m/ 230–1,200ft but occasionally as deep as 1,000m/3,300ft.
Food: Fish and squid, or crustaceans when young.
Size: 1.4m/4.5ft.
Breeding: Buoyant eggs shed into the water are fertilized externally; the larvae are planktonic.
Status: Not listed by IUCN.

SILVERSIDES, NEEDLEFISH, HALFBEAKS AND KILLIFISH

These fish belong to three closely related orders. Silversides such as grunion are atheriniforms, while the elongated snouts of needlefish and halfbeaked fish are typical of families within the order Beloniformes. Cyprinodontiforms, or killifish, are a diverse group comprising elongate, as well as tubbier, members.

California grunion

Leuresthes tenuis

This small herring-like fish is famous for its spawning behaviour. Instead of shedding its eggs into the water, where they are likely to be eaten, it spawns at night on sandy beaches, just after the higher-than-normal spring tides that occur at the full and new moon. Large numbers of grunion swim in with the waves until they are virtually stranded, and each female works her tail end into the wet sand to deposit her eggs. The male coils around the female to fertilize her eggs, then both fish slip back into the sea. The timing ensures that the eggs remain above water level for about two weeks until they are washed out by the next high spring tide. By this time they are ready to hatch, and the larval grunion emerge within two or three minutes and are swept out to sea.

Identification: A slender, sinuous fish with large eyes, pectoral fins set well forward, two small dorsal fins, an anal fin with an elongated base and a forked tail fin. It has a bluish-green back, silvery sides and belly, and a blue-tinged silvery band bordered with violet along each flank.

Distribution: Coastal eastern Pacific Ocean, from Monterey Bay, California (US) to northern Baja California, Mexico.
Habitat: Coastal waters and bays at depths of no more than 18m/60ft.
Food: Plankton.
Size: 20cm/8in.
Breeding: Eggs are deposited on beaches below the highest tide line, and fertilized externally.
Status: Not listed by IUCN.

Hound needlefish

Tylosurus crocodilus

Widespread in the tropical oceans of the world, this is one of more than 50 similar species of needlefish. It gets its common name from its elongated, cylindrical form and extremely sharp snout, and is notorious for the way that it leaps from the water when agitated or alarmed, perhaps by predators, or when attracted towards lights at night. The fish flies through the air like a spear and people have been impaled by flying needlefish – some being seriously injured or even killed. It also has a habit of skittering across the ocean surface at high speed to escape predators or to move out of the way of boats, using its rapidly vibrating tail rather like an outboard motor – a technique that is reminiscent of the take-off runs of the closely related flying fish. It is a predator of other fish, swimming very rapidly in pursuit of its quarry, although young needlefish feed on plankton.

Identification: A very elongated, cylindrical fish with a sharp, needle-like snout lined with many sharp teeth. This is the only species of needlefish in which the teeth protrude outwards in juveniles, although they are straighter in adult fish. The dorsal and anal fins are set well back on the body, long-rayed at the front and with short-rayed extensions towards the tail fin, which is deeply forked. Body is dark blue above and white below, with silvery sides.

Distribution: Tropical Indo-Pacific Ocean from the Red Sea and South Africa to Polynesia and Japan; also Indonesia and northern Australia; tropical Atlantic range from New Jersey, USA, and Brazil to West Africa.
Habitat: Coral reefs and associated lagoons, to depths of 13m/40ft.
Food: Smaller fish.
Size: 1.5m/5ft.
Breeding: Eggs shed in the water are fertilized externally, and attach to corals and other objects.
Status: Not listed by IUCN.

Sheep's head minnow

Cyprinodon variegatus

Distribution: North and South America, from north-eastern USA to Mexico, the West Indies and Venezuela.
Habitat: Near muddy bottoms in fresh, brackish and saltwaters, including shallow, cloudy, virtually stagnant pools and ditches.
Food: Plant material, insect larvae, smaller fish, algae and detritus.
Size: 5cm/2in.
Breeding: Eggs shed into nest pits are fertilized by the male, which then defends them until they hatch.
Status: Not listed by IUCN.

This small, stumpy fish is one of the killifish, a large and widespread family found mainly in warm climates. It is extremely hardy and adaptable; it can live in muddy puddles that are too shallow for other species, tolerate a wide range of salinities, and survive in warm, virtually deoxygenated water by gulping air at the surface. The sheep's head minnow eats a wide variety of foods, including mosquito larvae, and is eaten in turn by other fish, turtles and wading birds. Its main defence is to travel in schools, but it also burrows into sediments to hide. Before spawning – which can occur at any time of year in warm waters – the males dig nest pits in the bottom mud and entice females to lay their eggs in them. Each female may lay several batches of eggs, each of up to 300, and the male defends the nest until the eggs hatch.

Identification: A short, deep-bodied fish, with a single, tall dorsal fin and a squarish caudal fin. Mainly silvery, with a dark marginal band on the tail, but males glow a bright blue colour when spawning.

Ballyhoo (*Hemiramphus brasiliensis*): 55cm/21.6in
The ballyhoo is a subtropical Atlantic member of the halfbeak family, a group closely related to the needlefish and flying fish. The name refers to the way the upper jaw is very much shorter than the lower; in other respects it resembles a silver-coloured needlefish, with three black stripes extending the length of its back. It lives in schools in shallow inshore waters, where it feeds on seagrasses and small fish.

Hardhead silverside (*Atherinomorus stipes*): 10cm/4in
A relative of the California grunion (*Leuresthes tenuis*), the hardhead silverside is a small, large-eyed, silver-coloured fish that swims in schools and feeds on small crustaceans and other zooplankton. It is an adaptable species that lives on coral reefs and soft seabeds in the tropical and subtropical western Atlantic and Caribbean, and in brackish mangrove creeks and even in freshwater streams.

Sand-smelt (*Atherina presbyter*): 20cm/8in
The slender-bodied sand-smelt has a clear green back and sides, with a broad, bright silver line running along each flank from head to tail. It lives in schools in shallow coastal waters and estuaries in the eastern North Atlantic and western Mediterranean, catching small crustaceans and fish larvae with its strongly protrusile jaws.

Four-eyed fish

Anableps anableps

This bizarre killifish is specialized for life at the water's surface, with eyes that are adapted to see well both above and below the surface. Each eye has a divided retina and two pupils that permit light to pass through the lens in different directions. The lens is ovoid, so light from below the water surface is projected through its longer dimension, while light from above the surface passes through its width. The contrast between the length and width of the lens provides the different optical qualities necessary for seeing well in both water and air. The adaptation allows the fish to target aerial and aquatic prey, and during the day it spends most of its time poised at the surface with its eyes bisected by the water line. It can also survive on mud exposed at low tide in coastal mangrove swamps.

Identification: An elongated, brownish coloured fish with large, rounded pectoral fins, a single dorsal fin set well back on the body, and a rounded tail fin. Each high-set, protruding, frog-like eye is laterally divided into two parts.

Distribution: North-eastern South America, from Trinidad and Venezuela to the Amazon delta in Brazil.
Habitat: Shallow, muddy freshwater streams and brackish mangrove channels and lagoons.
Food: Insects, crustaceans, molluscs and other types of small creature.
Size: 15cm/6in.
Breeding: Males and females mate side-to-side; females bear live young.
Status: Not listed by IUCN.

DORIES, BERYCIFORMS AND SCORPIONFISH

Dories, a well-known commercial food fish, and boarfish, are dominant in the order Zeiformes. They have narrow deep bodies, and large mouths with distensible jaws. Beryciforms include big-eyed members such as the pineconefish and species of squirrelfish, some of which have evolved light organs beneath the eye area. Scorpionfish, such as lionfish and gurnards, are an attractive, though often venomous, family of scorpaeniforms.

John dory

Zeus faber

Identification: Very deep, narrow body; high-set eyes and protrusile jaws. Two dorsal fins, the first with 9–11 strong spines with extended rays; two anal fins. Generally grey with yellow and brown stripes and blotches; yellow-ringed black spot on each flank.

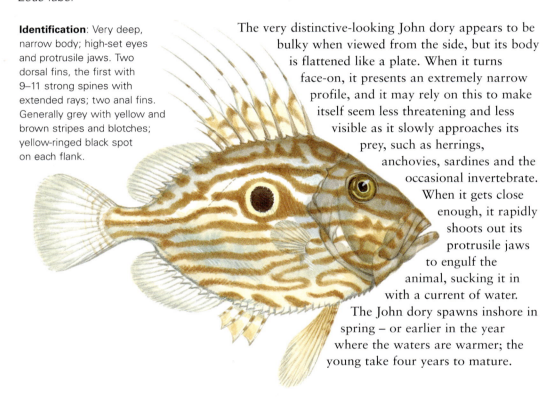

The very distinctive-looking John dory appears to be bulky when viewed from the side, but its body is flattened like a plate. When it turns face-on, it presents an extremely narrow profile, and it may rely on this to make itself seem less threatening and less visible as it slowly approaches its prey, such as herrings, anchovies, sardines and the occasional invertebrate. When it gets close enough, it rapidly shoots out its protrusile jaws to engulf the animal, sucking it in with a current of water. The John dory spawns inshore in spring – or earlier in the year where the waters are warmer; the young take four years to mature.

Distribution: Widespread in shallow temperate seas, including the eastern North Atlantic Ocean, the Mediterranean and Black Seas, western North Pacific Ocean around Japan and Korea, and the western South Pacific Ocean around Australia and New Zealand.
Habitat: Inshore waters close to the seabed, at depths of 5–400m/ 16–1,310ft.
Food: Schooling fish, plus occasional crustaceans, octopus and cuttlefish.
Size: 65cm/25.5in.
Breeding: Eggs are shed into the water where they are fertilized externally.
Status: Not listed by IUCN.

Pinecone fish

Monocentris japonica

This tropical Indo-Pacific fish is heavily defended by an armour of very large, sturdy, ridged plates, and a set of extremely strong dorsal and pelvic spines. It is nocturnal, emerging at night to feed on small planktonic animals. It has big eyes for locating its prey in the dim light, and a pair of small light organs on its lower jaw that may act as lures. The light is produced by symbiotic bacteria within each organ, and the colour of the light varies from orange by day to blue-green at night.

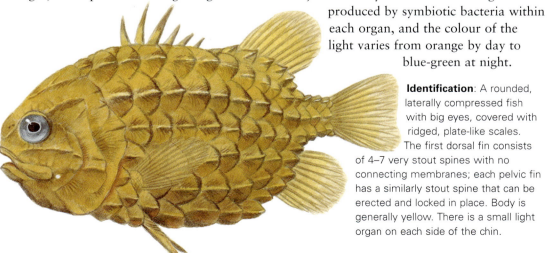

Identification: A rounded, laterally compressed fish with big eyes, covered with ridged, plate-like scales. The first dorsal fin consists of 4–7 very stout spines with no connecting membranes; each pelvic fin has a similarly stout spine that can be erected and locked in place. Body is generally yellow. There is a small light organ on each side of the chin.

Distribution: Tropical Indian and western Pacific Oceans, from the Red Sea and eastern Africa to southern Japan, Australia and northern New Zealand.
Habitat: Rocky reefs below the tide line, in caves and crevices at depths of 10–200m/33–655ft.
Food: Mainly small planktonic crustaceans.
Size: 15cm/6in.
Breeding: Eggs are shed into the water where they are fertilized externally.
Status: Not listed by IUCN.

Red lionfish

Pterois volitans

The red lionfish is one of eight members of the *Pterois* genus native to the coral seas of the Indo-Pacific. Its extravagant dorsal fin is equipped with grooved spines linked to venom glands, making it very dangerous, and its dramatic appearance may act as warning to potential predators. The fish is mostly nocturnal, spending the day almost motionless in a cave or crevice with its head inclined downwards; it counters any threat by advancing with its dorsal spines facing forward. It emerges at night to hunt for smaller fish and shrimps, using its widespread pectoral fins to corner a victim and then striking very rapidly to seize it in its jaws.

Distribution: Native to the western tropical Pacific Ocean, from southern Japan to northern New Zealand, and west to Sumatra. Also eastern Indian Ocean; introduced to western Atlantic.
Habitat: Mainly coral reefs and lagoons, from 2–50m/ 6.5–165ft.
Food: Small fish, shrimps and crabs.
Size: 38cm/15in.
Breeding: Eggs are shed in buoyant mucous containers; they are fertilized externally and the larvae are planktonic.
Status: Not listed by IUCN.

Identification: Long fin rays on pectoral and dorsal fins, and bold stripes of red to black. Adults often have white spots along the lateral line. There is usually a leaf-like tentacle above each eye.

Striped redcoat squirrelfish (*Sargocentron rubrum*): 20cm/8in
Named for the longitudinal red and silver stripes on its deep flanks, this big-eyed subtropical and tropical species (above) has strong spines in its first dorsal fin, on each cheek, and in front of its anal fin. It lives on Indo-Pacific coastal reefs and wrecks, hiding by day and emerging at night to feed on crabs, shrimps and some small fish.

Common boarfish (*Capros aper*): 30cm/12in
Usually deep red with yellowish markings, this deep-bodied fish is equipped with long, stout dorsal and pelvic spines, and shorter anal fin spines. It lives in schools in the shelf seas of the eastern North Atlantic and western Mediterranean, mainly over rocky reefs, and uses its protrusile mouth to capture crustaceans, marine worms and molluscs.

Sable fish (*Anoplopoma fimbria*): 80cm/31in
At first glance, this scorpionfish looks more like a trout, with a long, sleek body and greenish, spotted back. It occurs in the North Pacific, from the Bering Sea to Southern Japan and Mexico, and migrates over long distances. It feeds on crustaceans, marine worms and small fish, and is the basis of a commercial fishery.

Flying gurnard

Dactylopterus volitans

Despite the wing-like proportions of its enlarged pectoral fins, the flying gurnard cannot actually fly. It spends most of its time exploring the seabed, creeping over soft sediments with its pectoral fins expanded so that it resembles a foraging ray. It uses the detached front lobes of these fins like legs, both to propel itself and probe for prey, such as buried bivalve molluscs or small crabs. In the process, it flushes small mobile animals into open water, and the gurnard is often shadowed by opportunist predatory fish that snap up any escapees.

Identification: A large-eyed fish with a big, blunt, armoured head and a long backward-pointing spine on each cheek. Two dorsal fins, the first with two free spines at the front. Greatly enlarged, fan-like pelvic fins, with the front six rays separated to form a mobile lobe. Mainly orange-red with some blue spots on the back; paler below. Pelvic fins mainly brown, with lighter and darker spots.

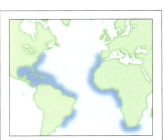

Distribution: Subtropical and tropical Atlantic Ocean, from the US to Argentina, and from France to the Azores. Also found in brackish estuarine waters.
Habitat: Sandy or muddy seabeds, often near reefs, in shallow water to depths of 100m/330ft.
Food: Crabs, shrimps, clams and small bottom-living fish.
Size: 38cm/15in.
Breeding: Eggs are shed into the water where they are fertilized externally.
Status: Not listed by IUCN.

PERCHLIKE FISH

The sheer breadth of this order of ray-finned fish has already been noted. Among the large-bodied, mostly warm-water and tropical perciforms covered on the following pages are representatives from significant food fish families such as the Serranidae, sea bass and groupers, as well as the Letherinidae, made up of bream and emperor species, and many other colourful reef fish and scavengers.

Snook

Centropomus undecimalis

The big, silvery common snook is widespread in the warm waters of the Caribbean region and adjacent Atlantic, and the most abundant species in its family Centropomidae. It occurs in shallow coastal areas of salty and brackish water, usually at depths less than 20m/65ft, where it preys on smaller fish and crustaceans such as shrimps and crabs. It has few predators apart from human sport fishers, for whom it is a prize catch. It spawns in salt water near river estuaries between May and September, and the young larvae then move upriver to live in freshwater tributaries.

Identification: A streamlined, hump-backed fish with a sharp snout, protruding lower jaw and sloping forehead. It has two dorsal fins – the first spiny – a forked tail fin and a prominent black lateral line. It is dull grey in colour above with a yellow or green tinge, and silvery on the sides and belly. In some populations of fish many of the fins are yellow.

Distribution: Western central Atlantic, Gulf of Mexico and Caribbean, from the Carolinas south to Rio de Janeiro, Brazil.
Habitat: Coastal waters, lagoons and mangrove-lined estuaries, penetrating into brackish and fresh water.
Food: Fish and crustaceans, such as shrimps.
Size: 1.4m/5ft.
Breeding: Eggs shed in salt water, where they are fertilized externally. Larvae migrate to brackish and fresh waters.
Status: Not listed by IUCN.

Royal gramma

Gramma loreto

Identification: Small, with a long-based dorsal fin and elongated pectoral fins. It is bluish-purple at the front, fading through pink to yellow at the back. Oblique black stripe through eye; black spot at front of dorsal fin.

This small, brightly coloured, rainbow-patterned reef fish lives in caves and crevices among the coral, often hanging upside down from the roof of a cavity with just its head protruding. Like many reef fish, the royal gramma changes sex as it ages, starting out as a female and becoming a male. It is territorial, and when a territory-holding male dies, a female will change sex in order to take over the role. Breeding males lure females to spawn by preparing nursery sites in small crevices and then lining them with pieces of seaweed and coral. When the eggs are laid, both sexes defend them until hatching, about seven days later.

Distribution: Caribbean and western central Atlantic Ocean from Bermuda to Venezuela.
Habitat: Crevices in coral reefs.
Food: Small planktonic crustaceans, such as copepods; also picks skin parasites off other fish, such as snappers.
Size: 8cm/3in.
Breeding: Eggs shed into a crevice where they are fertilized by the male and tended by both parents.
Status: Not listed by IUCN.

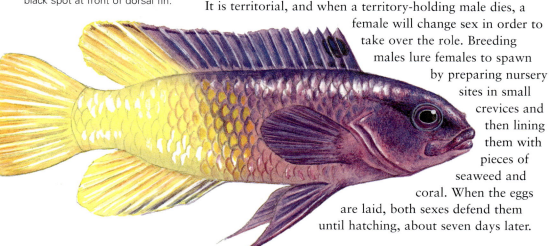

Giant sea bass

Stereolepis gigas

Distribution: Eastern Pacific from California to Mexico.
Habitat: Rocky reefs with kelp beds, in depths of about 5–46m/16–150ft.
Food: Mainly bottom-dwelling fish, squid, octopus, lobsters and crabs.
Size: 2.5m/8.2ft.
Breeding: Eggs are fertilized externally and float to the surface of the water where they hatch within 1–2 days. Larvae are planktonic.
Status: Listed as Critically Endangered by IUCN.

Now extremely scarce throughout its restricted range, the giant sea bass is a bottom-feeding predator that targets slow-moving rays, flatfish, crabs and cephalopods. Cruising through the rocky reefs that are its favoured habitat, it approaches its prey and rapidly opens its huge mouth to create a suction current, drawing the victim in. As an adult, its only natural enemies are large sharks, but it has been intensively exploited as a commercial and sports fish. As a slow-breeding species it has been unable to make good the losses. Its bottom-feeding habits also make it vulnerable to pollution, since the sea bed off California is badly contaminated with toxic chemicals.

Identification: A very large, stout-bodied fish with a big head and a huge mouth, an arched back, and a spiny, long-based first dorsal fin. Bright orange with black spots when juvenile, it turns bronze-purple and then grey or black with age. Adults can change colour rapidly, from jet black to light grey, and hide or display black spots at will.

Orange sea perch (*Anthias squamipinnis*): 15cm/6in
With its lyre-shaped tail, this small, blunt-nosed, spiny-finned, plankton-eating fish from the tropical Indo-Pacific forms large schools on coral reefs. Like many reef fish, it changes sex with age, the orange-yellow female turning into a more reddish male, and develops an elongated spine at the front of the dorsal fin.

Coney (*Cephalopholis fulva*): 40cm/15.75in
Identifiable by the two black spots on its lower lip, the coney is a variably coloured grouper found on coral reefs in the tropical west Atlantic, Gulf of Mexico and Caribbean. It feeds on small fish and crustaceans, favouring water at least 45m/145ft deep.

Florida pompano (*Trachinotus carolinus*): 60cm/23.6in
The Florida pompano is a deep-bodied, laterally compressed fish with a deeply forked tail. It lives in schools in the open coastal waters of the Atlantic and Caribbean from Massachusetts, USA, to Venezuela. Silvery with a yellow throat and belly, it has yellowish pelvic and anal fins. It feeds on molluscs, crustaceans and small fish.

Oriental sweetlips

Plectorhinchus orientalis

Also known as grunts, because of their ability to make sounds by grinding their pharyngeal teeth, the 175 species of sweetlips are bottom-feeding predators that prey mainly on invertebrates buried in the sediments. They use their loose, rubbery lips to suck up the sand – which is ejected through the gills in a cloud – and any animals that it conceals. The oriental sweetlips is one of the biggest and most colourful species, well known for its lack of timidity when approached by divers. It usually feeds by night, often in groups, and shelters in caves during the day.

Identification: A stout-bodied fish with a large, blunt head and a big, low-slung mouth with thick, loose, rubbery lips. The first dorsal fin has up to 15 spines and is joined to the second dorsal fin. The pectoral and pelvic fins are relatively small, and the tail fin is shallowly forked. Very colourfully marked, with longitudinal blue and white stripes on the body, a yellow and black face and eye, and yellow fins spotted and striped with black.

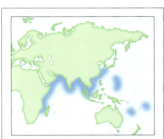

Distribution: Indo-Pacific: East Africa to Samoa, north to Ryukyu Islands, south to New Caledonia; Palau to eastern Caroline and Mariana Islands in Micronesia.
Habitat: Seabed on rocky and coral reefs, to depths of 25m/80ft.
Food: Worms, molluscs, crustaceans, such as crabs and shrimps, and small fish.
Size: 85cm/33.5in.
Breeding: Eggs shed and are fertilized externally.
Status: Not listed by IUCN.

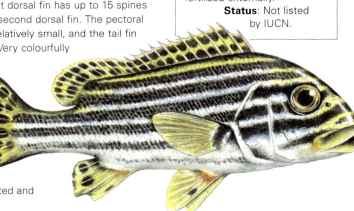

Sweetlip emperor

Lethrinus miniatus

Known by a variety of names, including trumpet emperor, longnosed emperor and red-throat emperor, this bulky species is usually to be found on coral reefs by day, lurking among the coral heads for protection from larger predators, such as sharks. By night, it moves out over the open sand of coral lagoons and similar areas to forage for food, often in small schools. It will take a variety of prey, but favours crabs and sea urchins, which it is able to crack open with its strong jaws. It is regularly caught by both commercial and sport fishers, but if it evades capture, or being eaten by other animals, it may live for 20 years or more.

Identification: A deep-bodied fish with a large head and big mouth, high-set eyes and a moderately long snout. The lips tend to be red in colour, giving this species its common name. Body is silver-grey in colour with about eight indistinct vertical dark bars. The spiny dorsal fin, anal fin and tail are often bright red, and the pelvic and pectoral fin bases and the area around the eye are red-orange.

Distribution: Western Pacific, from northern and western Australia to New Caledonia and Ryukyu Is.
Food: Crustaceans, sea urchins, starfish, molluscs and fish.
Habitat: Favours coral reefs during the day; may move into nearby sandy lagoons at night to feed. Found at depths of about 30m/100ft.
Size: 90cm/35.5in.
Breeding: Eggs are released into the water where they are fertilized externally.
Status: Not listed by IUCN.

Common sea bream

Pagrus pagrus

Usually found on or near rocky reefs and wrecks, the common sea bream is a bottom-feeding fish that preys mainly on crabs, brittlestars, molluscs and small fish. Despite its name, it is now far less common than it once was, having been overexploited by commercial fisheries. Larger, older fish are now rare, and since this is a species that changes sex with age – from female to male – the selective removal of larger fish seriously unbalances the sex ratio. However, like many warm-water fish, the common sea bream tends to accumulate toxins in its body, through eating filter-feeding animals that have themselves ingested mildly toxic microorganisms. The risk of becoming a victim of such poisoning, known as 'ciguatera poisoning', may make humans regard the species less favourably as a food source, and improve its chances of survival.

Identification: A deep-bodied, laterally compressed fish with a large, blunt head, big eyes, a spiny dorsal fin and a forked tail. Silvery red with reddish dorsal, pectoral and tail fins, and faint yellow spots on each scale giving a yellow-striped effect.

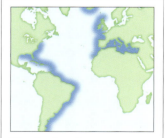

Distribution: Eastern Atlantic: Strait of Gibraltar to Madeira and the Canary Is; also Mediterranean and northward to the British Isles. Western Atlantic: New York, USA and northern Gulf of Mexico to Argentina.
Habitat: Rocky or sandy sea beds to a depth of about 250m/820ft.
Food: Crustaceans, echinoderms, molluscs and fish.
Size: 90cm/35in.
Breeding: Eggs are fertilized in the water.
Status: Listed as Endangered by IUCN.

Distribution: Indo-Pacific, including waters off New Zealand, Australia, Indonesia, China, Taiwan and Japan.
Habitat: Rocky and coral reefs, and sandy and muddy brackish estuaries, including seagrass beds.
Food: Bottom-dwelling animals, including crustaceans, marine worms, sea urchins, starfish, molluscs and fish.
Size: 1.3m/4.25ft.
Breeding: Eggs are released into the water where they are fertilized externally.
Status: Not listed by IUCN.

Snapper

Chrysophrys auratus

Widespread in the coastal waters of the western Pacific, but forming several separate populations, the snapper, or squirefish, is a bottom-dwelling species that is most abundant near rocky reef areas on the inner continental shelf. Groups of young snappers are often encountered in shallow inshore areas such seagrass beds, but the older, larger fish tend to stay out on the reefs. It feeds on a variety of hard-shelled animals, such as crabs, sea urchins and topshells, crushing them with its strong teeth, but it will also attack schooling fish and take fish fragments when schools are being targeted by other species. It is a valued food fish, caught in large numbers by commercial fishers.

Identification: Deep-bodied and laterally compressed with a large head, typically with a rounded profile but developing a high forehead with age. It has a fairly small mouth, a spiny dorsal fin and forked tail fin. Pale pink with blue-tinged fins and a scattering of iridescent bright blue spots on back and flanks.

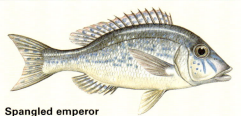

Spangled emperor
(*Lethrinus nebulosus*): 87cm/34.25in
The largest of the emperors, the spangled emperor is very like the sweetlip emperor (see opposite), but yellow-olive with pearly blue spots and streaks, giving a spangled effect. It lives on Indo-Pacific coral reefs and seagrass beds and among mangroves, feeding on sea urchins, molluscs, crustaceans, marine worms and fish.

Jolthead porgy (*Calamus bajonado*): 60cm/24in
Common in the waters of the Caribbean and off southern Florida, USA, as well as the western central Atlantic from South Carolina, USA, to Brazil, this is a deep-bodied, silvery-brown fish with a high, rounded forehead. It has strong, flattened teeth for crushing sea urchins, crabs and molluscs, and its name may refer to its habit of using its head to dislodge shellfish from rocks.

Gilthead bream (*Sparus aurata*): 70cm/27.6in
A shallow-water species that lives in schools over sandy seabeds, it is a deep-bodied fish with a strongly arched, dark grey back, a dark blotch on each gill cover and a golden stripe across its forehead. It preys heavily on mussels and oysters, using the long, pointed teeth in the front of its mouth to prise them from rocks before crushing them with its flattened cheek teeth.

Scat

Scatophagus argus

This very flattened species is common in the brackish waters of the tidal mangrove swamps that fringe estuaries in the tropical Indo-Pacific. It will eat almost anything, including the faeces of other fish – the name *Scatophagus* means 'faeces-eater' – so it has no trouble finding food in the rich, if malodorous, waters of the muddy swamps. The tangled mangrove roots also give it protection from larger predators, so the habitat makes an excellent nursery for the young fish. As they mature, they become less tolerant of brackish water, and move out on to marine coral reefs where they eventually spawn. The larvae then drift back inshore to develop in the relative security of the mangroves.

Identification: A squarish, laterally compressed fish with a small head and mouth, and a steep forehead. The spines in its dorsal, anal and pelvic fins are mildly venomous. Young fish are silvery green or silvery brown with large black spots. As they age, they turn a dull silver, retaining the spots.

Distribution: Tropical Indian Ocean and western Pacific Ocean, from Kuwait to Fiji and north to Japan.
Habitat: Shallow bays, brackish estuaries and freshwater streams, especially among tidal mangroves.
Food: Worms, crustaceans, insects, plant material and organic detritus.
Size: 35cm/13.75in.
Breeding: Eggs are released and fertilized externally in salt water, and larvae migrate to brackish estuaries.
Status: Not listed by IUCN.

Copperband butterflyfish

Chelmon rostratus

It is not surprising that butterflyfish are valued commercially for their dazzling colouration, which looks conspicuous in an aquarium. In the wild, however, the colour pattern has a greater purpose: against the background of a coral reef it acts as a disruption pattern, breaking up the fish's outline and making it more difficult to see. If a predator does target it, it is likely to be attracted to the prominent eyespot on the dorsal fin rays. This may give the butterflyfish a chance to escape, even if its dorsal fin is shredded in the process. This common species occurs both on coral reefs and in estuaries, singly or in pairs that defend a territory against other fish of the same species.

Identification: A very striking species, which appears taller than it is long because of its compressed, deep-bodied form, long dorsal and anal fins, and vertical yellow stripes on a white background. The snout is long and slender, and the dark eye is less conspicuous than the dark eye-spot on the dorsal fin. There is also a dark band at the base of the tail. Similar in shape to its relative *Chelmon marginalis*, the margined coralfish, although the latter has just one prominent copper-coloured stripe and fewer dorsal rays.

Distribution: Western tropical Pacific Ocean, from the Andaman Sea to the Philippines and Australia.
Habitat: Rocky shores, coral reefs and estuaries, to a depth of 25m/80ft.
Food: Small marine crustaceans and encrusting animals.
Size: 15cm/6in.
Breeding: Eggs are shed in the water where they are fertilized externally; the larvae are planktonic. Pairs usually mate for life.
Status: Not listed by IUCN.

Royal empress angelfish

Pygoplites diacanthus

Identification: A deep-bodied, compressed fish with a short snout. Basically yellow – or orange when young – with black-edged vertical white bars on the body and front part of the dorsal fin. The rear of the dorsal fin is deep blue, and the anal fin has yellow and blue stripes. Juvenile fish have an eye-like dark spot of colour at the base of the dorsal fin, which fades as they mature.

Closely allied to the butterflyfish, and equally spectacular in appearance, angelfish are more bulky creatures with shorter snouts and a heavy spine at the base of each gill cover. The royal empress angelfish is a particularly colourful species, but the visually disruptive effect of its vertical stripes may make it harder for a potential predator to pick it out clearly in its natural habitat. It feeds on the encrusting animals that live among the corals, and it is usually seen singly or in pairs near caves and overhanging ledges, which the animal uses as refuges. As with butterflyfish fish, the royal empress is often exported as an aquarium species, but will rarely achieve long life under these conditions.

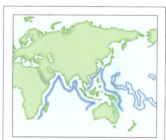

Distribution: Tropical Indo-Pacific Ocean, from Red Sea and East Africa to the Tuamoto Islands, north to the Ryukyu Islands, and south to the Great Barrier Reef.
Habitat: Coral reefs and associated coral-rich lagoons; may seek refuge in underwater caves if threatened by predators.
Food: Sponges, sea squirts and similar animals.
Size: 25cm/10in.
Breeding: Eggs are shed in the water and fertilized externally, developing into planktonic larvae.

Orange clownfish

Amphiprion percula

Distribution: Western South Pacific, New Guinea and Solomon Islands.
Habitat: Coral reefs.
Food: Small planktonic crustaceans and similar animals, and algae.
Size: 8cm/3in.
Breeding: Eggs are laid in a nest site prepared by the male, which he then fertilizes and defends.
Status: Not listed by IUCN.

One of five species with similar habits, this tropical reef fish lives in association with large sea anemones, sheltering within their stinging tentacles as a defence against other fish. It is apparently immune to the stings, being protected by a coating of mucus that it secretes in response to its first contact with the tentacles. It always chooses one of three species of anemone, suggesting that it may not be immune to the stings of other species. It lives in small groups consisting of a breeding pair and up to four non-breeding males. The breeding female is the largest; if she dies, the male of the pair changes sex to take over as egg-layer, and one of the younger fish is promoted to the role of breeding male.

Identification: A plump, blunt-nosed fish, nearly always found sheltering among the tentacles of an anemone. It is orange with three irregular black-bordered vertical white bands. The rounded fins are orange and edged in black. Often confused with the clown anemone fish, *A. ocellaris*, although the latter lacks the black borders between coloured stripes.

Four-eye butterflyfish (*Chaetodon capistratus*): 6cm/2.3in
Named for the large, white-ringed black eyespot on the rear end of its disc-shaped, dove-grey and pale yellow body, this elegant little fish lives on shallow reefs in the Caribbean, Gulf of Mexico and nearby western Atlantic. Its real eye is normally masked by a dark stripe. Their common name of 'butterflyfish' refers to the flitting action of these fish as they feed delicately on the reef.

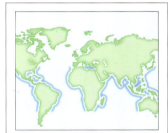

Forceps butterflyfish (*Forcipiger longirostris*): 15cm/6in
Widespread but generally uncommon on the coral reefs of the tropical Indo-Pacific Ocean, this butterflyfish has a highly elongated snout with a very small mouth at the tip. It uses this to pick tiny invertebrates from among the spines of sea urchin and in coral crevices. It is mainly bright yellow, but its head is black above and off-white below, and it has a grey-green tail.

Sergeant major (*Abudefduf saxatilis*): 15cm/6in
One of the most widespread damselfish, the sergeant major is a tropical Atlantic and Caribbean species with black vertical bars on its deep, yellowish-green body. It lives mainly on reefs, where it forms large schools that feed on algae, small crustaceans, invertebrate larvae and small fish. Some populations also scavenge floating offal, and juveniles may pick parasites from the skin of larger animals, most notably green turtles.

Striped mullet

Mugil cephalus

This sleek fish is one of about 80 species of mullets found mainly in salty and brackish water. Typical of its family, it has a muscular, gizzard-like stomach and a long intestine for processing vegetable foods as well as more easily digested animals. It can also ingest detritus and absorb the nutrients that it contains, making it flexible in its eating habits. In addition, it can tolerate variations in salinity that enable it to range upstream in rivers and return to the sea. Young fish exploit this by spending their early years in estuaries, where they are less vulnerable to predators. However, this makes the striped mullet easy to raise in fish farms, and it is widely cultivated in Southeast Asia.

Identification: A streamlined, round-bodied fish with an upturned mouth, two small triangular dorsal fins, the first with spines, and a large, shallowly forked tail. Bluish grey or greenish above, with silver sides and a white belly.

Distribution: Widespread in tropical and subtropical oceans and seas.
Habitat: Coastal and shallow waters to depths of 120m/390ft, favouring muddy areas; also estuaries and rivers.
Food: Small planktonic animals, bottom-living worms and microorganisms, small algae and detritus.
Size: 1.2m/4ft.
Breeding: Females typically spawn between 5 and 7 million eggs. Eggs shed and externally fertilized offshore; larvae then move inshore to develop in estuaries.
Status: Not listed by IUCN.

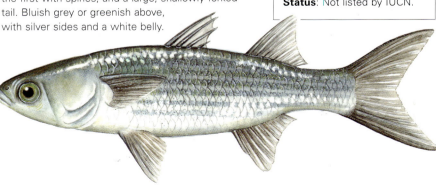

Giant kelpfish

Heterostichus rostratus

The giant kelpfish is the largest of the blennies. Like all true blennies, it has a continuous dorsal fin of which the first part is spiny and the remainder is soft, and a pelvic fin which is situated under the throat. The giant kelpfish spends its life among the submerged 'forests' of giant kelp – a type of large seaweed – that grow along the Pacific coasts of North America. The giant kelpfish's body colour varies to match that of the local kelp, and its elongated form blends in well with the strap-like kelp fronds. The bottom-feeding adults prey on a variety of shellfish and small fish. As adults they are solitary by habit, but the young occur in schools.

Identification: A large blenny with a long head and body, long dorsal and anal fins with prominent rays and a small tail fin. Often found among rocks often associated with giant kelp. Usually brownish or greenish in colour, mottled with silvery white, and often with darker vertical bars along the flanks. Adults solitary, young swim in schools.

Distribution: Coastal eastern Pacific from central California, USA, to southern Baja California, Mexico.
Habitat: Among rocks in coastal kelp forests, to depths of 40m/130ft.
Food: Crustaceans, molluscs and small fish.
Size: 60cm/24in.
Breeding: Released eggs attach to coral-like seaweeds, where they are fertilized and guarded by the male.
Status: Not listed by IUCN.

Moorish idol

Zanclus cornutus

This is one of the most spectacular of all reef fish, thanks to its bold, striped colour scheme and its elongated, sickle-shaped dorsal fin. Sometimes the extended tip of the fin is cut short, presumably when in conflict with predators or prey. It lives mainly on tropical coral reefs, where it uses its long snout to probe cracks and crevices for coralline seaweeds and encrusting animals such as sponges to eat. It occurs in a variety of reef habitats, from cloudy lagoons and sheltered reef flats to exposed reef faces, and down to considerable depths. Usually found in small groups, it occasionally swims in large schools of a hundred or more individuals. Young exist as free-swimming larvae for a considerable period after hatching, and may cover great distances, accounting for the lack of variation seen in this species over its widespread geographical distribution.

Identification: A deep-bodied, laterally compressed fish with an extended, tube-like snout, a short projection over each eye, and a backswept dorsal fin extended into a very long filament. It has two broad, vertical black bars on its yellow and white body, another black bar on its small tail, and an orange or yellow saddle-like patch on top of its tubular snout. The small mouth is lined with elongate teeth which act as bristles.

Distribution: Subtropical and tropical Indo-Pacific from East Africa to Polynesia, Hawaii and Japan, and coastal eastern Pacific from Gulf of California to Peru.
Habitat: Coral reefs, from shallow water to depths of more than 180m/590ft. Also favours the slightly turgid waters of inland lagoons.
Food: Small encrusting animals and coralline algae.
Size: 20cm/8in.
Breeding: Eggs are released into the water where they are fertilized externally. The larvae drift for a considerable period before settling.
Status: Not listed by IUCN.

Golden damselfish

Amblyglyphidodon aureus

Usually found at depths of 12–24m/40–80ft on the steep outer coral reef slopes and in deep channels, this delicate-looking fish favours waters with strong currents where there are plenty of sea fans and gorgonian sea whips growing. The fish lays its eggs on the stems of these organisms, and then the male guards them against egg predators until they have hatched. Adults feed on the small animals of the zooplankton, typically alone or in small groups, quite close to the bottom or the reef face. The young have a similar diet to the adults, but they live in schools close to the feeding polyps of soft corals for defence.

Identification: A small, deep-bodied, laterally compressed fish with long-based, backswept dorsal and anal fins. Body colour is golden yellow with small bluish to purplish spots on its face and belly, and often blue-tinged fins.

Distribution: Tropical eastern Indian Ocean and western Pacific Ocean.
Habitat: Coral reefs, in deeper zones with gorgonian corals and strong currents, at depths of 3–45m/10–150ft.
Food: Small planktonic crustaceans.
Size: 10cm/4in.
Breeding: Lays eggs on coral-like sea whips and sea fans, where they are fertilized and guarded by the male.
Status: Not listed by IUCN.

Achilles tang (*Acanthurus achilles*): 30cm/12in
A striking coral reef fish from the tropical west Pacific, the Achilles tang is a deep-bodied, laterally flattened species with a largely black body outlined with white, a bright orange tail and orange patch towards the rear of each flank. It is common on Hawaiian reefs, where it favours rocky areas with large cracks, caves and crevices in the shallower, well-oxygenated surge zones.

Rainbow parrotfish (*Scarus guacamaia*): 1m/3.25ft
This is one of at least 80 species of parrotfish, named for the strong beak-like jaws they use to scrape algae from stony corals. The rainbow parrotfish is one of the largest, and lives on reefs in the tropical west Atlantic and Caribbean. The multicoloured adults are very variable, but typically greenish blue with orange fins. The young live among mangroves. The species is under threat because of habitat destruction.

Unicorn fish (*Naso lituratus*): 50cm/20in
Also known as the lipstick tang because of its prominent yellow lips, this greenish grey, Indo-Pacific reef fish has a black and grey dorsal fin, a yellow anal fin, a crescent-shaped tail with a black band, and a prominent 'unicorn' bump on its steep forehead. Two yellow patches on each side of the tail base mark the positions of sharp spines.

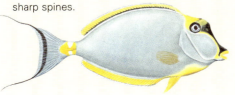

Blue tang

Acanthurus coeruleus

The beautifully coloured blue tang is one of the surgeonfish, named for the sharp, scalpel-like spine on each side of the caudal peduncle, or tail base. These spines fit into horizontal grooves, but can be extended to make effective defensive weapons, capable of inflicting slash wounds. Juveniles are yellow rather than blue. In the intermediate phase before reaching maturity, they are blue anteriorly with a bright yellow tail (as shown). In addition to grazing algae, juveniles pick dead skin and skin parasites from green turtles, often forming 'cleaning stations' with other reef species such as sergeant major fish.

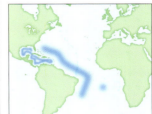

Distribution: Tropical western Atlantic Ocean, Gulf of Mexico and Caribbean. Also near Ascension Island in southeastern Atlantic.
Habitat: Coral and rocky reefs, and seagrass beds from 2–40m/6.5–130ft.
Food: Mainly small marine algae from rocks and reefs.
Size: 30cm/12in.
Breeding: Eggs are shed into the water where they are fertilized externally.
Status: Not listed by IUCN.

Identification: Laterally compressed body, large head with protruding mouth, and long-based dorsal and anal fins. Adults deep blue with narrow stripes of paler blue on body, and a pale yellow spine on each side of tail base. Juveniles yellow, may retain yellow tail until fully mature.

FLATFISH

Flatfish (Pleuronectiformes) are flattened laterally and, as adults, they swim and rest on their sides, one eye migrating around the head during their metamorphosis from the larval form. It is interesting to note that some species have both their eyes on the right side, others on the left side. Another feature of flatfish is that their eyes are protrusive – an adaptation to living partially buried on the sea bed.

Turbot

Psetta maxima

Identification: An almost circular flatfish, with a large head and both eyes on the left side. The dorsal and anal fins form a fringe around the scaleless body. Usually dull sandy brown.

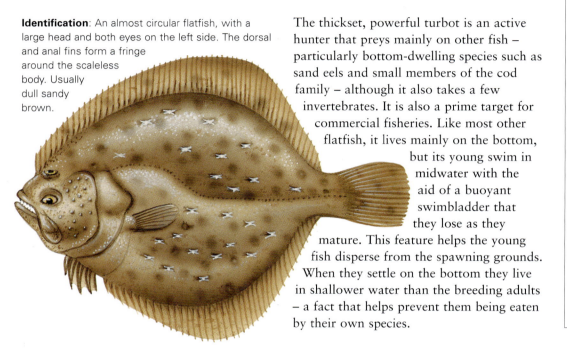

The thickset, powerful turbot is an active hunter that preys mainly on other fish – particularly bottom-dwelling species such as sand eels and small members of the cod family – although it also takes a few invertebrates. It is also a prime target for commercial fisheries. Like most other flatfish, it lives mainly on the bottom, but its young swim in midwater with the aid of a buoyant swimbladder that they lose as they mature. This feature helps the young fish disperse from the spawning grounds. When they settle on the bottom they live in shallower water than the breeding adults – a fact that helps prevent them being eaten by their own species.

Distribution: North-east Atlantic Ocean from Arctic Circle to North Africa, plus Mediterranean and Black seas, and most of Baltic Sea.
Habitat: Sandy or rocky seabeds, including brackish waters, in depths from 20–70m/65–230ft.
Food: Smaller fish, such as sand eels, herring, whiting and gobies, plus large crustaceans and bivalve molluscs.
Size: 1m/3.25ft.
Breeding: Eggs are shed in the water and are fertilized externally.
Status: Not listed by IUCN.

European plaice

Pleuronectes platessa

Identification: A medium-sized flatfish with an approximately diamond-shaped body and a small head, with both eyes on the right-hand (upper) side, and a row of bony knobs between the eyes and the upper gill opening. Upper side of fish is brown with red or orange spots; lower side is white.

The plaice is one of the most familiar of the flatfish, because it is widely caught and sold whole for food. It is also one of the commonest species to be seen alive by recreational divers in northern Europe, and young plaice may even be disturbed by people paddling on holiday beaches. This is because it favours sandy shores, where it swims in with the rising tide to prey on buried molluscs and worms as they emerge to feed. It often nips off the siphon tubes of burrowing clams and other bivalves, and grazes the tentacles of fanworms, using the well-developed teeth on the left-hand, lower side, of its mouth. It is most active at night, typically spending the day lying on the sea bed partially buried by sediment.

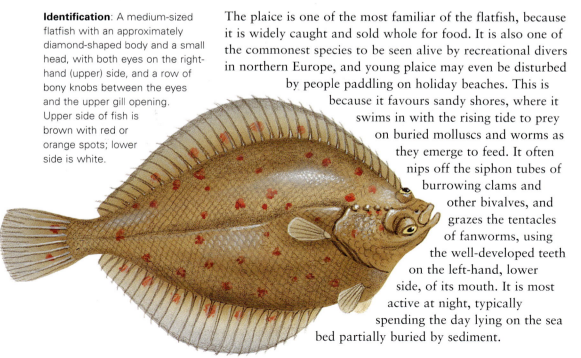

Distribution: North Atlantic coastal waters from southern Greenland and Iceland to Scandinavia and southern Europe, Barents Sea, western Baltic, Mediterranean and southern Black Sea.
Habitat: Sandy or muddy seabeds at depths of 10–50m/30–165ft.
Food: Bottom-dwelling molluscs, crustaceans, worms and small fish.
Size: 50cm/20in.
Breeding: Eggs released into the water are buoyant; they develop into larvae living near the surface.
Status: Not listed by IUCN.

Panther flounder

Bothus pantherinus

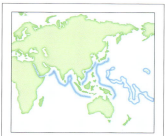

Distribution: Tropical Indo-Pacific Ocean, from Red Sea to Tahiti and southern Japan.
Habitat: Sandy and silty areas associated with coral reefs.
Food: Bottom-dwelling invertebrates and small fish.
Size: 25cm/10in.
Breeding: Eggs are shed in the water and are fertilized externally.
Status: Not listed by IUCN.

Named for its spots – and also known as the leopard sole – the tropical panther flounder spends most of its time on shallow sandy sea beds among coral, half hidden by sediment that it flicks over its camouflaged body until only its rather protuberant eyes are visible. This helps it avoid the attentions of most of the large predators that patrol the reef, although hunters such as sharks may detect it. It feeds on the small animals that live in the sand, such as crustaceans, molluscs and worms, and also preys on the larval fish. This may explain why its own young are often found in intertidal pools, where the adults are unlikely to encounter them.

Identification: A small flatfish with an oval profile and protruding eyes on the left (upper) side. The rays of its very long-based dorsal and anal fins are elongated to form a spiny fringe, and the male's pectoral fin rays are extended into long filaments. Its colouration is highly variable, but generally mottled brown with a pattern of dark spots surrounded by pale spots, and a dark blotch on the lateral line.

Starry flounder (*Platichthys stellatus*): 80cm/31in
This North Pacific flatfish lives in cold coastal waters from the Bering Sea south to Korea and California, USA. It gets its name from the bold pattern of yellow or orange bars on its blackish dorsal, anal and tail fins; these seem to radiate from the point in the middle of its roughly diamond-shaped body, like rays. Otherwise it is dark brown with darker, blotches. It lives in a wide range of salinities from salty to fresh water, feeding on bottom-dwelling invertebrates.

Small-headed sole (*Soleichthys microcephalus*): 20cm/8in
Known only from the Pacific waters off New South Wales, Australia, the small-headed sole is a subtropical species of estuaries and shallow bays, where it partly buries itself in sandy or muddy sediments. It is vividly coloured for a flatfish, being orange-brown with a series of darker bars and a bright blue fringe formed from the dorsal, anal and tail fins.

Atlantic halibut (*Hippoglossus hippoglossus*): 2m/6.5ft
This big, elongated, dull green-brown flatfish lives in North Atlantic and Arctic waters, where it preys on other fish such as cod, haddock and skate. There are records of it reaching 4m/13ft. This large fish is now rare due to overfishing, and the species has been classified as Endangered.

Dover sole

Solea solea

The Dover sole is distinguished by the way its small, curved mouth is set to one side of its extremely rounded snout. It is largely nocturnal, but may be active on dark days or in cloudy water. It usually spends the day partly buried in the sediment, emerging at night to feed largely on small bottom-dwelling invertebrates. It sometimes swims well clear of the bottom to take small fish. As with all flatfish it begins life looking like a normal fish, and lives near the surface, but its eyes move to one side as it metamorphoses into a small flatfish. It is an important food-fish and is often sold whole like the plaice.

Identification: An elongated flatfish with both eyes on the right-hand (upper) side of its head, a very blunt snout, a small mouth and a small pectoral fin. Medium to dark brown with irregular, indistinct dark patches on its upper side, and a dark spot on the upper pectoral fin; white below.

Distribution: Coastal north-eastern Atlantic Ocean from Norway to Senegal and Cape Verde Islands, western Baltic, Mediterranean and southwestern Black Seas.
Habitat: Sandy and muddy seabeds at depths of 10–100m/33–330ft, moving to deeper waters in winter.
Food: Mainly bottom-dwelling worms, molluscs and crustaceans, plus small fish.
Size: 70cm/27.5in.
Breeding: Eggs are released into the water and fertilized externally.
Status: Not listed by IUCN.

TRIGGERFISH, BOXFISH AND PUFFERFISH

The fish on the following pages belong to the order Tetradontiformes – a term which is derived from the Greek for 'bearing four teeth'. Members have two pairs of sharp teeth set at the front of the jaw, which may be visible even when the mouth is closed. These fish also lack pelvic fins. Puffers and porcupine fish can rapidly inflate their bodies to deter predators, and many are also venomous.

Clown triggerfish

Balistoides conspicillum

Identification: An oval-bodied fish with high-set eyes and two dorsal fins. Basically black, it has white spots on its belly, flanks and caudal peduncle, a yellowish, reticulated pattern on its back, pale bluish-white dorsal and anal fins with black tips, a yellow band on its caudal fin, and bright orange lips.

This reef fish owes its name to the 'clown' effect of its broad orange lips set off by the flamboyant, spotted, black and white pattern on its belly. Like all triggerfish, the first dorsal fin has three strong spines. The first, especially strong, spine can be erected at will and locked in place with the second dorsal spine, which acts as a trigger, engaging the locking mechanism. The spines cannot be lowered while the mechanism is locked. The fish uses this adaptation to wedge itself in a reef crevice when it is not feeding, and thus make itself safer from predators. When the danger has passed, the mechanism is 'unlocked' and the spines lowered. The skin also has a protective covering of tough scales.

Distribution: Tropical Indo-Pacific Ocean from Africa to Samoa, and north to Japan.
Habitat: Coral reefs, on the deep seaward reef slopes. May also venture into clear coastal waters.
Food: Sea urchins, crustaceans, molluscs and sea squirts.
Size: 50cm/6in.
Breeding: Eggs are released into the water and fertilized externally.
Status: Not listed by IUCN.

Scrawled file fish

Aluterus scriptus

The file fish are close relatives of the triggerfish. Each species has a single, long dorsal spine that is typically saw-toothed on its rear edge, like a file. This is the largest species in its family, found in warm seas where it lives mainly on coral reefs and in their associated lagoons. It uses its small mouth to graze algae and plant-like animals from hard corals and rocks, and is often seen at a variety of angles using its pointed snout to probe into crevices. It can also be found sheltering beneath floating objects in open oceans well away from reefs, having been swept from its usual range by the current.

Identification: A moderately deep-bodied fish with a large head, long snout and large, high-set eyes. It has two dorsal fins, the first of which is reduced to a single spine, and its long caudal fin – about one-third the length of its body – is often folded so it seems to be pointed. Its second dorsal and anal fins are yellow, and its greenish brown or tan body is covered with numerous black or blue spots and lines.

Distribution: Tropical and subtropical oceans worldwide.
Habitat: Coral and rocky reefs to depths of 120m/395ft.
Food: Algae, seagrasses, corals and encrusting animals such as colonial anemones and sea squirts.
Size: 40cm/15.75in.
Breeding: Eggs are released into the water and fertilized externally.
Status: Not listed by IUCN.

Longhorn cowfish

Lactoria cornuta

Distribution: Tropical Indian Ocean and Red Sea, north to southern Japan and south to the north-eastern tropics of Australia.
Habitat: Sandy areas with algae (seaweeds) near coral reefs.
Food: Bottom-dwelling invertebrates.
Size: 30cm/12in.
Breeding: Eggs are released into the water and are fertilized externally.
Status: Not listed by IUCN.

The boxfish, or trunkfish, have bodies that are encased in an angular, box-like defensive armour formed from thick, fused scales. This protective armour acts like a shell, preventing all body movement, so the fish have to move themselves laboriously through the water with just their small fins. The longhorn cowfish has the additional feature of very long fleshy horns above its eyes. It feeds by swimming head-down over sandy seabeds among coral, and blowing jets of water into the sand to disperse it. This exposes any small buried animals, which it then sucks into its mouth.

Identification: Very distinctive-looking fish, with cuboid body armour made of fused scales and long 'horns' above the large, high-set eyes. It has a small, low-slung mouth and a relatively long tail. Body colouration varies – from green or yellow to orange with blue spots – depending on habitat.

Blotched porcupine fish (*Diodon liturosus*): 40cm/15.75in
The porcupine fish are similar to pufferfish, but are covered with spines that bristle out when the fish is inflated. This Indo-Pacific reef species forages at night for crustaceans and molluscs, hiding away by day in crevices and caves. It is named for the large black blotches on its yellowish body.

Queen triggerfish (*Balistes vetula*): 30cm/12in
Found in the waters of the west Atlantic and Caribbean, the queen triggerfish (below) is a deep-bodied, large-headed tetradontiform, and has particularly sharp teeth for feeding on invertebrates such as starfish and sea urchins. Its colour varies with its habitat, but it always has iridescent bluish-purple stripes around its mouth, and fringing its dorsal, anal and caudal fins.

Blue-spotted boxfish (*Ostracion tuberculatus*): 30cm/12in
A relative of the longhorn cowfish (see above), this Indo-Pacific reef species has the same body form. Young fish are a clear, bright yellow with black spots, but as they get older the yellow turns bluish. It feeds on seaweeds and small animals taken from the water and sand.

Fugu pufferfish

Takifugu niphobles

Pufferfish are famous for two features: the way they can inflate their bodies with water or air to discourage enemies and make themselves hard to swallow, and the fact that their internal organs contain poisons called tetrodotoxins that can be fatal if eaten by humans. Despite this, some species are considered delicacies in Japan, where they are known as *fugu*. They are normally prepared by chefs trained to remove the toxic organs, but fish prepared incompetently cause several deaths every year. This is one of the smaller species, found in shallow waters where it uses its strong beak to crack the shells of the crabs, clams and other shellfish that form most of its diet.

Distribution: North-western Pacific Ocean, from Vietnam to Japan.
Habitat: Sandy seabeds.
Food: Hard-shelled molluscs and crustaceans.
Size: 10cm/4in.
Breeding: Eggs are released into intertidal water and fertilized externally.
Status: Listed as Data Deficient by IUCN.

Identification: Plump-bodied with a tough 'beak', high-set eyes and small fins. Greyish or brown above with paler spots, and a black blotch on its flank just above the pectoral and another just below the dorsal fins. When inflated, the body becomes rounded.

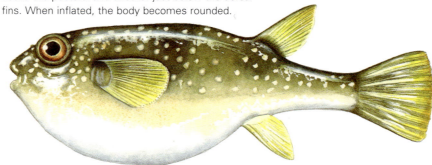

LIZARDS, SNAKES, CROCODILIANS AND AMPHIBIANS

As well as the turtles, many other species of reptiles also live in the world's oceans. Some are adapted to a life spent entirely at sea, whereas others live part of their life on the land. The marine toad is an example of an amphibian that lays its eggs in brackish water.

Marine iguana

Amblyrhynchus cristatus

Identification: Large lizard with a spiny dorsal crest running from the back of the head to the tip of its flattened tail. Squarish head with blunt snout; covered with horny protuberances around the eyes and nose. Feet are long and clawed. Colour dark greyish-brown to black; sometimes featuring a greenish crest and reddish flanks.

The marine iguana is the only living lizard to use the sea as its main habitat. This reptile is a strange sight basking on the wave-swept rocks of its Galapagos home, but to see it dive and swim in the cold sea is even more unexpected. But it is perfectly adapted for its lifestyle; it has a powerful, flattened tail for swimming – at which time it normally holds its limbs close to its body to aid streamlining. It cannot breathe under water, but during diving its heart rate slows, reducing blood flow and conserving oxygen. Special nasal glands remove excess salt from the body ingested with its food, which consists of marine algae. Highly territorial, males fight to defend small areas of the shore and attract females, often indulging in head butting fights to ward off rival males.

Distribution: Seas around the Galapagos Islands.
Habitat: Coastal rocks and waters.
Food: Marine algae.
Size: 1.5m/5ft.
Breeding: Two to three eggs laid in a sandy area, where they incubate for more than 100 days.
Status: Listed as Vulnerable by IUCN.

Saltwater crocodile

Crocodylus porosus

Identification: Large head with powerful jaws and large, conical teeth. Rows of bony plates run from behind the neck to the tip of the tail. Juveniles tan with black stripes and spots on the body and tail. Adults are darker, with tan or grey areas on back and flanks, creamy white or yellow.

Also known by several other common names including the estuarine crocodile, this is the largest species of living crocodile. Once widely hunted for its hide and because of its large size, this species has been the subject of extensive conservation programmes since the early 1970s, and numbers have now dramatically recovered. As its common name suggests, it frequents marine environments, although it is also encountered in freshwater rivers and swamps. The saltwater crocodile spends little time on land, and is a long-distance traveller with a wide distribution, swimming with the aid of its flattened tail. Prey varies according to the size of an individual – full-grown specimens can take prey as large as buffalo. Breeding territories are formed in freshwater sites and eggs are laid in a mound constructed from mud and vegetation. The female guards the nest until the eggs hatch. Then, alerted by their calls, she releases them from the nest.

Distribution: Indo-Pacific: South-east Asia to New Guinea and Australia.
Habitat: Brackish and coastal waters; also rivers and swamps.
Food: Invertebrates, such as crustaceans, and vertebrates, including fish, amphibians, seabirds and large mammals.
Size: Up to maximum of 6.3m/20.7ft; males more often reaching 5m/16.4ft; females about 3m/10 ft.
Breeding: 40–60 eggs laid in mound during the November–March wet season, hatching about 90 days later.
Status: Listed as Low Risk by IUCN.

Broad-snouted caiman

Caiman latirostris

This highly aquatic crocodilian frequents a range of habitats including swamps, marshes and mangroves, in addition to freshwater river systems. It also occurs around the mangrove regions of small coastal islands in southern Brazil. It is a medium-sized species, characterized by its exceptionally broad snout. It has a preference for eating aquatic snails, although it also takes other invertebrates and vertebrates, such as frogs and fish. By the time the broad-snouted caiman is adult, its jaws are strong and wide enough to crush turtle shells, so these also figure on the menu. In the breeding season, nests are often constructed on remote river islands. The young hatch after about 70 days and may be assisted in leaving the nest and reaching the water by their mother. It is estimated that there are about 250,000 to 500,000 individuals alive in the wild today.

Distribution: Argentina, Bolivia, Brazil, Paraguay and Uruguay.
Habitat: Brackish and coastal waters; also rivers and swamps.
Food: Snails and other invertebrates; also turtles, fish and amphibians.
Size: Up to maximum of 3.5m/11.5ft; usually about 2m/6.6ft.
Breeding: 20–60 eggs laid in mound during the wet season, hatching about 70 days later.
Status: Low Risk.

Identification: Head very broad and relatively short with a central ridge. Jaws lined with conical teeth. Body and legs scaly. Adults are often pale olive-green in colour.

Turtle-headed sea snake (*Emydocephalus annulatus*): 80cm/31in
Most species of sea snake are highly venomous, but the turtle-headed sea snake is an exception and its venom is mild. A shallow coral-reef species, it has evolved to feed on the eggs of fish, using its hard, pointed snout to dislodge the eggs from crevices before swallowing them. Found from Indonesia to the Philippines and northern Australia.

Olive sea snake (*Aipysurus laevis*): 1.8m/6ft
This large, short-headed, highly venomous sea snake inhabits the waters of coastal coral reefs, and is common in the seas around northern Australia and southern New Guinea. It belongs to the group of hydrophiid sea snakes, which evolved from venomous terrestrial Australian snakes about 30 million years ago. Unlike the kraits, which lay their eggs on land, hydrophiid snakes spend their entire lives in the sea, and even give birth to live young in the water.

Marine toad (*Bufo marinus*): up to 24cm/9.5in
Also called the cane toad, this is one of the largest of all amphibians. Although it often lays its eggs in brackish water, its natural habitat is tropical swampy forest. It ranges from Texas, USA, to Peru, although it has been introduced to other parts of the USA and Australia to control pests. Its skin glands contain a powerful toxin, although it is often preyed on by snakes.

Banded Sea Snake

Laticauda colubrina

Like other sea snakes, the banded sea snake, or sea krait, is a highly venomous reptile adapted to a life at sea. Many species of sea snakes never leave the water, but the banded sea snake comes ashore to mate and lay its eggs. Although it is an extremely capable swimmer and diver, it breathes surface air, and special valves on its nostrils close when it submerges, preventing water entering the nasal cavity. The banded sea snake also has a laterally flattened, oar-like tail, which it uses to propel itself through the water. Sea snakes shed their skin frequently – about every two to six weeks – and this helps rid them of aquatic parasites. Not generally aggressive to humans, the banded sea snake can nevertheless deliver a highly toxic venom in its bite – unwary divers and people fishing are the most common victims. However, the venom is usually used to subdue quickly its natural prey of invertebrates and fish, which it most often hunts at night.

Distribution: Oceanic waters of Australia, New Guinea, Pacific Islands, the Philippines, Southeast Asia, Sri Lanka and Japan.
Habitat: Coastal waters and coral reefs.
Food: Crabs, cuttlefish, squid, fish and fish eggs.
Size: 2m/6.6ft.
Breeding: Viviparous; up to 14 young.
Status: Not listed.

Identification: This is a long, narrow-bodied snake. The head is small and its eyelids have been replaced by modified scales. The tail is laterally flattened and terminates in a rounded tip. The body colour is pale blue with rings of black bands running the length of the body.

WHALES, DOLPHINS AND PORPOISES

The whales, dolphins and porpoises are air-breathing mammals totally adapted to a life spent entirely in an aquatic environment – even the young are born in the water. These animals swim by using powerful up-and-down movements of their horizontal tail flukes. These are most often social animals living in groups from a few individuals up to many hundreds.

Beluga

Delphinapterus leucas

Often known as the white whale because of its gleaming white skin when adult, the beluga is a northern species favouring coastal waters and, in winter, the edge of the floating pack ice. It is gregarious, normally travelling in groups of ten or more. Groups are either all males or all females and their darker-skinned young. All-male herds of more than 100 are known. Belugas feed mainly on fish, such as herring, cod and salmon, but also dive to the seabed for crabs and molluscs. They communicate with whistles, squeaks and belching sounds, and have an echo-location system that is probably used when feeding. Like many whales they are threatened by hunting and, in some areas, pollution.

Identification: A relatively small whale with a stocky frame, a bulbous forehead and a mobile face. It has gleaming white skin when mature, but is darker skinned when young. The dorsal fin has been replaced by a dorsal ridge, which is more prominent in males. The males are some 50 per cent heavier than the females.

Distribution: Arctic Ocean and adjoining seas, including the Sea of Okhotsk, Bering Sea, Gulf of Alaska and Hudson Bay, plus a small population in the Gulf of St Lawrence, Canada.
Habitat: Fjords, estuaries, and shallows in summer; near ice edge in winter.
Food: Fish and squid, plus crabs, octopus and other bottom-living invertebrates.
Size: 4m/13ft.
Breeding: One calf born after a 12-month gestation; birth interval 2–3 years.
Status: Listed as Vulnerable by IUCN.

Narwhal

Monodon monoceros

Related to the beluga (*Delphinapterus leucas*) described above, the narwhal is famous for the single, long 'unicorn' tusk of the adult male. This is a modified tooth, which grows to a length of 2m/6.5ft or more, and has a pronounced left-hand spiral. The function of the tusk is not certain: it is extremely well supplied with nerve endings that make it sensitive to water temperature and pressure, but it is not clear why this sensitivity is not shared by females. Since narwhals are social animals, usually seen in small groups that sometimes associate in larger herds, the tusk may act as an indicator of male status – like the antlers of deer. Both sexes take the same prey, often feeding at depth on bottom-living invertebrates as well as fish taken in open water.

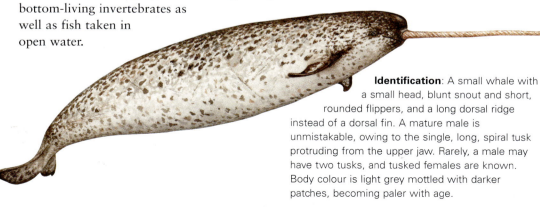

Identification: A small whale with a small head, blunt snout and short, rounded flippers, and a long dorsal ridge instead of a dorsal fin. A mature male is unmistakable, owing to the single, long, spiral tusk protruding from the upper jaw. Rarely, a male may have two tusks, and tusked females are known. Body colour is light grey mottled with darker patches, becoming paler with age.

Distribution: Ranges widely throughout the Arctic Ocean, from north-eastern Canada and Greenland to northwestern Siberia.
Habitat: Mainly deep water near pack ice, following the ice edge as it advances and retreats with the seasons.
Food: Mainly fish, squid and shrimps.
Size: 4.5m/14.75ft.
Breeding: A single calf (rarely twins) born after a 15-month gestation; birth interval 2–3 years.
Status: Listed as Data Deficient by IUCN.

Humpback whale
Megaptera novaeangliae

Distribution: All oceans, but seasonally resident in cold polar waters in summer, and warm subtropical or tropical waters in winter.
Habitat: Feeds and breeds in relatively shallow waters, but crosses deep oceans on migration.
Food: Schooling fish and krill.
Size: 14m/46ft.
Breeding: Single calf born every 2 years or so, in warm-water wintering areas.
Status: Listed as Vulnerable by IUCN.

This is probably the most familiar of the big rorqual or baleen whales, thanks to its spectacular acrobatic displays. Despite its immense weight, it may leap right out of the water, falling back with a huge splash: a behaviour known as breaching. Both sexes also slap their tail flukes and flippers on the water, and males communicate with a complex repertoire of whale 'songs'. They are social animals, travelling and feeding in small groups that often form part of larger aggregations. They have a cooperative feeding technique that involves swimming around and below fish or krill while releasing a rising curtain of bubbles to concentrate the school. Each whale then lunges upwards to scoop up a vast volume of prey and water. It expels the water through the sieve-like baleen plates lining its mouth.

Identification: A large whale with a pronounced hump in front of its dorsal fin, a stout body and very long flippers – the longest of any whale. There are rounded knobs on top of the large head, beneath the jaw, and on the front edges of the flippers. These are often encrusted with barnacles. Some 12–36 grooves extend from the chin to the belly. Body colour is basically black, with a variable pattern of white patches below and on the flippers and tail flukes.

Southern right whale (*Eubalaena australis*): 17m/56ft
Found only in the waters around Antarctica, between 30 and 50 degrees south, this large whale was considered the 'right' whale to catch by whalers. It has a very big head, no dorsal fin, and no throat grooves, and is basically brown to black in colour with white horny growths on its head. It feeds on planktonic crustaceans such as copepods and krill.

Grey whale (*Eschrichtius robustus*): 14m/46ft
This north Pacific Ocean whale has a very coastal distribution, since it feeds by sieving small animals from the bottom sediments, usually in water that is less than 50m/164ft in depth. The whale feeds in Arctic waters during the summer months, migrating to the subtropics for the winter season. It has a relatively small head, and its grey skin is encrusted with variable paler patches of barnacles.

Bryde's whale (*Balaenoptera edeni*): 12m/39ft
Identifiable by the three ridges located on top of its head, prominent sickle-shaped dorsal fin, dark-grey back and pale-coloured throat, Bryde's whale occurs worldwide in warm tropical or subtropical oceans. It is an opportunistic feeder, taking mainly schooling fish and crustaceans by straining water through the baleen plates lining its mouth.

Long-finned pilot whale
Globicephala melas

The pilot whales are basically big dolphins, and this species has the same habit of living in large groups, or 'pods', of between 10 and 50, and occasionally 100 or more. It is essentially oceanic, roaming nomadically in search of schools of squid or, failing that, fish. Its preference for the deep ocean means that it is poorly adapted for shallow coastal waters, and it is prone to becoming stranded on tidal shores. Its social bonds are so strong that one disoriented whale is followed by others, and mass strandings are common. The long-finned pilot whale also has a long history of exploitation in the North Atlantic, particularly in the Faeroes where a traditional hunting practice involves driving whole pods ashore to be killed. Some 1,200 pilot whales are killed in this way each year.

Identification: A medium-sized whale with a very bulbous head, especially in males. It has long, backswept flippers and a round, slightly hooked dorsal fin. It is black or dark grey with a white diagonal stripe behind the eye, and greyish areas on the belly and chin.

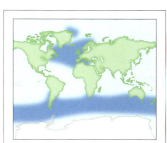

Distribution: Temperate to sub-polar waters of the North Atlantic Ocean, entering the western Mediterranean Sea, and the southern Pacific, Atlantic and Indian Oceans.
Habitat: Mainly the deep oceans, but may stray into shallower coastal waters in search of food.
Food: Mainly squid, plus schooling fish.
Size: 5m/16.4ft.
Breeding: A single calf is born after a gestation of 15–16 months. Birth interval 3–4 years.
Status: Not listed by IUCN.

OPEN OCEAN AND DEEP WATER

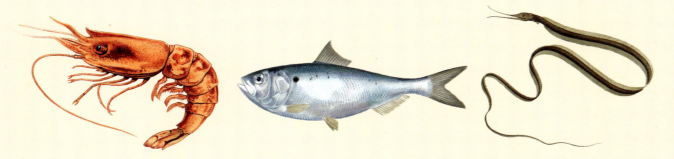

Despite its enormity, the open ocean supports surprisingly few species. Life in the 'big blue' tends to be concentrated in small areas, with one species attracting another to create small and often ephemeral communities – for example, a drifting object, or organism, will attract zooplankton, plankton feeders and spawning fish, which in turn attract filter-feeding fish and larger predators.

At the edge of the continental shelves, the sea floor slopes steeply away and a strange, alien world begins. The residents of this still largely unexplored environment continue to amaze scientists, with new species and novel ways of life discovered on almost every journey to the depths.

Amazingly enough, there are representatives of almost all major marine groups living in deep water – bony fish and sharks, crustaceans, echinoderms, molluscs and various worm phyla are all present and all have found ways to cope with the low light and low energy conditions. Even mammals, such as the sperm whale, although tied to the surface by the imperative to breathe air, make it to extraordinary depths.

*Above, left to right: Deep water peaked shrimp (*Acanthephyra curtirostris*); Atlantic menhaden (*Brevoortia tyrannus*); slender snipe eel (*Nemichthys scolopaceus*).*

*Right: Freckled driftfish (*Psenes cyanophrys*) shelter under an abandoned plastic oil can in the open ocean.*

HYDROZOANS, JELLYFISH AND COMB JELLIES

The free-swimming members of the phylum Cnidaria include some of the most admired and feared animals in the sea. All are armed with stinging cells, some of which are lethal to humans. The mysterious comb jellies of the phylum Ctenophora look rather similar, but do not sting.

Portuguese man-o-war

Physalia physalis

The Portuguese man-o-war is a floating cluster of individual hydrozoan animals that work together so closely they appear to be a single organism. The colony drifts at the water surface supported by a large medusa, or swimming bell, which is modified into a gas-filled float. Dangling from the float is a stem bearing clusters of polyps specialized for performing different tasks, such as feeding, reproduction or defence. Feeding polyps are armed with fine, stinging tentacles that trail in the water to snare and paralyze prey, such as small fish or shrimp. Any food that is caught is shared with other non-feeding polyps – all are connected by a common central cavity that serves as a gut. Reproductive polyps bud off new individuals, which usually remain part of the colony. The polyps with the largest stinging tentacles are concerned exclusively with defence of the colony. Hundreds of thousands of people swimming in the sea receive unpleasant stings from man-o-war tentacles every year, although a few marine animals are able to tolerate them.

Identification: The large float bears a tall sail and supports a cluster of tentacled feeding polyps, small reproductive polyps and defensive polyps with very long tentacles. Polyps may be pink, lilac or bright blue in colour.

Distribution: Tropical and temperate waters of Atlantic, Pacific and Indian Oceans and adjoining seas.
Habitat: Surface.
Food: Small fish and larvae, shrimps and other plankton.
Size: 30cm/12in; tentacles 50m/164ft in length.
Breeding: Colonies grow by asexual budding of member polyps. Hermaphrodite reproductive zooids release eggs and sperm into the water, fertilized eggs develop into planula larvae that may found new colonies.
Status: Common; not listed by IUCN.

Purple jellyfish

Pelagia noctiluca

Also known as the mauve stinger, this dainty jellyfish has fine tentacles that grow up to 3m/10ft long. There are eight tentacles in all, growing from the rim of a mushroom-shaped swimming bell. Beneath the bell, four large, frilly arms surround the central mouth, creating a funnel-like opening called the manubrium. Both the swimming bell and tentacles are well-endowed with stinging cells, though to humans the sting is more a nuisance than a serious hazard. The scientific name *noctiluca* means 'night light'. Purple jellyfish may produce a bioluminescent glow when disturbed and secrete a glowing mucus when handled. Larvae of the purple jelly develop directly into miniature jellyfish, called ephyrae. There is no sessile polyp stage. The species occasionally occurs in great numbers – these 'jellyfish plagues' can pose a major nuisance to fishermen and on tourist beaches.

Identification: Mushroom-shaped swimming bell is covered in pink or purple warts. The bell has eight lobes, with a single, long tentacle and sense organ growing from the notches in between. The four oral arms are well developed and have elaborate frills.

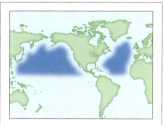

Distribution: Warm-temperate waters of the North Atlantic and North Pacific and adjoining seas.
Habitat: Warm surface waters in coastal areas and over deep water.
Food: Small fish and plankton-dwelling invertebrates.
Size: 60cm/24in in diameter.
Breeding: External fertilization; fertilized eggs develop via ephrya larvae to juvenile medusae with no polyp phase.
Status: Common; not listed by IUCN.

Lion's mane jelly

Cyanea capillata

Distribution: Arctic, Atlantic and Pacific Oceans, north of 42°, and adjoining seas.
Habitat: Cold and cool waters.
Food: Mainly other jellyfish.
Size: Occasionally 2m/6.6ft across; tentacles 30m/100ft.
Breeding: Little is known about reproductive behaviour, but individuals mature within a few months.
Status: Not listed by IUCN.

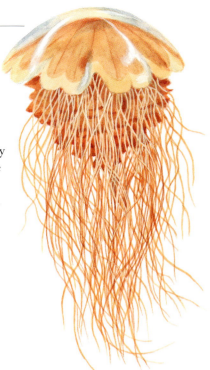

The lion's mane jelly is named for the dramatic tangle of brownish-orange frills associated with the four food-gathering arms surrounding the mouth in the underside of the bell. The bell is divided into eight lobes, and there is a cluster of between 60 and 150 thread-like tentacles associated with each lobe. The tentacles are sticky and easily snare smaller jellies – the species' main prey. In humans, the tentacles usually cause a moderately painful sting similar to that of a severe nettle rash, which in very extreme cases can be life-threatening. Lion's mane medusae live only a single year. In the summer they reproduce sexually, with fertilized eggs that develop into tiny larvae. These sink to the sea floor where they develop into over-wintering polyps, which begin budding off tiny new medusae in the spring of the following year. The largest specimens are found in the far north in the autumn.

Identification: Yellow or orange saucer-shaped bell with deeply scalloped edges; four short, very frilly arms and eight clusters of very long, fine, sticky tentacles.

By the wind sailor (*Velella velella*): 6cm/2.4in in diameter
This is another surface-dwelling oceanic colony, like the Portuguese man-o-war. Also known as the bluebottle on account of striking indigo pigmentation of the large float and associated tissues. The float bears a fin-like sail, allowing the colony to be carried long distances aided by wind and current. It is found in tropical and temperate Atlantic, Pacific and Indian waters.

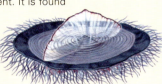

Hula skirt jelly (*Physophora hydrostatica*): 40cm/15.75in in diameter
This colony floats in mid-water to depths of 1,000m/3,280ft or more, controlling its buoyancy by secreting gas into a float. The float supports an elongated stem, which bears polyps specialized to the tasks of feeding and breeding. As with the by the wind sailor, it is found in tropical and temperate zones of the Atlantic, Pacific and Indian oceans.

Venus' girdle (*Cestum veneris*): 1.5m/5ft long
A highly unusual comb jelly that grows widthways to form a delicate, belt-like body, with the mouth in the middle of the leading edge. The animal normally swims with the long leading edge forwards, but can perform worm-like undulation that propels it quickly sideways. It occurs widely throughout the temperate and tropical waters of the Atlantic, Pacific and Indian oceans, and adjoining seas.

Giant comb jelly

Beroe forskalii

Like most other comb jellies, *Beroe* species are slightly elongate jellyfish-like animals with eight rows of comb-like structures running the length of the body. Unlike their relatives the sea gooseberries, they lack tentacles of any sort. The 'body' comprises a sac with a large cavity with a single, large opening – the mouth. For such delicate-looking animals, they are surprisingly voracious predators. The jelly relies on luck to encounter prey, mainly other jellies, which are engulfed whole by the particularly sizable mouth. Comb jellies drift about in open water, propelled weakly by the rhythmic, wave-like beating of the cilia (hair-like structures) lining their comb-rows. Under certain illumination, the rows refract white light to create spectacular displays of shimmering rainbow colours. This is not bioluminescence, although some related animals are able to produce light, usually a pale blue glow.

Distribution: Warm-temperate north Atlantic and Mediterranean waters.
Habitat: Open water.
Food: Other comb jellies.
Size: 15cm/6in.
Breeding: Hermaphroditic; eggs and sperm released into the water develop into cydippid larvae and then into adult jellies.
Status: Not listed by IUCN.

Identification: Elongate body with eight parallel rows of light-splitting comb-rows. The mouth is particularly large, opening directly into the digestive cavity, which, in turn, branches into eight interconnected canals that run alongside the comb-rows.

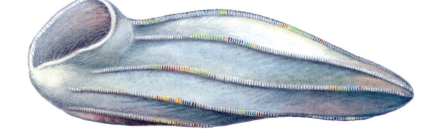

CEPHALOPOD MOLLUSCS

The cephalopods rank among the most highly evolved and intelligent invertebrates. Several species of octopus and squid have adapted to life in the open ocean, and some live at extreme depths. Biologists are only just beginning to learn the secrets of these mysterious deep-sea molluscs, some of which have famously evaded human observation for decades, existing only in legend.

Nautilus

Nautilus pompilius

Identification: The shell is an expanding spiral, with brown bands above, but pure white below. The opening of the shell is shielded by a tough hood. Two prominent eyes and a cluster of small tentacles protrude from the large living chamber.

The genus *Nautilus* is all that remains of a once great order of molluscs. They are the closest living relatives of another vast but wholly extinct group, the ammonites. Nautili are considered very primitive – they have retained a large external shell and their movements are slow – more like that of snails than of other cephalopods. The shell contains a series of sealed chambers – the body of the animal occupies the largest of these, which is also the most recently made. The others contain gas for buoyancy, as well as the gas-producing organ. The nautilus propels itself by weak jet propulsion or crawls over the sea floor using its tentacles. It spends the day in deep water but rises to shallower areas at night. Food is collected by the tentacles around the mouth. Nautili are long-lived by cephalopod standards, but breed slowly – females produce a dozen or so large eggs in a year, which hatch into nautili 2cm/0.75in across.

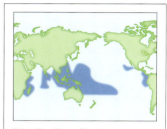

Distribution: Tropical areas of Indian and Pacific Oceans.
Habitat: Deep water close to reefs down to 800m/2,600ft.
Food: Small fish, crustaceans and dead animals.
Size: Up to 25cm/10in.
Breeding: Internal fertilization; large eggs develop directly into miniature versions of the adult, reaching maturity in 5–10 years.
Status: Feared to be in decline; not listed by IUCN.

Giant squid

Architeuthis dux

The giant squid has all the hallmarks of a mythical sea monster – enormous size, fearsome weapons in the form of powerful arms and tentacles and a beak that could bite though steel cable. Until recently, it was known only from dead specimens washed up on beaches, but in 2005 Japanese scientists published video footage of a giant squid taken from a research submersible. Their observations showed the squid to be an active and aggressive predator. Giant squid have few enemies – sperm whales and sleeper sharks eat smaller specimens, but it is quite possible for larger individuals to fight back successfully. Little is known about the life history of giant squid. The larvae were once thought to belong to an entirely different genus, *Rhynchoteuthis*.

Identification: Front of the animal's body bears eight arms with rows of powerful serrated suckers and two long tentacles with suckers at their clubbed ends. The fins, positioned at the end of the body, are small. The eyes are the largest in the animal kingdom at up to 30cm/12in across. Two large gills are located inside the mantle cavity.

Distribution: Temperate and deep waters of tropical oceans worldwide.
Habitat: Deep water, often associated with continental and island slopes of 200–1,000m/650–3,300ft in depth.
Food: Mostly deep-sea fishes and smaller squid species.
Size: Up to 18m/59ft in length
Breeding: Little known; fertilization is internal; larvae and juveniles sometimes found in shallower water.
Status: Unknown. Strandings may be result of changing ocean currents. Not listed by IUCN.

Football octopus (Pelagic tuberculate octopus)

Ocythoe tuberculata

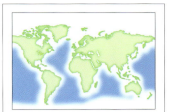

Distribution: Temperate and deep waters of tropical oceans worldwide.
Habitat: Surface waters of open oceans.
Food: Smaller pelagic animals.
Size: Up to 1m/3.25ft.
Breeding: Ovoviviparous.
Status: Thought to be rare but not listed by IUCN.

Female football octopus rise to feed in surface waters at night. By day, it seems they sink to deeper water. They are strong swimmers. A unique feature is the presence of a gas bladder, like that seen in many bony fish, which helps the animal control its buoyancy. Males are tiny, about one-tenth the size of females. Males and juvenile females sometimes seek shelter inside the gelatinous body of salps (pelagic tunicates). The species is the only living cephalopod known to give birth to live young, which hatch from their eggs while still inside the mother. It is not yet known quite how the tiny males manage to fertilize the females' eggs, but the process probably involves passing a packet of sperm (a spermatophore) to the female. Football octopus are eaten by many large fish and marine mammals.

Identification: Upper and lower pairs of arms longer than those that spread to the sides. The body and arms are highly muscular and the skin of the upper surface of the mantle is covered in small bumps, or tubercles.

Colossal squid (*Mesonychoteuthis hamiltoni*): may exceed 30m/100ft
Potentially far exceeding even the giant squid in size, the colossal squid is a relatively recent discovery. Known only from abyssal depths of the icy seas around Antarctica, it must rank among the greatest living predators. Its tentacles are armed with saw-edged suckers and hooks capable of tearing through flesh and hide.

Firefly squid (*Watasenia scintillans*): 10cm/4in
A pelagic species so far only known from the sea around eastern China and Japan where it is commercially fished. Photophores on the mantle and arms emit a bright blue luminescence.

Deep-sea finned octopus (*Staurotheuthis syrtensis*): 15cm/6in
A delicate-finned octopus from the deep Atlantic, with arms linked by a web of skin forming a bell or balloon shape, depending on the posture of the arms. Two rounded fins give the impression of large, flapping ears. The small suckers are modified into luminescent organs.

Bigfin squid (*Magnapinna pacifica*): Adult size unknown
Known from just three young individuals, the Pacific bigfin squid has a small body, eight small arms and two slightly larger tentacles. The back of the body bears two enormous membranous fins, several times longer than the body itself.

Vampire squid

Vampyroteuthis infernalis

The scientific name of this species is rather unflattering. It means 'Vampire squid from hell' – a little melodramatic considering the animal is no larger than a human hand. The vampire squid is a small, nimble swimming deep-water squid. The eyes are large – relative to the animal's size, perhaps the largest in the animal kingdom. The arms bear rows of sharp spines with which the squid grasps its prey. The arms are connected by an extensive web. The second pair of arms are retractile, and can be extended to several times the length of the body. There are numerous light-producing organs all along the arms and the tips. It can secrete clouds of glowing fluid, which may be used to confuse predators in much the same way as other squids use ink.

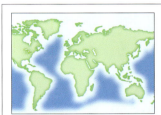

Distribution: Tropical and temperate oceans worldwide.
Habitat: Typically found at depths of 600–1,200m/ 2,000–4,000ft.
Food: Copepods, prawns and cnidarians.
Size: 13cm/5in.
Breeding: Internally fertilized eggs, up to 4mm across, are released into the water, where they drift within small, free-floating masses.
Status: Threatened, becoming endangered.

Identification: Gelatinous body with spiny arms connected by a web and two oval fins resembling flapping ears. Has very large eyes.

OSTRACODS, COPEPODS, ISOPODS AND AMPHIPODS

The taxa on these pages are representatives of the most abundant group of animals in the ocean – the crustaceans. Many members of these groups are small and cryptic, but they occur in stunning variety and in such numbers that without them, the entire marine food web would collapse.

Mussel shrimps (Subclass Ostracoda)

Ostracods are also known as pea shrimps or mussel shrimps on account of their hinged carapace, which forms a delicate spherical case into which the entire body can be withdrawn. The body plan is amazingly successful and more than 8,000 species of ostracod have been described. Most, however are less than 2mm in diameter, with *Gigantocypris* the giant of its kind. Ostracods swim in mid-water using rowing actions of the large antennae. The other appendages remain tucked inside the carapace. Movement of the antennae generates a feeding current, drawing tiny prey, such as algae or copepods, close enough to snare on the bristly appendages.

Identification: Ostracods live within a pair of hemispherical carapace valves. These open slightly to allow antennae and other appendages to emerge to allow feeding and locomotion.

Right: The giant ostracod Gigantocypris agassizii grows up to 3cm/1.2in across and lives inside a near spherical translucent carapace.

Distribution: All oceans.
Habitat: Pelagic and benthic from coasts and surface to depths; also fresh water.
Food: Algae, bacteria, other small invertebrates and fish larvae.
Size: Up to 3cm/1.2in.
Breeding: Female ostracods brood young inside carapace; many species reproduce by parthenogenesis (virgin birth).
Status: Abundant; not listed by IUCN.

Copepods (Subclass Copepoda)

Above: The deep-water copepod Euaugaptilus hyperboreus *is a tiny, colourless copepod that lives in the deep, cold waters beneath the Arctic pack ice.*

Copepods are tiny crustaceans and are among the most numerous animal on Earth. They are on the menu for hundreds of species of plankton feeders, from jellyfish whales, which filter them from the sea at a rate of trillions per day. However, copepods are not wholly helpless. With reaction times among the fastest of any aquatic animals, these tiny animals can respond to changes in water pressure that might signal an approaching predator. They react by making sudden darting movements generated by powerful flicks of the antennae. When threatened, many deep-water species emit puffs of bioluminescent dye to divert possible predators. The risk of being eaten is also reduced by avoiding sunlit surface waters during the day – copepods are among the multitude of vertical commuters that rise from deeper water to feed at night. The group includes a number of larger parasitic species that live attached to the bodies of larger species.

Identification: Tiny crustaceans with a single eye in the middle of the head, or cephalosome.

Left: The pelagic copepod Undinula vulgaris. *This common species of tropical waters worldwide forms a large part of the diet of many filter-feeding animals.*

Distribution: All oceans and seas worldwide.
Habitat: Mostly pelagic from coasts and surface to depths.
Food: Algae and particles of organic matter; some are parasitic.
Size: 1mm–1cm/0.04–0.4in.
Breeding: Females carry fertilized eggs in one or two large clusters attached to the abdomen.
Status: Abundant; not listed by IUCN.

Left: The deep-sea Pleuromamma xiphias *is one of the species known to produce bioluminescence in response to the threat of predation.*

Sea lice (Order Isopoda)

The isopods are one of the largest and most diverse groups of crustaceans, with more than 10,000 species. Of these, the majority live in deep water and are rarely seen. Each segment of the body is covered with a curved plate, or tergum. Many species can roll into a ball like a woodlouse (a terrestrial member of the same group). There are eight pairs of thoracic legs, the first of which (the maxillipeds) assist the mouthparts, while the others are used for crawling. The abdominal appendages are used for swimming and also serve as gills. Isopods are good parents. Females brood their young in a pouch called the marsupium (similar in function to the pouches of marsupial mammals). The brooding phase can last several months, during which time the female is often especially cautious, sometimes remaining hidden in a burrow or lair where she and her young are relatively safe.

Identification: As a general rule, isopods are flattened animals, with a segmented body lacking a carapace.

Above: The deep-sea louse Bathynomus giganteus *grows up to 30cm/12in in length and is one of the largest of the isopods. This carnivorous crustacean is reminiscent of the long-extinct trilobites.*

Right: The pelagic sea slater Idotea metallica *is a common species of sea louse from tropical and warm-temperate waters.*

Distribution: All oceans and seas worldwide.
Habitat: Mainly benthic, some live associated with flotsam (there are also freshwater and terrestrial species).
Food: Small fish and a wide range of invertebrates.
Size: 5mm–40cm/0.2–15.75in.
Breeding: Mating occurs after a partial moult; females brood eggs and larvae; young are released at late larval stage or as miniature adults.
Status: Common; not listed by IUCN.

Whale parasites and commensals

Commensalism refers to a particular type of parasitism, where one organism benefits, and the other is neither aided nor afflicted.

Whale barnacles

Many species of whale barnacle are highly specialized and will only grow on certain species of whale. Mature larvae settle on the skin of a whale and attach themselves with a special cement. They use the whale as transportation while filtering plankton as food.

Whale lice

Whale lice are amphipods belonging to the genus *Cyamus*. They are about 1–2cm/0.4–0.8in long. Superficially spider-like, they live nestled in among the clusters of barnacles on the heads of great whales. Like other amphipods, they eat a mixture of plankton and detritus, including flakes of dead skin shed by their huge hosts. They do not appear to do the whales any harm, and are passed from whale to whale, most often from mother to calf, by physical contact.

Copepods

Whales are among the list of vertebrates targeted by parasitic copepods. These animals are equipped with a long mouth tube and a set of serrated jaws, which they use to burrow through the host's skin. They remain attached there, the ribbon-like body trailing alongside the host, while feeding directly on its blood.

Amphipods (Subclass Amphipoda)

Amphipods are a diverse group of animals. Most of the 8,000 or so species bear seven pairs of thoracic appendages and, on the abdomen, three pairs of swimming legs and three pairs of stiff appendages. However, one group, known as skeleton shrimps, is very spindly, with body and appendages of more or less equal thickness. The lifestyles of amphipods are extremely diverse, with pelagic, bottom-dwelling, burrowing, tube-building and parasitic examples (there are also many freshwater and even some terrestrial species). They move by walking on the thoracic legs or swimming using the abdominal appendages or the antennae.

Identification: Diverse, though usually shrimp-like, with a laterally compressed body.

Above: The deep-sea amphipod Eurythnes gryllus *is a cosmopolitan scavenger found in water as deep as 6,500m/21,325ft.*

Right: The pram bug Phronima sedentaria *is a pelagic amphipod that seeks shelter inside the body of pelagic salps. It is allegedly the inspiration for the monster in the science-fiction film* Alien.

Distribution: All oceans and seas worldwide.
Habitat: All marine habitats (also in fresh water and on land).
Food: Particles of organic material, algae, smaller invertebrates; some species are parasitic.
Size: 1mm–30cm/0.04–12in.
Breeding: After mating, the female carries fertilized eggs in a brood pouch under body; the young emerge as miniature versions of their parents.
Status: Abundant; not listed by IUCN.

KRILL AND SHRIMPS

The class Malacostraca includes some of the world's most abundant species, and some of the most exploited. Apart from being a great natural spectacle, swarms of krill and shrimp are a vital resource for larger animals and increasingly a target of commercial fisheries. Research is underway in various oceanic locations to verify the impact of over-fishing on numbers and breeding.

Deep water opossum shrimp

Gnathophausia ingens

The order Mysidacea includes about 800 small shrimp-like crustaceans named for the pouch-like marsupium in which females brood their larvae – which is a little like the pouch of marsupial mammals such as opossums. By the time the young emerge from the pouch they have developed into miniature versions of their parents. The group also includes the extremely delicate-looking fairy shrimps. Opossum shrimps live in large swarms, usually close to the sea floor. They are eaten by many kinds of fish, and many species seek sanctuary among stinging anemones, moving carefully between the stinging tentacles. Deep-sea species such as *Gnathophausia* produce bioluminescence when disturbed, presumably in an attempt to confuse potential predators. They feed mainly on plankton and other organic material filtered from the water using their bristly thoracic legs.

Identification: Usually distinguished by its large size and bright red colour, *Gnathophausia* is a primitive opossum shrimp, in which only the first pair of appendages on the thorax are modified into mouthparts. The other thoracic legs and abdominal appendages are used for swimming.

Distribution: Likely to be present in all oceans.
Habitat: Benthic, from near surface to deep water.
Food: Mainly algae and detritus drifting down through the water.
Size: 0.1–35cm/0.04–13.75in.
Breeding: Eggs fertilized and develop into larvae within the female's brood pouch.
Status: Common; not listed by IUCN.

Antarctic krill

Euphausia superba

Identification: Elongate, translucent, segmented body, with a head dominated by large, round eyes. Of eight thoracic appendage, two are modified into mouthparts, six are long, bristly legs used for catching food. Abdomen has five pairs of appendages.

Dense swarms of this phenomenally abundant shrimp-like crustacean may stretch over several square kilometres of ocean to a depth of 5m/16ft or more. These vast aggregations contain billions, even trillions of small, shrimp-like animals with a segmented body, two pairs of long antennae, and six to eight pairs of thoracic appendages, five pairs of abdominal swimming legs and two pairs of tail appendages either side of long tail segment. Antarctic krill are eaten by all kinds of other animals, most notably the world's largest animal, the blue whale, which in the Southern Hemisphere feeds almost exclusively on this species at a rate of up to 4,000kg/4 tons a day during the summer. Krill are filter feeders, and use long bristles on their thoracic appendages to form a basket under the body that sieves plankton and organic matter from the water or sediment.

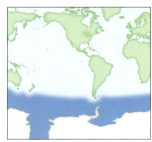

Distribution: Southern Ocean.
Habitat: Surface waters of open ocean down to about 100m/330ft.
Food: Algae and small zooplankton.
Size: 5cm/2in.
Breeding: Spawns several times over the summer period; fertilization is external; no parental care.
Status: Abundant but declining under increasing pressure from commercial fishing interest. Not listed by IUCN.

Deep water peaked shrimp

Acanthephyra curtirostris

Distribution: Tropical and subtropical oceans worldwide.
Habitat: Deep mid-water, from 200–2,200m/660–7,200ft.
Food: Small pelagic animals.
Size: Up to 8cm/3in.
Breeding: External fertilization; larvae develop in mid-water without any parental care.
Status: Common; not listed by IUCN.

This bright-red shrimp spends its entire life in the mid-water zone, never once touching the bottom or reaching the surface. The striking red colour helps it to remain invisible, even in the upper reaches of its depth range where a small amount of blue and green light from the surface penetrates, but no red light. Under these conditions the body appears to be entirely black. It swims using broad, paddle-like appendages on its abdomen known as pleopods. The thoracic legs, which benthic shrimps use for walking, also assist with swimming, but are used mainly for catching food. The species is carnivorous, and preys on smaller members of the mid-water community – principally other small crustaceans – in which it lives.

Identification: Scarlet body, carapace forms a peak over the head; two pairs of antennae – one short, one very long; thoracic legs are delicate, abdominal appendages much more robust, and biramous (branching in two).

Northern shrimp (*Pandalus borealis*): up to 12cm/4.75in
This predatory shrimp is among the most heavily exploited of all the crustaceans and is a familiar food item. It is present in cold parts of the Atlantic and Pacific oceans, and has a variety of common names, some of which refer to its reddish-pink colour. In far northern waters, most individuals start off as males, becoming females when they have grown large enough to produce eggs.

Deep-water krill (*Bentheuphausia amblyops*): up to 5cm/2in
This North Atlantic bottom-dwelling species lives in water more than 1,000m/3,300ft deep and, unlike all its close relatives, lacks bioluminescent body markings. It also has much smaller eyes, suggesting that it depends more heavily on other senses to find food and mates and to detect predators.

Icelandic boxer shrimp (*Spongicoloides profundus*): size unknown
This shrimp lives at depths of up to 1,500m/4,900ft in the North Atlantic and is often associated with glass sponges, in which it may live. Boxer shrimps are named for their greatly enlarged walking legs, which are often carried in front of the head, in the manner of a boxer taking guard. New species of the *Spongicoloides* genus are now being discovered in the Pacific.

Pelagic red crab

Pleuroncodes planipes

The red crab belongs to a group of crustaceans know as squat lobsters. The body appear short because of the small carapace and a characteristic posture in which the abdomen and tail are tucked up under the body. Of the five pairs of walking legs, the first are very large and bears robust claws. There are no specialized swimming appendages, but red crabs still swim, using powerful flicks of the abdomen. For most of the year, they live and feed on the sea bed, but in spring they swim to the surface to moult and breed. They form aggregations numbering millions or even billions of animals, and provide a food resource for both grey and blue whales, loggerhead turtles and predatory fish such as tuna. From time to time – especially in El Niño years – red crab swarms are washed ashore.

Distribution: Pacific Ocean.
Habitat: Benthic most of the year, rising to surface waters of open ocean to breed.
Food: Plankton.
Size: 2–8cm/0.75–3in.
Breeding: Females brood developing eggs attached to their abdomen; larvae develop though several moult stages.
Status: Common; not listed by IUCN.

Identification: Small lobster-like crustacean with bright-red body. First pair of walking legs bear long claws. All legs have bristles to help gather small food items from the water.

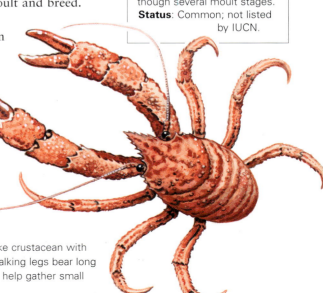

CRABS, LOBSTERS AND SEA SPIDERS

Despite appearing to slot into a rather natural-looking group, the similarities between these bottom-dwelling marine scuttlers are limited. Crabs and lobsters are decapod crustaceans, while sea spiders belong to a small and entirely separate branch of the arthropod tree, the class Pycnogonida. Despite the Pycnogonids' superficial resemblance to land spiders, their anatomy is quite different.

Alaskan king crab

Paralithodes camtschaticus

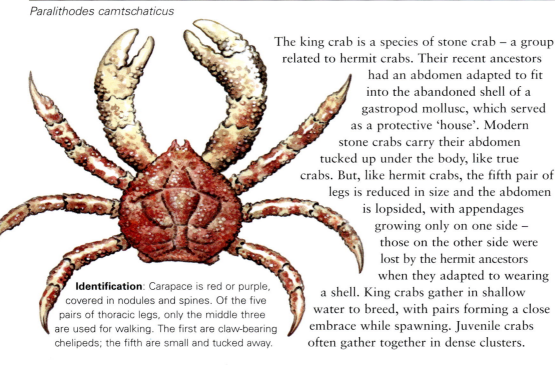

The king crab is a species of stone crab – a group related to hermit crabs. Their recent ancestors had an abdomen adapted to fit into the abandoned shell of a gastropod mollusc, which served as a protective 'house'. Modern stone crabs carry their abdomen tucked up under the body, like true crabs. But, like hermit crabs, the fifth pair of legs is reduced in size and the abdomen is lopsided, with appendages growing only on one side – those on the other side were lost by the hermit ancestors when they adapted to wearing a shell. King crabs gather in shallow water to breed, with pairs forming a close embrace while spawning. Juvenile crabs often gather together in dense clusters.

Identification: Carapace is red or purple, covered in nodules and spines. Of the five pairs of thoracic legs, only the middle three are used for walking. The first are claw-bearing chelipeds; the fifth are small and tucked away.

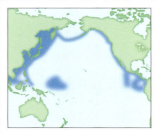

Distribution: Continental shelves in the North Pacific Ocean.
Habitat: Benthic, on sea floor 200–300m/650–1,000ft down.
Food: Echinoderms, molluscs and other bottom-dwelling invertebrates.
Size: Legspan 1m/3.25ft; carapace 25cm/10in across.
Breeding: Spawns in spring.
Status: Highly commercial; not listed by IUCN.

Vent crab

Bythograea thermydron

Identification: Unremarkable-looking crab with adults having an all-white body. Delicate carapace, five pairs of slightly bristly walking legs, of which first pair bear robust pincers that are used for tearing up food.

Vent crabs live at enormous depths, typically favouring the waters around hydrothermal vents – places where scalding hot water from deep inside the Earth is expelled into the sea along with dissolved chemicals that most marine life would find toxic. The crabs live among the clusters of tube worms that grow alongside the vents, in water temperatures that vary widely depending on proximity to the vent itself. Vent crabs move about by crawling or swimming. They are carnivorous – feeding on other specialized animals with which they share their extreme habitat, mainly tubeworms, shrimps and mussels. Juvenile vent crabs are bright orange – but their colour fades with successive moults until they attain the white colour of adults.

Distribution: Pacific Ocean, restricted to thermal vents.
Habitat: Close to thermal vents at an average depth of 2,700m/8,850ft.
Food: Other vent invertebrates.
Size: Up to 13cm/4.75in.
Breeding: Little known – planktonic larvae probably provide means of dispersal from vent to vent.
Status: Thought to be common; not listed by IUCN.

Japanese spider crab

Macrocheira kaempferi

Distribution: Continental shelves of North Pacific.
Habitat: Benthic, at depths of 150–200m/480–650ft.
Food: Bottom-dwelling molluscs, other crustaceans and dead animals.
Size: Legspan as much as 4m/13ft.
Breeding: Ventures into shallower water to spawn.
Status: Common; not listed by IUCN.

The world's largest living arthropod, the Japanese spider crab is a deep-water giant, with a carapace measuring up to 37cm/14.6in across. Its longest appendages, the great pincer legs, or chelipeds, are up to 2m/6.6ft long. An individual of this size will weigh up to 20kg/44lb. They are able to attain such proportions only with the aid of water to help support the weight of their legs. The length of the legs is an adaptation to moving about on soft marine sediments – by spreading its weight over a wide area the crab avoids sinking into the choking silt. On land, they are all but helpless. They can live up to 100 years.

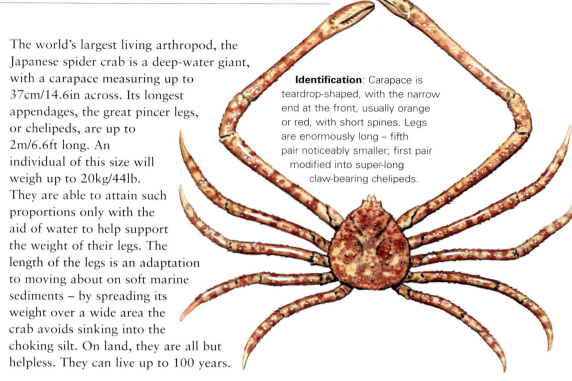

Identification: Carapace is teardrop-shaped, with the narrow end at the front, usually orange or red, with short spines. Legs are enormously long – fifth pair noticeably smaller; first pair modified into super-long claw-bearing chelipeds.

Crustacean larvae as plankton

For the most part, crustacean larvae look nothing like their parents. In the course of their development from fertilized egg through to juvenile, they pass through a number of larval stages, or 'instars' – a term that is perhaps more often associated with insect development. The names vary between the different groups, but in most taxa the earliest larval form is a microscopic but rotund little creature known as the nauplius. Nauplii have two pairs of large antennae, a set of mandibles (jaw-like mouth parts) and a single eye positioned in the middle of the head. From these humble beginnings, the larva passes through several more instars, acquiring more body segments and appendages at each new stage, and growing to look more and more like the adult parent. Like insects, crustaceans must shed their rigid exoskeleton in order to grow larger, and so each instar is separated from the next by at least one moult.

Below: A nauplius larva of the goose barnacle group.

Giant deep sea spider

Colossendeis colossus

This bizarre-looking animal is not a true spider, but belongs to a sister group of the chelicerates (spiders and scorpions) called the Pycnogonida. Sea spiders appear to be all legs – the body is reduced to a small trunk, the head is virtually nonexistent and the abdomen is a tiny stump, like a short tail. The animal's body is so small that most of the vital organs are located in the leg bases. Sea spiders feed on soft-bodied prey, mainly 'grazing' on organisms such as hydras and bryozoans (sea mosses), which encrust rocks and firm surfaces on the sea bed. Food is sucked up through the proboscis at the front. The giant sea spider is the largest species known: usually 30–40cm/12–15.75in long; occasionally 70cm/27.5in.

Distribution: Likely to be present in all oceans.
Habitat: Benthic in deep water down to 3,000m/9,750ft.
Food: Mainly benthic sessile invertebrates.
Size: Up to 70cm/27.5in.
Breeding: Males carry fertilized eggs in clusters on specialized legs.
Status: Unknown; not listed by IUCN.

Identification Tiny trunk section bears four pairs of walking legs. A fifth pair grows from the head section of females, and in males there is a sixth pair of legs used for carrying eggs.

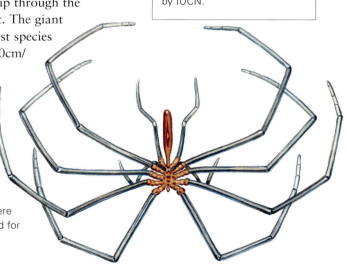

CHIMERAS AND RAYS

The species described here are deep water and oceanic cartilaginous fish. Modern chimeras (of the order Chimaeriformes) are a small group consisting of just a few dozen species. Rays and skates (Rajiformes), on the other hand, exhibit a wide variety of physical forms and lifestyles, from sluggish bottom-dwellers to graceful predators of mid-water habitats.

Chimera/Rabbit fish

Chimaera monstrosa

The common chimera is one of about 40 species belonging to the subclass Holocephali. Of these, many are deep-water specialists about which little is known. The common Atlantic species, however, is familiar to the local fishing industry. It is most active at night, when it migrates to shallower waters to feed. Chimeras, like the agnathans, have a persistent notochord – a flexible supporting rod running the length of the body. Males have a clasping structure on the forehead which may help to hold the female while mating.

Identification: Elongate, ventrally flattened body tapering to a very fine tail, with large pectoral fins held at right angles to the sides of the body. Dorsal fin has prominent spine; eyes large; body patterned with irregular longitudinal brown and white stripes and spots.

Distribution: Eastern Atlantic range, from tropical waters to northern temperate zone; also Mediterranean Sea; may be present in western Pacific, but not widely confirmed.
Habitat: Deep water of the continental slope descending to sea floor, at depths of 1,000m/3,300ft.
Food: Benthic invertebrates.
Size: Up to 1.5m/5ft.
Breeding: Oviparous, with internal fertilization; young hatch fully formed; no parental care.
Status: Common; not listed by IUCN.

Blind electric ray

Typhlonarke aysoni

Identification: A small, drab-looking ray with a rather floppy disc and poorly developed tail. The pelvic fins, not shown here, are modified into limb-like appendages.

Electric rays are also known as numbfishes because of their ability to deliver electric shocks large enough to stun prey or leave a potential predator with an unpleasantly tingling sensation. The shock is the result of electric discharge from specialized muscle cells, called electrocytes, situated mainly in the animal's 'wings'. This small species is known only from New Zealand waters, where it is considered rare. It turns up occasionally as bycatch, and there are concerns that it may be threatened by fisheries using bottom-trawling techniques. Little is known of its ecology, but anatomical studies suggest that it is a poor swimmer, and usually moves by 'walking' along the sea floor using its modified pelvic fins. It feeds mainly on polychaete worms collected from the sea bed. Its lifespan is not known.

Distribution: Endemic to New Zealand. Distribution is likely to extend to south-western Pacific, but range and extent is not certain due to confusion with a similar species, *T. tarakea*.
Habitat: Sea floor in water that is as deep as 900m/3,000ft.
Food: Benthic invertebrates, mainly worms.
Size: Up to 38cm/15in.
Breeding: Probably ovoviviparous.
Status: Listed as Data Deficient on IUCN.

Pelagic stingray

Pteroplatytrygon violacea

Distribution: Tropical and subtropical oceans and seas worldwide.
Habitat: Open water down to 240m/800ft.
Food: Fish and pelagic invertebrates.
Size: Up to 1.6m/5.25ft.
Breeding: Ovoviviparous, litters of 4–9 pups born after gestation of 2–4 months, with probably 2 litters a year.
Status: Common; not listed by IUCN.

Identification: Pectoral fins give the body a diamond-shaped outline; tail almost twice as long as the body with one or two large spines. Eyes are slightly sunken. Colour varies from brown to bluish green on dorsal surface and purplish below, but there are no markings. Dorsal area bears numerous spines.

The only ray adapted to truly open-water existence, the pelagic ray is a large, graceful swimmer able to swim upside down when attacking prey from below. It eats pelagic cephalopods, crustaceans and jellyfish, sometimes using its pectoral fins to help manipulate them to the mouth on the underside or the head. The sting is a defensive weapon, capable of inflicting a painful wound – not life-threatening to humans, but sufficient to deter most fish. Young of the species hatch from eggs while still inside the uterus and continue to grow here, nourished by a secretion from the uterine walls.

Distribution: Temperate northern Pacific Ocean.
Habitat: Sea floor in deep water down to 3,000m/ 9,842ft.
Food: Deep-water shrimp, amphipods and squid.
Size: Up to 91cm/36in.
Breeding: Oviparous.
Status: May be at risk from deep-water trawling, but not currently listed by IUCN.

Spotted ratfish
(*Hydrolagus colliei*): 97cm/38in
A native of the eastern Pacific Ocean this relatively common species has a venomous spine at the front of the dorsal fin. Sometimes taken as bycatch, it has limited economic value and the risk of injury from the sting and its powerful bite mean it is not targeted by fishing.

Long-nosed chimera (*Harriotta raleighana*): 1.2m/4ft
Found in deep tropical and temperate waters around the world, the long- or narrow-nosed chimera has a long, flattened upturned snout and a tail tapering to a long thread.

Deep sea skate (*Bathyraja abyssicola*): 1.4m/4.6ft
Like so many deep-sea species, very little is known about the ecology of this large ray. It is a predator feeding mostly on deep-water shrimp, amphipods and squid. It turns up in bottom trawls off Japan, Canada and the USA.

Sandpaper skate (*Bathyraja interrupta*): 86cm/34in
Also known as the Bering skate, this species feeds mainly from the sea floor – burrowing invertebrates, such as polychaete worms and amphipods, make up most of its diet. It may be at risk from bottom-trawling fisheries.

Alaska skate

Bathyraja parmifera

Very little is known about the ecology of this deep-sea ray. It is a predator feeding mostly on deep-water shrimp, amphipods and squid. The same bottom-trawling techniques that bring up individual Alaska skate off the coasts of Japan and North America also sometimes bring up eggs. These are tough, leathery pouches with horns projecting from the corners that help anchor them in the sand or sediment of the sea floor. This type of egg is fairly typical of the skate family and is known colloquially as 'mermaid's purse'.

Identification: Body wider than it is long. Snout pointed, body outline follows convex then concave curve from mouth to pectoral fin tip. Upper surface is brown with variable spots and blotches. Pelvic fins of male modified into very large claspers. Two small dorsal fins on tail.

SIX-GILLED AND DOGFISH SHARKS

These primitive-looking sharks belong to the orders Hexanchiformes and Squaliformes. They lack the sleek lines and athleticism of their more documented relatives, the requiem sharks. Hexanchiforms include the six- and seven-gilled sharks: fossils suggest that the latter may bear a striking resemblance to Jurassic ancestors. 'Dogfish sharks' is a colloquial term for a small group that live in northerly oceans.

Six-gilled shark

Hexanchus griseus

This large shark is usually found swimming in water as deep as 1,800m/5,900ft and is therefore rarely seen. However, between July and November the blunt-nosed six-gilled shark migrates into some shallow water locations, allowing divers a rare glimpse of it. A robust, elongate shark with a long caudal fin and a single dorsal fin, it gets its common name because it has six gill openings on each side of the head; most sharks have five pairs of gill openings. This species is a member of the order Hexanchiformes, known as the frilled sharks and cow sharks – all of the sharks in this order have six or even seven pairs of gill openings. Although a predator of small sea creatures, it will also scavenge on the carcasses of larger marine animals.

Identification: Body robust with a single dorsal fin set well back, close to the caudal fin. Caudal fin has a long upper lobe and a short lower lobe. Pectoral fins broadly triangular in shape. Head with blunt snout and large eyes set far forward on the head. Has six gill slits. Teeth in upper jaw are saw-like, those in the lower jaw are more pointed in shape.

Distribution: Widespread in tropical and temperate seas.
Habitat: From the intertidal zone (occasionally) down to 1,875m/6,150 ft but usually about 90m/300ft.
Food: Varied diet includes crustaceans, other fish, whale carcasses and seals.
Size: Up to 4.8m/15.8 ft.
Breeding: Ovoviviparous, with litters of over 100 pups; gestation may take up to 2 years or more.
Status: Listed as Lower Risk by IUCN.

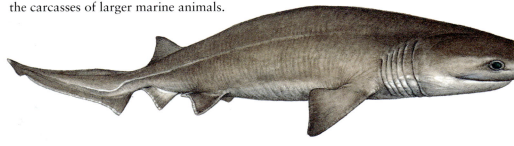

Frilled shark

Chlamydoselachus anguineus

This deep-water species looks more like an eel than a shark. The frilled shark is the only surviving member of its family and is something of an evolutionary relic. Frill sharks live mostly in deep water and were only discovered in the late 1800s. The name refers to the first of the six pairs of gill slits, which forms a continuous, frilly edged opening that runs right around the throat from one side of the head to the other. Each of the hundreds of teeth that develop and are shed in a lifetime is shaped like a trident, with three sharp points – other species with teeth like this are known only from the fossil record. The teeth are suitable for gripping prey but not for slicing or tearing, so victims are swallowed whole. The jaw opens very wide to allow this.

Identification: Body is long and slender with six pairs of frilly gill slits, the first of which extends right around the throat. The mouth opens at the front of the head – it is not underslung as in most other sharks. The eyes are large, the skin is pale brown. The tail fin is asymmetrical, lacking a lower lobe.

Distribution: Eastern Atlantic populations off north-eastern Europe and southern Africa; in Pacific it inhabits waters off Japan and New Zealand.
Habitat: Cold waters of the continental shelf and slope down to 1,600m/5,250ft.
Food: Smaller fish, including sharks and rays.
Size: Up to 2m/6.6ft.
Breeding: Ovoviviparous; young hatch from eggs inside female and are born as independent sharks.
Status: Not listed by IUCN.

Sleeper shark (Greenland shark)

Somniosus microcephalus

Distribution: Northern Atlantic and Arctic Ocean, occasional records from the Southern Hemisphere.
Habitat: Cold, deep water of the continental shelf down to 1,200m/3,950ft.
Food: Varied diet includes other fish, smaller marine mammals, squid, octopus and carrion.
Size: Up to 7.3m/24ft.
Breeding: Ovoviviparous, with litters of a dozen or more pups.
Status: Probably common, but not listed by IUCN.

These huge members of the dogfish order are so named because of their somewhat sluggish movement, despite which they are effective predators and scavengers, occupying the top of the deep-sea food chain. Recent research suggests that sleeper sharks are one of very few predators capable of tackling giant squid. Sleeper sharks are not fished commercially but they turn up regularly as bycatch and are targeted by Inuit subsistence fisheries. The flesh contains high levels of urea and trimethylamine oxide. If eaten fresh it is toxic, inducing a condition similar to drunkenness, but it can be dried or carefully cooked to make it fit for human consumption. Sleeper sharks develop and grow slowly and females give birth to live young that hatch from eggs inside the uterus.

Identification: A very large, heavy-set shark with five pairs of gill slits that are small in relation to the animal's size. The dorsal and pectoral fins are also small, and the tail fin is asymmetrical with a notch in the upper lobe. They are generally brown, black or grey in colour, with some having dark lines or white spots along the flanks.

Bramble shark (*Echinorhinus brucus*): up to 2.75m/9ft
A large, deep-water shark with dark grey-brown metallic-looking skin and a scattering of spiky scales. The tail fin is highly asymmetrical. The species is best known from the Mediterranean region and the continental shelves of the north-eastern Atlantic, but has been recorded in all oceans, with the possible exception of the Indian Ocean.

Spined pygmy shark (*Squaliolus laticaudus*): up to 21cm/8.25in
This is a miniature deep-water shark that migrates to shallower depths at night to prey on small fish, squid and crustaceans. There is a characteristic spine – common to most of the 130 or so species of squaliform shark – in front of the first dorsal fin, and it has a bioluminescent patch on the belly.

Goblin shark (*Mitsukurina owtsoni*): up to 5m/16.4ft
This is a bottom-dwelling species found in tropical oceans. Its exaggerated facial features account for the shark's common name, and it is characterized by having a particularly long, pointed snout that overhangs the mouth, looking like a huge nose. It swims relatively slowly, but is able to project its jaws rapidly forward in order to snap up prey, such as cephalopods and crabs.

Cookiecutter shark

Isistius brasiliensis

This is a small shark, with a long, narrow, cylindrical body and a short, blunt snout. The lips can be formed into a sucker with which the shark attaches itself to much larger prey. The shark then bites into the flesh with saw-like rows of lower teeth and rotates its entire body to remove a neat circular chunk of meat. Cookiecutter scars are commonly seen on a variety of species of larger fish and marine mammals. The scientific name *Isistius* refers to Isis, the ancient Egyptian goddess of light. This is appropriate, as cookiecutters are bioluminescent, and the skin of the belly contains a great many photophores. These are cells containing chemicals that react with enzymes to produce an eerie, green glow. The arrangement of photophores enhances the counter-shading effect, making the fish extremely difficult to see from below. Cookiecutters lurk in deep water during the day, and migrate to shallower depths to feed at night.

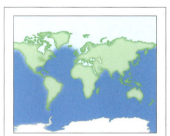

Distribution: Tropical and temperate Atlantic, Indian and Pacific Oceans.
Habitat: Open ocean and deep water down to 3,500m/11,500ft.
Food: Eats small fish and crustaceans whole; parasitic on larger fish and marine mammals.
Size: Up to 56cm/22in.
Breeding: Ovoviviparous with litters of up to 12 young.
Status: Not listed by IUCN.

Identification: Long, narrow body with an even brown colouring, except for dark collar. Dorsal and anal fins are small. Snout is short and conical; mouth has flexible, muscular lips for creating suction.

WHALE, REQUIEM AND MEGAMOUTH SHARKS

The gentle whale shark spends most of its time in the open ocean, along with several much smaller and more aggressive sharks, which make a living through speed, ferocity and superbly acute senses. The rarely-sighted megamouth is neither especially large, fast or fierce – but it is exceptional in other ways.

Whale shark

Rhincodon typus

This, the world's largest living fish, is only just beginning to be understood. Until recently it was known mainly from shallow seas, as a seasonal visitor to reefs and coasts. But for several months a year it disappeared. Studies have revealed it to be migratory and able to descend to great depths in search of food. Like other large marine organisms, it is a filter feeder, specializing in plankton and small fish. Where food is plentiful, whale sharks may temporarily gather in groups of up to 100 or more. They are hunted mainly for their fins. Left undisturbed, they can live to more than 100 years.

Identification: Vast, bulbous-bodied shark with square snout and large mouth. The body has several longitudinal ridges, is dark grey to brown above, white below, marked with a pattern of white spots and horizontal stripes on back and flanks. Of its two dorsal fins, the second is very small; the pectoral fins are triangular, the pelvic and anal fins small. Its tail is large with a longer upper lobe.

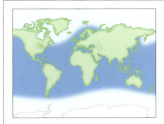

Distribution: Tropical and warm temperate oceans worldwide.
Habitat: From coastal reefs to deep open ocean, down to 1,000m/3,300ft or more.
Food: Plankton and small fish.
Size: Up to 20m/66ft.
Breeding: Ovoviviparous, with large litters of up to 300 pups.
Status: Listed as vulnerable by IUCN.

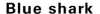

Blue shark

Prionace glauca

Identification: Long, narrow body with asymmetrical caudal fin. Dorsal fin is not particularly large, but pectoral fins are very long. Eyes appear large on conical, flattened head. Body is strikingly counter-shaded – dark blue on the back, bright blue on the flanks and paler in colour underneath.

Also known as the blue whaler because of its frequent association with dead whales, the blue shark is a species whose future may be under threat due to increased commercial exploitation – more than 10 million are killed annually for food. Blue sharks are curious and opportunistic and readily investigate any possible source of food, including divers and shipwreck victims, thus earning a reputation as one of the more dangerous shark species. However, more usual food sources include squids and small fish, such as herrings – schooling species are especially favoured in the open ocean, where feeding opportunities can be few and far between. Female blue sharks can produce a great many young. One female was recorded carrying 134 embryos, though it is unlikely all would have survived to birth.

Distribution: Tropical and temperate oceans and seas worldwide.
Habitat: Open water to 350m/1,150ft deep.
Food: Smaller fish and invertebrates, including octopus and squid; may also scavenge carcasses of larger animals.
Size: Up to 4m/13ft. There have been unconfirmed reports of larger individuals being sighted.
Breeding: Ovoviviparous, 4–80 pups born per litter; there is no parental care.
Status: Listed as Near Threatened by IUCN.

Oceanic white tip shark

Carcharhinus longimanus

Distribution: Tropical and subtropical waters of all oceans.
Habitat: Surface waters of open ocean down to about 150m/500ft.
Food: Mainly bony fish, but this opportunistic feeder will eat virtually anything.
Size: Up to 4m/13ft.
Breeding: Ovoviviparous; litters of 1–15 pups.
Status: Abundant at present, but suffering from exploitation for its fins and as bycatch. Listed as Near Threatened by IUCN.

The oceanic white tip is a solitary wanderer and an opportunistic feeder. It spends most its time cruising the warm surface waters of open oceans, with its acute senses alert to the possibility of food. Temporary aggregations may form around plentiful food resources, and the species is often involved in feeding frenzies. It is intensely curious and will eat almost anything, including medium to large fish, especially tuna and dorados, as well as other sharks, rays, squid, turtles, sea birds and even human garbage. It will also eat humans, and it is often among the first of the large scavengers to gather at the scene of a disaster at sea. However, attacks close to shore are less likely. It is often accompanied by remoras, a species of fish that it seems not to eat.

Identification: A stout shark with a very large dorsal fin. The rest of the body is brownish grey above and pale coloured below. Pectoral fins are long and tapering; tail fin lobes are asymmetric. All but the smallest fins are tipped with white. Often seen in association with remoras, which may hitch a ride by attaching themselves to the shark's body.

Megamouth shark

Megachasma pelagios

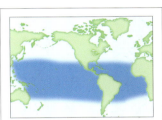

Distribution: Tropical waters of Pacific and Atlantic Oceans.
Habitat: Pelagic in open ocean, from surface waters possibly down to 1,000m/3,300ft.
Food: Larger planktonic animals, small fish and jellyfish.
Size: Up to 5.5m/18ft.
Breeding: Ovoviviparous.
Status: Listed as Data Deficient by IUCN.

This bizarre-looking species is known only from 27 confirmed sightings and just six landed specimens, the first of which was taken off Hawaii in 1976. Named for its enormous jaws, which can be protruded forwards, the megamouth sounds intimidating, but the jaws are lined with very tiny hooked teeth and the species is at least a partial filter feeder, taking nothing larger than shrimps, jellyfish and small pelagic fish. It migrates vertically on a daily basis, rising to surface waters at dusk along with the planktonic animals it feeds on. When the jaws are protruded, a bright-white band of tissue is exposed between the upper lip and jaw. This is highly conspicuous, even in gloomy water, and may play some role in feeding or in individual recognition.

Identification: Large rounded head and large mouth. Dark bluish-grey above, paler below. One large and one small dorsal fin; pectoral fins very large, as is the asymmetrical tail, fins usually tipped with white.

Silky shark (*Carcharhinus falciformis*): up to 3.5m/11.5ft
This is a long, slender, deep-water specialist found in subtropical and tropical waters as deep as 4,000m/13,100ft, but equally at home in surface waters, where it is regarded as dangerous to humans. In fact, the reverse is much more often the case, as this is one of the most intensively fished shark species, and is exploited for meat, hide, fins and liver oil.

Night shark (*Carcharhinus signatus*): up to 2.8m/9ft
A slender brown shark with a long pointed snout. Night sharks lurk in waters off Atlantic continental shelves, often in schools. They are nocturnal and eat small fish and squid. They pose no threat to humans.

Spinner shark (*Carcharhinus brevipinna*): up to 3m/10ft
This grey-coloured shark of the tropical and subtropical Atlantic, Indian and Indo-Pacific has a very pointed snout and a highly asymmetric tail with a greatly elongated upper lobe. It is named for its feeding behaviour, which involves a spectacular open-mouthed vertical ascent – complete with rapid spinning motion – through schools of fish. This is conducted at such speed that the shark may leap clear of the water.

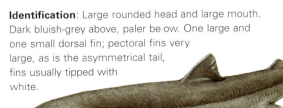

LOBE FINS AND EELS

The cumbersome coelacanth is an iconic reminder of our own origins – fish like this are believed to have given rise to all terrestrial vertebrates. Their modern distribution is limited to part of the Indian Ocean, while that of eels and their relatives is enormous. Several species of eel spend part of their lives in both freshwater and marine environments.

Coelacanth

Latimeria chalumnae

Coelacanths are perhaps the world's most famous 'living fossil'. Before a specimen turned up in 1938 as bycatch of a trawler from the Indian Ocean port of East London, South Africa, scientists thought fish like this had been extinct since the time of the dinosaurs. A second species, from Sulawesi, was discovered in 1999. The structure and action of the flexible lobe-like pectoral and pelvic fins suggest a likely means by which four-legged land animals might have evolved from a fish ancestor. The fish appears to use them for propelling itself slowly over the sea floor. The fins support no weight, but their movement is similar to walking in quadrupeds. The second dorsal and anal fins are also lobate and are used for swimming, performing slow sculling movements. Coelacanths invest heavily in their young. The eggs are among the largest known for ovoviviparous fish, at up to 10cm/4in across.

Identification: Chunky fish with dark bluish-brown heavy scales. The fins are fleshy lobes with hollow rays. The eyes and mouth are large, and the tail is a symmetrical, muscular paddle, with a continuous fringing fin.

Distribution: Western Indian Ocean off South Africa, Mozambique, Madagascar and the Comoros Islands.
Habitat: Rocky sea bed at depths of 150–700m/ 500–2,300ft
Food: Deep-sea fish and invertebrates.
Size: Up to 2.5m/8.2ft.
Breeding: Ovoviviparous; up to 20 young – over 30cm/12in long – born after a 13-month gestation period. Life span of individuals up to 50 years.
Status: Critically Endangered. Species is of enormous scientific significance.

Slender snipe eel

Nemichthys scolopaceus

The snipe eel's elongated, outwardly curving jaws are lined with tiny backward-pointing teeth. The fish cannot really bite, or even properly close its mouth. It hunts by swimming with its mouth open, sweeping the water. Once snagged by the teeth, small prey finds itself in a position it can only move in one direction – down the eel's throat. The eel is particularly efficient at catching shrimp, whose long antennae are easily snagged. The tactic can backfire and snipe eels have been found clinging to the tails of fish too large to swallow from which they are unable to disengage. The body is thin, ending in a thread-like tail. A dorsal fin runs halfway along the body, and is replaced by a row of short spines running to the tail. The anal fin is a little taller than the dorsal and soft rayed all the way to the tail.

Identification: The strange, almost bird-like head is by far the thickest park of the body, with large eyes and long, slender outwardly curving jaws. The skin is dark brown above, almost black on the belly.

Distribution: Tropical and temperate seas and oceans worldwide.
Habitat: Deep mid-water down to 2,000m/ 6,560ft.
Food: Pelagic crustaceans and small fish.
Size: Up to 1.3m/4.25ft.
Breeding: Oviparous, with planktonic leptocephali larvae typical of eels; no parental care; spawns only once in its lifetime.
Status: Not listed by IUCN.

American eel

Anguilla rostrata

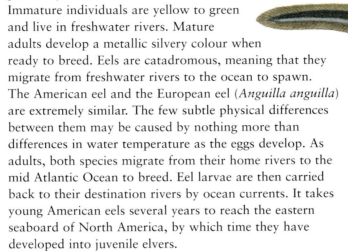

The American eel is a long, snakelike predatory fish. Immature individuals are yellow to green and live in freshwater rivers. Mature adults develop a metallic silvery colour when ready to breed. Eels are catadromous, meaning that they migrate from freshwater rivers to the ocean to spawn. The American eel and the European eel (*Anguilla anguilla*) are extremely similar. The few subtle physical differences between them may be caused by nothing more than differences in water temperature as the eggs develop. As adults, both species migrate from their home rivers to the mid Atlantic Ocean to breed. Eel larvae are then carried back to their destination rivers by ocean currents. It takes young American eels several years to reach the eastern seaboard of North America, by which time they have developed into juvenile elvers.

Distribution: Eastern Atlantic Ocean and Caribbean and from rivers of eastern North and Central America and West Indies to mid-Atlantic.
Habitat: Freshwater and marine, from estuaries to open ocean.
Food: Smaller fish and invertebrates
Size: Up to 1.5m/5ft; females slightly smaller
Breeding: Oviparous; no parental care; adults complete single spawning migration to the Sargasso Sea and then die.
Status: Common; commercially fished; not listed by IUCN.

Identification: Long, snake-like body with a small, pointed head. The skin of the eel appears to be scaleless, but there are minute scales in the adult. The skin produces a slimy mucilage in response to stress, such as being handled. Pelvic fins absent, dorsal and anal fins form a continuous fringe around the rear two-thirds of the body.

Spiny eel
(*Notacanthus chemnitzii*):
up to 1.2m/4ft
Spiny eels are large, elongate fish distinguished by a row of spines along the back and another row on the belly in front of the anal fin. They live in deep, temperate waters of all oceans and feed mainly on bottom-dwelling invertebrates, especially sea anemones.

Bobtail eel (*Cyema atrum*): up to 15cm/6in
A rather obscure relative of the snipe eel, found in very deep mid-water of all oceans. The bobtail has a moderately elongated body and long, narrow, outwardly curving jaws.

Longneck eek (*Derichthys serpentinus*):
up to 40cm/15.75in
A cosmopolitan, deep-dwelling eel with a long, snake-like black body. The head is separated from the body by a narrow neck, behind which the dorsal and anal fins form a continuous fringe running the entire length of the body and around the tail. Longneck eels eat small fish and planktonic crustaceans.

Japanese eel (*Anguilla japonica*): up to 1.5m/5ft
A highly valuable food fish and close relative of the American and European eels. Like these eels, it develops in freshwater rivers and migrates to the open ocean to spawn. Japanese eels are thought to spawn near the Marianas Islands of the Pacific Ocean.

Gulper eel (pelican eel)

Eurypharynx pelicanoides

It is not difficult to see why the gulper eel is so named – this fish has a huge, gulping mouth. The jaws are greatly extended and the soft tissues of the mouth are highly elastic, giving the fish a truly gargantuan gape and allowing it to take in enormous quantities of water from which prey is filtered out and then swallowed whole. Not surprisingly, the gulper is not a particularly fussy eater and will take anything unlucky enough, and small enough, to come within range – in practice this means mostly deep-water shrimps and other crustaceans, small fish and squid. There is no tail fin as such – the body tapers into a long whip-like tail with a swollen tip containing light-producing cells. Adult gulper eels appear to enter a rapid decline and die shortly after spawning. Fertilized eggs develop into planktonic larvae, like those of other eels, known as leptocephali.

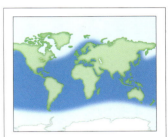

Distribution: Temperate and tropical oceans and seas worldwide.
Habitat: Very deep water down to 7,500m/24,600ft.
Food: Small fish and invertebrates.
Size: Up to 1m/3.25ft.
Breeding: Oviparous; no parental care; spawns only once in lifetime.
Status: Not listed by IUCN.

Identification: Gulper eels lack scales. The skin is smooth and slippery and that of the huge mouth is very stretchy. There is a single long dorsal fin running the length of the body and tail and a long anal fin. The long, narrow tail has terminal light organ.

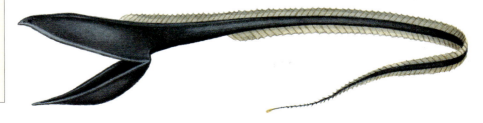

HERRINGS, ANCHOVIES AND RELATIVES

Clupeids are narrow-bodied, soft-finned, bony fish with oily flesh and a forked tail. Herrings, sardines, anchovies and shad are all clupeids. The two main families, herrings and anchovies, contain some 320 species, most of which are marine. They rely on the principle of safety in numbers, and form some of the most spectacular schooling formations in the oceans.

Atlantic herring

Clupea harengus

Herrings are adapted for long periods of rapid swimming and have a body plan that has not changed for million of years. Atlantic herrings live in large schools, mainly feeding by night either on individual items or on planktonic copepods strained from the water with specialized gill rakers. They retreat to deeper water by day. Vast schools of herring attract the attentions of predators, whose approach triggers a behaviour known as 'bait balling', in which every fish tries to hide in the middle of the crowd, creating a dense, swirling mass. This schooling behaviour is also exploited by trawlers, with almost certainly unsustainable numbers taken each year.

Identification: Slender fish with a triangular, pointed head and large mouth angled slightly upwards. There is a small dorsal fin halfway along the back, roughly level with pelvic fins; tail is large and forked. The body is covered in thin, silvery scales, with a row of thicker ones forming a keel along the underside.

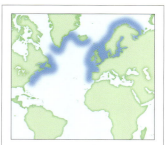

Distribution: Temperate waters of North Atlantic Ocean.
Habitat: Mainly coastal waters, down to about 200m/650ft.
Food: Plankton.
Size: Up to 45cm/17.75in.
Breeding: Oviparous; spawns annually (timing varies), eggs sink and adhere to weed or the substratum.
Status: Almost certainly threatened by fishing on an industrial scale. Not listed by IUCN.

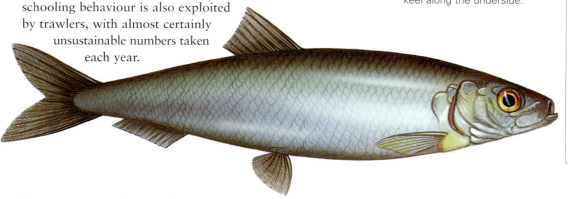

European pilchard

Sardina pilchardus

Identification: A small, spindle-shaped fish with a single, small, delicate dorsal fin and inconspicuous pectoral, pelvic and anal fins. The tail is deeply forked. The body is counter-shaded – steely grey above and bright silver below. Some fish display a series of dark spots on the flanks. Has typically oily skin which can give off a beautiful shimmer of colour when seen underwater.

A small cousin of the herring, the pilchard is intensively exploited by commercial fishing interests, and is eaten either fresh or canned as 'sardine'. Strictly speaking, a sardine is a young pilchard. As well as by humans, the species is also exploited by a large number of marine predators, including dolphins, sharks and larger bony fish such as tuna and mackerel. Pilchards feed close to the surface at night and retreat to deeper water by day. Different populations spawn at different times of year, with the main peaks in spring and summer. Females produce tens of thousands of small, floating eggs at a time, which hatch into larvae within 2 to 4 days. Like other schooling clupeids, pilchards spend their entire life in a school of similar aged and sized fish.

Distribution: Temperate waters of north-eastern Atlantic Ocean.
Habitat: Pelagic; in open oceans as well as close to shore, occasionally entering estuaries, from 10–100m/33–330ft.
Food: Plankton.
Size: Up to 25cm/10in.
Breeding: Oviparous; no parental care.
Status: Common, highly commercial; not listed by IUCN.

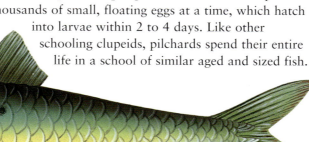

Wolf herring

Chirocentrus dorab

Distribution: Tropical and sub-tropical in-shore waters of the Indian and western Pacific Oceans.
Habitat: Pelagic, surface waters down to 120m/400ft.
Food: Other fish.
Size: 3.5m/11.5ft.
Breeding: Oviparous, but other details not known.
Status: Appears common; not listed by IUCN.

Named for their reputation for attacking anything that moves, wolf herrings are fast-swimming predators capable of leaping from the water, and 'porpoising' before the bow wave of boats. They swim in schools, searching out schools of smaller fish, in particular herrings and anchovies. Wolf herrings have rows of needle-like teeth at the front of the mouth, and smaller ones covering the roof of the mouth – once prey is snatched there is virtually no chance of escape. In addition to their teeth, wolf herrings also have gill rakers, which they can use to strain smaller prey from the water. Wolf herrings are sometimes used in Asian cooking, but tend not to be specifically targeted by fisheries – they fight hard and bite readily, and present a substantial risk of injury.

Identification: Long, narrow body with triangular head and large mouth armed with very sharp teeth; dorsal, anal, pectoral and pelvic fins are all small, caudal fins form large, deeply forked tail. The body is covered in small, silvery scales.

Anchoveta (*Engraulis ringens*): up to 20cm/8in
A diminutive fish that supports a vast fishing industry and provides the dietary mainstay of hundreds of predatory fish, birds and mammals. It lives in the south-east Pacific Ocean, where populations fluctuate alarmingly – crashes are usually associated with El Niño years.

Atlantic menhaden (*Brevoortia tyrannus*): up to 50cm/20in
A schooling, pelagic fish, deeper-bodied than other herrings but ecologically similar. Schools are generally restricted to warm surface waters where they provide an important food resource for larger fish and cetaceans.

Pacific herring (*Clupea pallasii*): up to 46cm/18in
A temperate species, less oceanic than its Atlantic equivalent and most common in waters of the continental shelves of the north Pacific. Adults venture into coastal waters to breed, sometimes entering estuaries.

Landlocked clupeids: The herring family includes a number of species found in coastal waters, some of which enter estuaries and can survive in brackish and fresh water. The American alewife (*Alosa pseudoharengus*), for example, thrives in the Great Lakes and in a number of other landlocked, freshwater habitats.

Pacific anchovy

Engraulis mordax

Anchovies spend their lives in huge schools, within which individuals move and react in unison. They use good eyesight and the lateral line organ to sense movement in their companions, and their reactions are so quick that the school appears to move as one. As with herrings, anchovies obtain most other food by filtering small animals, mainly copepods, from the water with their gill rakers, but they will also nibble at larger items. Spawning peaks in summer, but females continue to produce eggs in batches of a few hundred all year around. The eggs are unusual in being slightly oval rather than round. They hatch very quickly in warm water, in just a few days. This is just one of several anchovy species supporting large commercial fisheries.

Identification: Slender-bodied fish, almost circular in cross section; with small dorsal, anal and paired fins and deeply forked tail. The head appears chinless due to large snout and small lower jaw. Mouth is large, eye large and located well forward on head. Body bears silver scales on flanks that fade with age.

Distribution: Sub-tropical waters of north-eastern Pacific Ocean.
Habitat: Pelagic, surface waters of continental shelf down to 300m/1,000ft.
Food: Plankton.
Size: Up to 25cm/10in.
Breeding: Oviparous; spawns several times a year at the surface.
Status: Highly commercial; not listed by IUCN.

LIGHTFISH, HATCHETFISH AND RELATIVES

Members of the order Stomiiformes live in deep water, and they include some of the most bizarre-looking fish in the sea. Many species are bioluminescent, with colourful photophores arranged in a variety of striking patterns over the head and body.

Black dragonfish

Idiacanthus atlanticus

The species has marked sexual dimorphism – only females grow large, while males rarely exceed 5cm/2in long. Females are black in colour and are armed with large, fang-like teeth. They also have a single long, fleshy barbel, which dangles from the chin and serves as a fishing lure. The body and the lure bear a number of light-producing photophores that glow both blue and red. Female dragonfish migrate from the depths to shallower water to hunt at night. The tiny males are a paler shade of brown than females and lack impressive teeth, a barbel or pelvic fins. They rarely, if ever, venture above 1,000m/3,300ft and are apparently unable to feed, lacking a functional gut. They probably only live long enough to reproduce. Larval black dragonfish are even more peculiar than their parents. They are long, thin, and almost transparent, with eyes set on very long, thread-like stalks that can be almost half as long as the rest of the body.

Distribution: Sub-tropical and temperate waters of south Atlantic, south Pacific, southern Indian Ocean and Southern Ocean.
Habitat: Deep water to 2,000m/6,600ft.
Food: Females prey on smaller fish and invertebrates.
Size: Up to 40cm/15.75in.
Breeding: External fertilization results in unusual, glassy larvae.
Status: Not listed by IUCN.

Identification: Females of the species have a long, eel-like body with long, delicate dorsal and anal fins and a pair of feathery pelvic fins. The teeth are recurved and needle-sharp. There are bioluminescent cells along the flanks and concentrated in the tip of the long chin barbel, which probably acts as a lure.

Viperfish

Chauliodus sloani

Identification: Body long and gently tapering, covered with thin, iridescent scales that allow dark brownish-blue colouration to show through. First dorsal fin is soft but tall with a very long first ray. Paired pectoral and anal fins are long and narrow. Head relatively large, with large eye and mouth full of long, pointed teeth.

The viperfish has teeth so large that it cannot fully close its mouth. The teeth are adapted for impaling prey rather than for cutting or tearing flesh. Once the prey is caught, the teeth tilt inwards on slightly flexible roots to aid the swallowing process. The jaws can be dislocated and the stomach expanded in order to accommodate prey that is very nearly as large as the viperfish itself. A circular, light-emitting photophore situated under the eye serves to lure potential prey close to the animal's deadly fangs. Smaller light-emitting cells are arranged in rows along the belly and scattered over the body. The viperfish migrates from the depths to shallower water on a regular basis, rising at dusk from a daytime depth of about 2,000m/6,600ft or more to night-time hunting grounds at about 600m/2,000ft.

Distribution: Tropical and temperate waters of all oceans, and some adjoining seas.
Habitat: Deep water down to 2,500m/8,200ft.
Food: Smaller fish and pelagic crustaceans.
Size: Up to 35cm/13.75in.
Breeding: Oviparous, with external fertilization and no parental care.
Status: Not listed by IUCN.

Stoplight loosejaw

Malacosteus niger

Another deep-sea oddity, the stoplight loosejaw is named for the photophores under and behind the eyes, which glow red and green respectively. The lights probably serve to attract prey and to illuminate it so the loosejaw can aim its attack. Like other members of its family, the species has enormous jaws – far longer than the skull. When the fish open its mouth, the lower jaw dislocates and extends forward – a row of sharp, backward-pointing teeth hook into prey, which is then dragged back into the mouth. Rather than being enclosed within a sheath of flesh and skin, the skeleton of the lower law is exposed. This reduces drag and allows the lower jaw to shoot quickly forward without creating a pressure wave that might alert the prey.

Identification: The elongate body tapers to a tiny, laterally flattened tail fin. The paired fins are very narrow, the median fins are larger but very delicate. The fish is not a powerful swimmer and its jaws are longer than its skull. It has a red comma-like photophore under the eye and a green circular one behind the eye. Its head and body are black. The fish is shown here with mouth open, the exposed skeleton of the lower jaw swinging forward to its full extent and revealing the enormous gape between upper and lower jaws.

Distribution: Tropical and temperate zones of the Atlantic, Indian and Pacific Oceans.
Habitat: Deep water down to 2,500m/8,200ft.
Food: Bony fish and crustaceans, including deep-water shrimps and copepods.
Size: Up to 24cm/9.5in.
Breeding: Presumed to be oviparous, but details of its breeding are unknown.
Status: Not listed by IUCN.

upper jaw

lower jaw

Silver hatchetfish

Argyropelecus aculeatus

Hatchetfish are named for their body shape – they are flattened laterally, with a narrow tail and very deep front end, resembling the handle and blade of a hatchet. The species is able to hide even in open water thanks to a combination of shape, reflective scales and blue-emitting photophores that make its silhouette disappear when viewed from below. Hatchetfish lurk in the deeper part of their range during the day, rising at dusk to 100–300m/330–1,000ft to feed on a variety of small planktonic animals – copepods and the larvae of other crustaceans and fish are all taken, but best of all are ostracods.

Distribution: Tropical, subtropical and warm-temperate areas of the Atlantic, Indian and Pacific Oceans.
Habitat: Pelagic in open ocean at depths 100–600m/ 330–2,000ft.
Food: Zooplankton.
Size: Up to 8cm/3in.
Breeding: Fertilization is external; there is no parental care.
Status: Common; not listed by IUCN.

Jellynose (*Guentherus altivela*): up to 2m/6.6ft
The jellynose lives close to the sea floor of the continental slopes of the eastern Atlantic and eastern Pacific Oceans. It has a plump body that tapers to a pointed tail and feeds on other smaller fish. The second dorsal and anal fins form an almost continuous fringe around the tail.

Snaggletooth (*Astronesthes gemmifer*): up to about 20cm/8in
A long, black, scaleless fish found in all the world's oceans. It produces violet light from rows of light-producing organs on its flanks and two more close to each eye. The large mouth contains the intimidating array of very long, sharp teeth for which the species is named.

Pearlsides (*Maurolicus muelleri*): up to 8cm/3in
This small but striking fish lives in the Atlantic and Pacific at intermediate oceanic depths of about 1,500m/4,900ft, migrating vertically to shallower waters at night to feed on plankton-dwelling invertebrates, such as copepods. Its flanks are covered with gleaming silvery scales.

Lightfish (*Icthyococcus ovatus*): up to 5cm/2in
A deep-bodied fish, generally brownish-yellow with silvery flanks. The body tapers sharply to the tail and the caudal fin is small. Dorsal and anal fins are small, soft rayed and delicate. Photophores in two rows along underside. Found in all oceans, except northern Pacific.

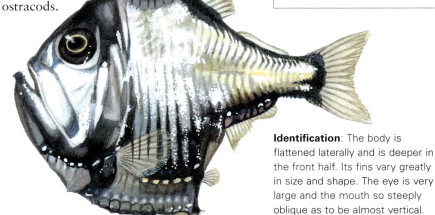

Identification: The body is flattened laterally and is deeper in the front half. Its fins vary greatly in size and shape. The eye is very large and the mouth so steeply oblique as to be almost vertical.

GRINNERS

Members of the order Aulopiformes are commonly known as 'grinners' on account of their exceptionally wide mouth and sharp, prominent teeth. The order consists of 13 living families of ray-finned marine fish, a number that includes a large number of deep-water specialists, many of which spend at least part of their lives as potentially self-fertilizing hermaphrodites.

Tripodfish

Bathypterois grallator

Among the deepest dwelling of all fishes, the tripodfish spends most of its time 'standing' on the sea floor, propped up on three elongated stiffened rays from the pelvic and caudal fins. Food is scarce at such great depths, and this characteristic posture, facing into the current, offers a low-energy alternative to swimming. The tripodfish can swim, and when it does so, the fin rays trail behind. The eyes are greatly reduced in size. Adult tripodfish live solitary lives in a habitat where it can be difficult to find a mate. As a result, they have evolved to be simultaneous hermaphrodites – both male and female reproductive organs mature in the same body at the same time, making it possible, if necessary, for a single individual to fertilize its own eggs.

Identification: Body has a diamond pattern of dark scales. The first ray of each pelvic fin and the last ray of the tail serve as tripod supports. The pectoral fins form streamers while the dorsal fin stabilizes the body.

Distribution: Tropical and temperate Atlantic, Indian and Pacific Oceans and deep adjoining seas.
Habitat: Deep-ocean floor to 3,500m/11,500ft.
Food: Nekton (deep-water plankton), mostly copepods.
Size: 40cm/15.75in.
Breeding: Simultaneous hermaphrodism.
Status: Not listed by IUCN.

Greeneye

Chlorophthalmus acutifrons

Identification: Has a tapering body which is at its widest at the head, dominated by large, green-coloured eyes. The fins are elongate, but soft rayed and delicate; the tail fin has a deep cleft. Body colour is green overall with patches of brilliant iridescence. The belly is paler in colour.

This is one of about 20 closely related species and the greeneye family has an almost global distribution. This particular species is commercially fished in Japan and the Philippines. Greeneyes live close to the sea floor, where they hunt smaller fish and invertebrates. They are named for their unusual eyes, which are very large and strikingly iridescent. There are further iridescent patches elsewhere on the head, while the rest of the body is drab by comparison. Like most members of this order, greeneyes appear to be hermaphrodites. They are thought to form schools for spawning. Greeneye larvae live in mid-water, sinking deeper and adopting a bottom-dwelling lifestyle as they reach adulthood.

Distribution: Western Pacific Ocean.
Habitat: Demersal (living close to the sea bed) in water down to 950m/3,100ft.
Food: Fish and invertebrates.
Size: Up to 30cm/12in.
Breeding: Hermaphroditic; oviparous; external fertilization; no parental care.
Status: Not listed by IUCN.

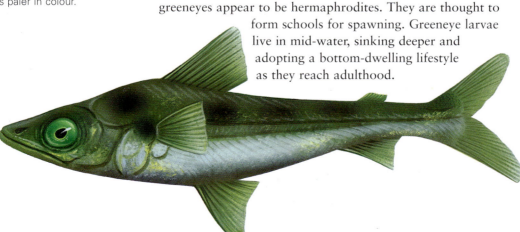

Telescope fish (*Gigantura chuni*):
up to 16cm/6.3in
A small relative of the larger grinner species, this tropical fish has a long, cylindrical body with large, rounded, soft-rayed pectoral, dorsal and anal fins and a deeply cleft, lopsided and ragged-looking tail fin with several overlong fin rays. It hunts smaller pelagic fish in deep water.

Daggertooth (*Anotopterus vorax*):
up to 1.05m/3.4ft
Adults of this long-bodied predatory fish live in deep mid-water in the chilly Southern Ocean. Having reached maturity, they make a one-way trip to warm temperate waters of the southern Atlantic, Pacific and Indian Oceans to spawn, after which they die. Two closely related species, *A. pharao* and *A. nikparini*, breed in the north Atlantic and Pacific, respectively.

White barracudina (*Arctozenus risso*):
up to 30cm/12in
Also known as the ribbon barracudina, this fast-swimming, silvery grinner favours the cold waters of the North Atlantic. It hunts alone or in large schools, using speed to ambush pelagic shrimps and smaller fish.

Grideye fish (*Ipnops agassizii*): up to 15cm/6in
This long, narrow-bodied relative of the tripod fish has large, short-based fins with soft rays. It, too, lives close to the sea floor at abyssal depths of 1,500–4,000m/5,000–13,000ft down.

Bombay duck (Bummalo)

Harpodon nehereus

The confusingly named and etymologically uncertain Bombay duck is an aggressive predator of smaller fish. The teeth are very sharp and curve slightly backwards. They also flex slightly so that prey, once caught, can easily be swallowed but much less easily released. Bombay duck are normally inhabitants of deep water, but at certain times of year (monsoon) they venture much closer to shore and may even enter estuaries in large schools. Adults spawn several times a year, releasing eggs and sperm that mingle in the water. There is no parental care and the larval fish are left to fend for themselves. They reach sexual maturity when they are about 13cm/5in long. Few ever reach the maximum size of 40cm/15.75in because the species is a highly commercial food fish. The fish is often dried and salted, and once processed like this, the odour is so strong that it has to be transported in air-tight containers.

Distribution: Indian Ocean and adjoining seas, including Indo-Pacific.
Habitat: Benthic in deeper waters of the continental shelf, down to 50m/160ft.
Food: Smaller fish.
Size: Up to 40cm/15.75in.
Breeding: Oviparous; external fertilization; no parental care.
Status: Not listed by IUCN.

Identification: Body is slightly flattened laterally. Has a very large first dorsal fin. Pale colour gives impression of tranlucency. An obvious lateral line of scales runs from the pectoral fins on each flank into a pointed middle lobe of the tail.

Longnose lancetfish

Alepisaurus ferox

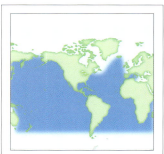

Distribution: Atlantic and Pacific Oceans and the adjoining seas.
Habitat: Deep mid-water down to 2,000m/6,600ft or more.
Food: Fish and invertebrates.
Size: Up to 2.15m/7ft.
Breeding: Oviparous; possibly asynchronous hermaphrodism; external fertilization; no parental care.
Status: Not listed by IUCN.

Identification: The body appears silvery, but all the fins are either black or dark brown. The first dorsal fin is very large, and the third, fourth and fifth dorsal fin rays may extend to form long, distinctive streamers. Second dorsal fin very small. The tail fin deeply forked, with an elongated first ray.

With its super-streamlined body and tall dorsal fin, the lancetfish is built for acceleration. Two or three fin rays in from the front, there are several over-long rays that form streamers. The mouth is armed with sharp teeth and two prominent fangs used for snatching prey – mostly smaller fish, but also invertebrates, from mid-water. Feeding adults may venture into sub-arctic waters, where prey can be abundant during the short summer, but they return to the tropics and sub-tropics to breed. Juveniles have undifferentiated gonads that may have the potential to develop into functional male or female sex organs, or perhaps both, although not at the same time.

LANTERNFISH, OPAH AND RIBBONFISH

The small order Myctophiformes contains about 250 species of lanternfish and blackchins, most of which are small, deep-dwelling and thus relatively little is known about them. The other species shown here all belong to the more diverse order Lampridiformes, which includes some of the most remarkable looking, and elusive, fish in the seas.

Blue lanternfish

Tarletonbeania crenularis

Identification: The mouth of the blue lanternfish is large, extending back past the eye. The body is counter-shaded – dark metallic blue on the back fading to silvery white on the underside. Even when not emitting light, the light organs on the belly and flanks can be seen as small, round spots (pimples).

Adult blue lanternfish spend their daylight hours at depth, rising much closer to the surface at night when they feed on plankton-dwelling crustaceans. Large eyes help the lanternfish to see in the gloom of deep water and in the dim light of moonlit surface waters. They, in turn, are eaten by larger predatory fish, such as albacore. Different species of lanternfish are distinguished largely by the pattern of the light-producing photophores found on their lower body. In the blue lanternfish, these photophores are arranged in sparse clusters and rows. Unlike their parents, larval lanternfish cannot afford to expend the energy required to retreat to deep water and so remain in surface waters for several weeks, feeding on smaller plankton, such as algae and fish and invertebrate larvae.

Distribution: Temperate and sub-arctic areas of the northern and eastern Pacific Ocean – off the coasts of North America, Russia and Japan.
Habitat: Deep mid-water down to 700m/2,300ft.
Food: Crustaceans.
Size: Up to 13cm/5in.
Breeding: Oviparous; external fertilization; spawning occurs in winter and spring; no parental care.
Status: Not listed by IUCN.

Opah

Lampris guttatus

Identification The opah is counter-shaded dark blue on the back to silvery on the belly, with many white spots. All the fins are a dramatic deep red. The first dorsal, pectoral and pelvic fins are pointed and curved slightly backwards; the second dorsal and anal fins form a fringe above and below the tail.

Also known as the spotted moonfish, the opah is a resident of open water with a laterally flattened body that appears almost round when seen in profile. Opahs grow very large – the heaviest individual on record weighed in at 270kg/595lb. Opahs are generally solitary but are often seen in the company of fast-swimming mackerel or tuna. Despite their ungainly proportions, opahs can produce a good turn of speed using a rigid flapping of their sharply tapering pectoral fins. They eat mainly small fish, crustaceans and small squid, which they swallow whole or tear into small pieces – the mouth is small and lacks teeth. Opahs are not targeted by fisheries, but they are considered a valuable bycatch, which may ultimately put them at risk.

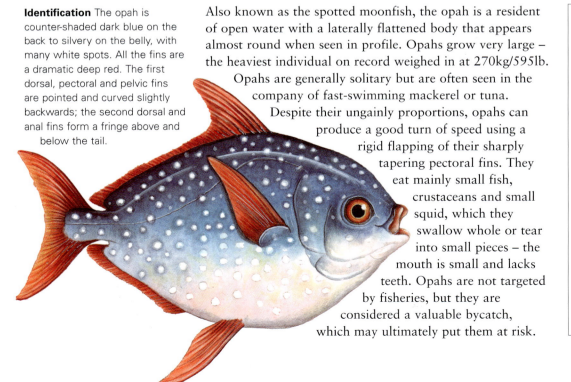

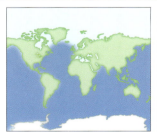

Distribution: Tropical and temperate Atlantic, Pacific and Indian Oceans, and some adjoining seas.
Habitat: Mid-water at 50–500m/150–1,600ft.
Food: Smaller fish, crustaceans and squid.
Size: Up to 2m/6.6ft.
Breeding: Oviparous; spawning occurs in spring.
Status: Not listed by IUCN, but may face exploitation in the future.

Blackchin (*Scopelengys tristis*): up to 20cm/8in
A small, drab-looking relative of the lanternfish, lacking light organs or metallic colouring. Blackchins are plankton eaters found throughout the tropics, and appear to spend their entire adult lives in water more than 400m/1,300ft deep.

Dealfish (*Trachipterus arctica*): up to 3m/10ft
One of several deep-sea ribbonfish species, the dealfish has a long, laterally flattened body that tapers steadily from head to tail. Confined to Arctic and north Atlantic waters, it eats smaller fish and squid and has a very slow reproductive cycle – taking 14 years to reach sexual maturity.

Scalloped ribbonfish (*Zu cristatus*): up to 1.2m/4ft
This tropical ribbonfish has an abruptly tapering body, is laterally flattened but it is less plank-like than its larger relatives, the dealfish and oarfish. Juveniles have an undulating, scalloped edge to the belly. The first rays of the dorsal fin and the pelvic fins form long streamers.

Sailfin (*Velifer hypselopterus*): up to 40cm/15.75in
A disc-shaped, laterally flattened fish with large, ragged-looking dorsal and anal fins. Thought to be rather rare, the species is restricted to tropical waters of the Indo-Pacific Ocean.

Oarfish

Regalecus glesne

The oarfish may well be the longest species of fish – specimens up to 17m/55.8ft long have been reported, though the largest reliable record is of a specimen 11m/36ft long. This extraordinary creature is thought to be the inspiration for many myths of sea monsters – even the Loch Ness monster. Oarfish are most often encountered washed up on land – sightings of live individuals are rare. Two recent accounts suggest that the fish maintains a vertical position in the water, propelling itself slowly with rippling movements of the dorsal fin, which runs the entire length of the body. The long, ribbon-like pelvic fins, meanwhile, are held out to the sides as stabilizers. Oarfish have no teeth and instead of scales their skin is covered with a fine coating of guanine, the material that gives all fish their silvery colour.

Distribution: Recorded in Atlantic Ocean and Mediterranean Sea, also in Indo-Pacific waters and eastern Pacific Ocean.
Habitat: Mid-water of open oceans from 20–1,000m/60–3,300ft.
Food: Pelagic crustaceans, small fish and squid.
Size: May exceed 11m/36ft in length.
Breeding: Oviparous; larvae known from surface waters.
Status: Not listed by IUCN.

Identification: Enormously long body is laterally flattened, silvery in colour with dark bluish-grey markings. The fins are crimson. The first dozen or so rays of the long fringing dorsal fin form a spectacular crest. Each of the pelvic fins comprises a single soft ray.

Tube-eye

Stylephorus chordatus

Distribution: All tropical oceans worldwide.
Habitat: Deep water.
Food: Small planktonic animals, mainly copepods.
Size: 30cm/12in.
Breeding: Not known.
Status: Not listed by IUCN.

A fish of deep tropical oceans, the tube-eye has upward-pointing goggle-eyes and a long, silver body that tapers to the tail. The lower lobe of the tail fin is elongated to form a whip-like extension. Like the oarfish (above), the species has a dorsal fin running the length of the body, and it swims vertically in the water. It migrates from the deep ocean to surface waters in order to feed each evening and it uses powerful suction to draw small crustaceans, such as copepods, into its small mouth. The buccal cavity (mouth chamber) can expand like a balloon to 40 times its resting volume to generate the necessary suction. Plankton is filtered from the water as it drains out through the gill slits. The details of its life history and breeding are virtually unknown.

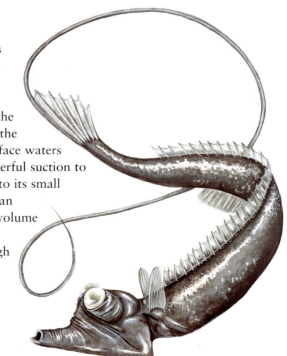

Identification: Long, tapering body ends in very long, whip-like tail fin, the rays of which are up to twice as long as the rest of the body. Large eyes are telescopic. The snout is tubular and the mouth is small.

BROTULAS, GRENADIERS AND COD RELATIVES

The large order Gadiformes includes many well-known species related to the familiar cods and hakes. Several of these live at great depths. The brotulas belong to a loosely related order, the Ophidiiformes, and they include the deepest living of all known fish species.

Abyssal brotula

Abyssobrotula galatheae

The abyssal brotula, discovered in the mid 1970s, is the deepest-living species of fish known to science. The record-breaking specimen was collected at 8,372m/27,467ft by a remotely controlled submersible in the deepest part of the Atlantic Ocean, the Puerto Rico trench. Unsurprisingly, very little is known of the species' behaviour or ecology – live specimens have been observed only on a handful of occasions. However, it is thought to be rather uncommon and its reproductive anatomy suggests that it is oviparous, although nothing is known of breeding ecology or larvae.

Identification: A short, rounded head is inclined slightly downward; body tapers steadily from pectoral region to tail. The dorsal and anal fins form a continuous fringe around the tail, and there is no caudal fin. Teeth are long and fang-like, and there is a short spur attached to the base of the lower jaw.

Distribution: Tropical seas and oceans worldwide.
Habitat: Deep and abyssal zones at 3,000–8,400m/ 10,000–27,500ft.
Food: Not known.
Size: Up to 17cm/6.7in.
Breeding: Not known.
Status: Not listed by IUCN.

Abyssal grenadier

Coryphaenoides armatus

Also known as rattails because of the way the body tapers to a long, narrow, pointed tail, grenadiers are among the most abundant fish of the deep oceans, with a collective biomass estimated at several million tonnes. Their abundance is a consequence of being very long-lived (60 years), as the rate of reproduction is actually very low. Grenadiers grow slowly – the rate of maturation depends on the availability of food. If necessary, a grenadier can go several months without feeding, but this inhibits development. It seems likely that the species is semelparous, meaning individuals have only one chance at reproduction – adults die soon after spawning for the first and only time. The sex ratio in some populations weighs heavily in favour of males. There is a small light-emitting organ on the animal's belly.

Distribution: Deep areas of all tropical and temperate oceans worldwide.
Habitat: Deep mid-water to 4,700m/15,400ft.
Food: Deep-sea crustaceans, sea cucumbers, squids and other fish.
Size: 1m/3.25ft.
Breeding: Oviparous; probably breeds only once in its lifetime.
Status: Very common; not listed by IUCN.

Identification: Large conical head with small chin barbel. Body tapers from pectoral region to very narrow tail. Dorsal fin has two long spines, followed by a short fringe of soft rays running the length of the body. Most of body is silvery brown or pink, becoming bluish on the belly.

Silver hake

Merluccius capensis

Distribution: Temperate waters of the south-eastern Atlantic.
Habitat: Close to the sea bed in water from 50–1,000m/ 150–3,300ft.
Food: Wide variety of smaller fish and invertebrate prey.
Size: 1.4m/4.6ft.
Breeding: Oviparous; spawns throughout the year.
Status: Some commercial harvesting; not listed by IUCN.

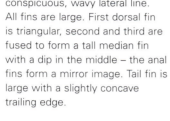

Identification: Elongate body, with tiny silver scales and conspicuous, wavy lateral line. All fins are large. First dorsal fin is triangular, second and third are fused to form a tall median fin with a dip in the middle – the anal fins form a mirror image. Tail fin is large with a slightly concave trailing edge.

Like other hakes and codfish, silver hakes are efficient predators. Their eyes and mouth are both large, reflecting indiscriminate, visual hunting habits. They will eat just about anything of manageable size, including smaller members of its own species. Breeding activity peaks in early spring (August and September), but continues to a lesser extent all year around. Given the species' cannibalistic tendencies, schools tend of contain fish of similar age and size. Adults perform an annual migration, heading south in the spring to take advantage of the abundant prey available in sub-Antarctic waters during the summer, returning to temperate waters in the autumn. The species is of minor commercial importance to fisheries based in southern Africa.

North Atlantic Codling (*Lepidion eques*): up to 45cm/17.75in
A medium-sized cod relative of temperate waters, with a large head and large, bulging eyes. The body tapers to a narrow tail with a small caudal fin. Codlings are predatory, feeding mainly on crustaceans and polychaete worms.

Bullseye grenadier (*Bathygadus macrops*): 50cm/20in
A moderately deep-dwelling fish of the tropical and subtropical north Atlantic. Occasionally caught and eaten, but not in large numbers.

Deep sea cusk eel (*Barathrites iris*): up to 65cm/25.6in
A deep-sea (5,300m/17,500ft) relative of the commercially important cusk eels, *Barathrites* has much the same shape – a small head and long, tapering body with a continuous dorsal-caudal-anal fin fringing the tail. Known Atlantic distribution; also present Indian and Pacific.

Gelatinous blindfish (*Aphyonus gelatinosus*): up to 15cm/6in
A relative of cusk eels and brotulas, specimens have turned up in bottom trawls of very deep water from tropical zones, but never in large numbers. The species has a pale body without scales or functional eyes, and bears live young.

Luminous hake

Steindachneria argentea

The luminous hake is a little-known relative of the cod, but unlike this more familiar species it is too small to attract the attentions of commercial fisheries. It lives at moderate depths, where very little daylight penetrates, and uses bioluminescence to help disguise its outline. There are light-emitting organs arranged in rows along the underside and on the head, and when these are glowing with their bluish light they make the fish very difficult to see from below. In addition, dark shading on its back helps to hide it from above. Luminous hake prey on smaller fish and invertebrates and are in turn targeted by larger species of hake, as well as by sharks. Juvenile fish tend to feed on crustaceans and small, deep-dwelling fish such as lanternfish.

Distribution: Tropical western Atlantic waters, from Florida, USA, and northern Gulf of Mexico through Central America to Venezuela.
Habitat: Close to sea floor in water 200–400m/ 650–1,300ft deep.
Food: Smaller fish and invertebrates.
Size: 30cm/12in.
Breeding: Ovoviviparous; details not known.
Status: Common; not listed by IUCN.

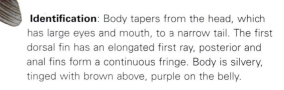

Identification: Body tapers from the head, which has large eyes and mouth, to a narrow tail. The first dorsal fin has an elongated first ray, posterior and anal fins form a continuous fringe. Body is silvery, tinged with brown above, purple on the belly.

ANGLERS AND TETRAODONTIFORMS

The grotesque-looking angler fish, many of which have evolved dorsal apparatus to 'lure' bait, are often used to illustrate the weird and wonderful life of the deep oceans, though many species actually live in shallow water. The order Tetraodontiformes is famous for another reason – it includes the world's largest bony fish, the magnificent ocean sunfish.

Sargassum fish

Histrio histrio

Identification: The body is in variable shades of brown with various flaps and frills to mimic the fronds of weed among which it usually lives. The dorsal fin ray is modified into a stout fishing lure to tempt prey close enough to ambush.

This unusual angler fish is a shallow-water, open-ocean specialist. It is usually associated with the floating seaweed *Sargassum*, but will also make use of other flotsam. The pelvic fins are specialized and able to grasp, rather like hands. The Sargassum fish is a relatively weak swimmer, but uses its fins to hold on to fronds of weed to avoid being swept away. Its camouflage makes it difficult to see among the weed. Breeding starts with courtship, with the male closely following the female. She then makes abrupt darts to the surface to spawn. The eggs are embedded in a jelly that expands on contact with seawater, creating a floating raft. The eggs may drift far from shelter and young fish are vulnerable.

Distribution: Ranges widely in Indian Ocean and Indo-Pacific; also found Western and Southern Pacific and Atlantic.
Habitat: Surface waters in drifts of *Sargassum* seaweed.
Food: Smaller fish and crustaceans (shrimps).
Size: 20cm/8in.
Breeding: Eggs fertilized externally, develop in floating mass with no parental care.
Status: Occasionally caught for food and aquarium trade; not listed in IUCN.

Giant sea devil

Ceratias holboelli

This is the original sea devil – the first and largest deep-sea angler to be described. Prey, in the form of smaller fish, is attracted by the sea devil twitching a fishing lure (the esca), formed from the modified first spine of the dorsal fin (the ilicium), and is then engulfed by the angler's huge mouth. Needle-like teeth ensure there is no escape. The other dorsal fin rays form distinctive knobbly protuberances, called 'caruncles', along the back. These fish are slow swimmers. Female sea devils produce eggs that float in rafts of jelly and hatch into tiny larvae that live as plankton. Males remain very small, and when mature seek out the larger mature females, which release chemical signals to guide suitors in the dark water. On finding a female, the male latches on to her body with sharp teeth and over time becomes permanently fused. He extracts what little nourishment he needs directly from her blood supply, through a placenta-like intermeshing of blood vessels, and produces sperm to fertilize her eggs.

Distribution: Tropical, sub-tropical and temperate oceans worldwide.
Habitat: Mostly deep water to 2,000m/6,562ft.
Food: Smaller fish.
Size: Females up to 1.2m/4ft long; males from 1–16cm/0.4–6.3in.
Breeding: Males form parasitic attachments to females. Eggs fertilized externally, develop in floating mass with no parental care.
Status: Not listed by IUCN.

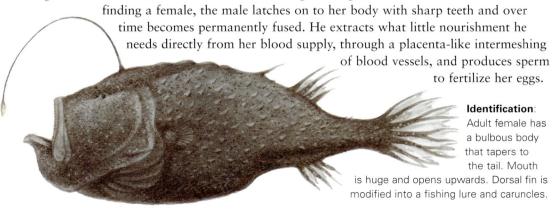

Identification: Adult female has a bulbous body that tapers to the tail. Mouth is huge and opens upwards. Dorsal fin is modified into a fishing lure and caruncles.

Toothy sea devil (*Neoceratias spinifer*)
6–7cm/2.4–2.8in
This mini-monster of the western central Pacific is the only known member of its family. Unusual among anglers in lacking a lure, it relies on a nightmarish array of moveable teeth mounted on the outer jaws.

Deep sea angler (*Linophryne macrodon*):
females 9cm/3.5in; males 2cm/0.8in
Females of this eastern central Pacific species have the most elaborate appendages of any angler species. They also bear a large barbel dangling from the lower jaw. Both lure and barbel are bioluminescent.

Whipnose (*Gigantactis elsmani*): females 38cm/15in
The fly fishermen of deep-sea anglers, the large upper jaw bears a highly elongated ilicium, or fishing rod, with a fleshy, tentacled lure at the tip. Recorded in various deep-water Pacific habitats, but full range still unknown.

Deep sea coffinfish (*Bathychaunax melanostomus*): up to 10cm/4in
This Indian Ocean species belongs to a family of anglers know as sea toads. Its bulbous body and narrow tail are covered with small spines. Lure rests in a groove on the head when not in use.

Spotted oceanic triggerfish
Canthidermis maculatus

Triggerfish are named for the shape of the first dorsal fin, which can be locked in an upright position, presumably as an anti-predation measure that makes the fish difficult to swallow. This species is characterized by a mainly blue or purple body, with some counter-shading. Unlike most other trigger fish, which are associated with reefs and coastal waters, the oceanic trigger is something of a nomad. It relies on the shelter of floating debris, such as detached fronds of weed, logs or pieces of floating wreckage and debris. This cover is essential – without it the trigger is exposed to predation. It eats other, smaller fish it finds there, but is especially intolerant of other triggers. It will dash at intruders aggressively, driving them away from its territory.

Distribution: Tropical and sub-tropical oceans worldwide.
Habitat: Surface dweller down to about 100m/330ft, associated with flotsam.
Food: Smaller fish and pelagic invertebrates.
Size: 50cm/20in.
Breeding: External fertilization, no parental care.
Status: Common, not listed by IUCN.

Identification:
Body is stout, with symmetrical tail fin and large, pointed, roughly equal second dorsal and anal fins. Marked with white or blue spots.

Giant oceanic sunfish
Mola mola

Distribution: Tropical to temperate waters of Pacific, Atlantic and Indian Oceans.
Habitat: Open ocean, close to surface, but may dive to 500m/1,600ft or more.
Food: Jellyfish, fish, molluscs, crustaceans and echinoderms.
Size: 3.3m/11ft long.
Breeding: Produces hundreds of millions of tiny eggs which are fertilized externally; these drift in the oceans with no parental care.
Status: Not listed by IUCN. Occasionally fished for meat and body parts used in Chinese medicine.

This is the world's largest bony fish, weighing in at anything up to 2,300kg/5,070lb. The vast, disc-shaped body is laterally compressed and stabilized by tall dorsal and anal fins. The name refers not to the fish's shape, but to its habit of 'sunbathing' while floating on its side near the surface. There is no tail; instead the body ends with a rounded rudder (the clavus) formed from the last few rays of the dorsal and anal fins. The skin is scaleless and tough. The sunfish has well-developed teeth, which are fused to form a sort of beak. The jaws are powerful enough to bite through shell and bone, but the mouth is small and the sunfish is not a fast swimmer, so it preys mostly on slow-moving or drifting animals. Mature females produce an astonishing number of tiny eggs, which drift the oceans – the chances of any one being fertilized and surviving infancy are small.

Identification: Very large truncated body, lacks tail. Caudal and pelvic fins are absent, dorsal and anal fins are tall, providing some stability and steering when swimming.

FLYING FISH AND SAWBELLIES

The 180 or so species of the order Beloniformes are mostly fast-swimming surface-dwellers, several of which can launch themselves out of the water to perform long glides. Members of the order Beryciformes, on the other hand, are far from streamlined – many have deep bodies with large heads, and spend their lives in moderate to deep water.

Cosmopolitan flying fish

Exocoetus volitans

This is the most common and widespread species of flying fish in the suborder Exocoetoidei. In preparation for take-off, it swims close to the surface and beats its tail up to 50 times a second. This causes the front of the body to lift from the water like an over-revved speedboat. Then, with a final flick of the tail, the fish leaves the water, accelerating rapidly as it breaks free of the surface tension.

Identification: Slender body, dark above and silvery below. Eyes are large. Pectoral fins greatly enlarged and can be opened out to the sides when gliding. Tail fin deeply notched and asymmetrical, with an enlarged lower lobe.

The pectoral fins spread wide to provide lift and it glides for 50m/164ft or more. This is a strategy for escaping predators, such as tuna and swordfish. These fast-swimming hunters can be left trailing once the flying fish leaves the water and speeds off through the air.

Distribution: Tropical and sub-tropical oceans and adjoining seas worldwide.
Habitat: Surface waters of open ocean, down to about 20m/66ft.
Food: Range of planktonic animals, mainly crustaceans.
Size: 30cm/12in.
Breeding: Oviparous; planktonic larvae; no parental care.
Status: Common; not listed by IUCN.

Needlefish

Belone belone

This is a fish of many common names – it is informally known as the garpike, sea pike, sea needle, greenbone and mackerel guide. This highly distinctive species is fished commercially as well as for sport – when hooked it fights hard, leaping clear of the water. It feeds mainly on schooling pelagic fish, such as smaller herrings and mackerel, and migrates along with these species – summering in the northern Atlantic and Baltic and retreating to warmer waters during the winter months. Female needlefish produce eggs that float at the water's surface, often becoming attached to floating weed or other debris by long tendrils. Needlefish of all sizes are eaten by a variety of fast-moving predators, including tuna, swordfish and seals.

Identification: Athletic fish with a greatly elongated, cylindrical body shaped by well-developed swimming muscles. Long, narrow snout and large eyes. Lower jaw is longer than upper jaw. Dorsal and anal fins set well back on body, close to the tail with a forked caudal fin. Silvery body. Sometimes confused with similiar species *Belone svetovidovi*.

Distribution: North-eastern Atlantic Ocean, also Mediterranean and Black seas.
Habitat: Open water close to surface; may occasionally enter estuaries.
Food: Smaller fish, especially sardines and anchovies.
Size: 95cm/37.5in.
Breeding: Oviparous; no parental care.
Status: Commercial game fish; not listed by IUCN.

Hairyfish (*Mirapinna esau*): up to 6cm/2.4in
Thought to be a relative of the tapetail, this strange-looking fish is known from only one specimen, which was collected near the Azores in the mid Atlantic.

Four-winged flying fish (*Cheilopogon furcatus*): up to 35cm/13.75in
This fish and its relatives have greatly enlarged pectoral and pelvic fins, well suited to 'flying'. They can glide for distances of up to 200m/660ft at speeds in excess of 80kmph/50mph. Found in tropical and sub-tropical oceans.

Alfonsino (*Beryx decadactylus*): up to 60cm/23.6in
A laterally flattened, deep-bodied, pelagic fish of tropical and temperate oceans. Has large eyes and a forked tail. The body is covered with small, comb-like scales, and is bright pink or red.

Tapetail (*Eutaeniophorus festivus*): up to 5cm/2in
A bizarre little fish belonging to the small order Cetomimiformes. Occurs in all tropical and temperate oceans but is not common in any of them. Body is elongate, with large fins. The pelvic fins are situated forward of the pectorals, at the throat. The tail ends in a long streamer.

Fangtooth

Anoplogaster cornuta

The common fangtooth, also know as the ogrefish, is named for its unpleasant gape full of needle-like teeth. It is a prickly customer in other ways, too – the body is covered in scales bearing short spines, giving it the feel of coarse sandpaper. The dorsal, anal, pectoral, pelvic and caudal fins all have conspicuously unwebbed fin rays. The lower fangs fit neatly into cavities in the palate when the mouth is closed. These cavities extend up inside the head, either side of the brain. The teeth are used for snagging smaller fish and invertebrates, but despite its fearsome appearance, it frequently falls victim to larger predators, especially tuna and albacore.

Identification: Head and mouth large, body short and deep with conspicuous lateral line lying within a groove that sweeps along the flank in a curve from eye level to the midline of the tail. Colour uniform dark brown to black.

Distribution: Tropical and temperate oceans worldwide.
Habitat: Close to sea floor in deep areas, from 500–5,000m/1,600–16,500ft.
Food: Smaller fish and invertebrates.
Size: 15cm/6in.
Breeding: Oviparous; larvae develop in surface waters; no parental care.
Status: Not listed by IUCN.

Orange roughy

Hoplostethus atlanticus

Distribution: Western Atlantic off Namibia and Pharoes, Pacific and Indian Oceans off Australia, New Zealand, Madagascar and southern Chile.
Habitat: Deep water from 200–2,000m/656–6,560ft.
Food: Crustaceans and smaller fish.
Size: 75cm/30in.
Breeding: Oviparous; no parental care.
Status: Protected by strict quotas in Australia and New Zealand, but not listed by IUCN.

The orange roughy grows exceptionally slowly, taking two or three decades to reach maturity. Examination of growth rings in otoliths (ear boxes) suggests that this species may live for up to 150 years – making it the longest-living fish species known to science. Orange roughy breed once a year, coming together in large schools to spawn near the surface. This behaviour is easily exploited by fishermen. The species' slow growth rates and sedentary nature are cause for great concern to conservationists. Populations have been greatly diminished by overfishing in recent times and numbers are very slow to recover.

Identification: A large head takes up about one-third of body length. Body is deep, laterally flattened and covered with small scales. In life, body is brick red, fading to orange when dead. Well-developed dorsal and anal fins, deeply notched tail fin. Pelvic fins set almost as far forward as pectoral fins.

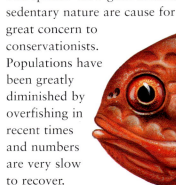
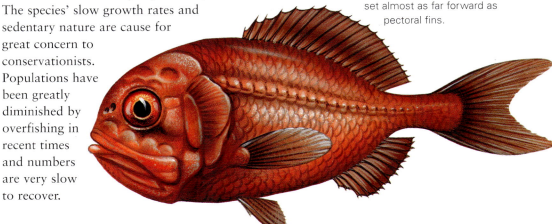

JACKS, REMORAS AND RELATIVES

These members of the large order Percifomes reflect just some of the diversity within this vast group. They all possess spiny fin rays, pelvic fins located well forward at the throat and thin, bone-like scales with a serrated edge. Most are fast-swimming predators, but a few are positively sluggish and some even resort to hitching rides on other fish.

Yellowtail amberjack

Seriola lalandi

Yellowtail amberjacks are a familiar sight on reefs and in coastal waters, but they also live in open ocean – juveniles, in particular, often live in schools far out to sea, having been carried with ocean currents as larvae. Large adults are more often solitary. All jacks are efficient swimmers – the carangiform mode of swimming, where the head stays still and the tail sweeps from side to side, is named after this family. The tall, forked tail fin offers powerful thrust without excessive turbulence. Amberjacks are predators of smaller fish species and invertebrates, which are ambushed and caught with a burst of speed.

Identification: Long, torpedo-shaped body with large, forked tail. Body is dark blue above and white below; tail fin is yellow or dark with yellow trailing edge. Single dorsal and anal fins are small with a triangular leading portion and an elongate fin base reaching nearly to the tail.

Distribution: Tropical and warm-temperate waters worldwide.
Habitat: Coasts, reefs and open ocean, usually close to sea floor, from shallows to 825m/2,700ft.
Food: Small fish, cephalopods and crustaceans.
Size: 2.5m/8.2ft.
Breeding: Oviparous; no parental care.
Status: Minor commercial importance, a popular gamefish; not listed by IUCN.

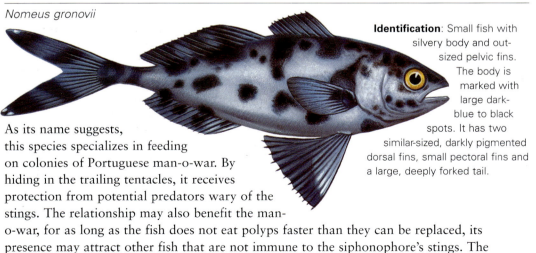

Man-o-war fish

Nomeus gronovii

Identification: Small fish with silvery body and out-sized pelvic fins. The body is marked with large dark-blue to black spots. It has two similar-sized, darkly pigmented dorsal fins, small pectoral fins and a large, deeply forked tail.

As its name suggests, this species specializes in feeding on colonies of Portuguese man-o-war. By hiding in the trailing tentacles, it receives protection from potential predators wary of the stings. The relationship may also benefit the man-o-war, for as long as the fish does not eat polyps faster than they can be replaced, its presence may attract other fish that are not immune to the siphonophore's stings. The man-o-war fish alternative name, 'driftfish', equally describes its lifestyle – it is not a powerful swimmer and apparently spends most of its life seeking or sheltering beneath its prey, drifting wherever ocean currents take it. This is certainly the case for juveniles, although it is thought that adults may descend into much deep waters later in life. Its absence from the eastern Atlantic Ocean and Mediterranean Sea has not been fully explained.

Distribution: Tropical and sub-tropical waters of Indian, Pacific and western Atlantic Oceans.
Habitat: Juveniles and sub-adults, surface waters from coastal areas to far offshore; adults may live near sea bed.
Food: Jellyfish and siphonophores.
Size: 39cm/15.4in.
Breeding: Oviparous; details not known.
Status: Not listed by IUCN.

Pilotfish (*Naucrates ductor*): up to 70cm/28in
The pilotfish (above) is a boldly patterned relative of the jacks. Its body is a dark-blue colour or black with seven or eight broad, evenly spaces white vertical bands. It lives in the surface waters of tropical and subtropical seas worldwide, and it is associated with floating objects, such as seaweed and jellyfish.

Halfmoon fish (*Medialuna californiensis*): up to 48cm/19in
A Pacific chub, from the perciform family Kyphosidae, the halfmoon is found around coasts and rocky reefs. Further out to sea, it habitually associates with floating kelp or sargassum weed or other flotsam. It is a popular food fish and is caught both commercially and for sport.

Horse mackerel (*Trachurus trachurus*): up to 70cm/28in
A widespread pelagic (a fish favouring the open ocean) carangid, the horse mackerel is a medium-sized, schooling fish of the Atlantic and western Pacific Oceans. The body is a greenish-grey colour above and silvery below, and it has large keeled (ridged) scales on the flanks. It is fished commercially in the eastern Atlantic Ocean and the North Sea.

Remora

Remora remora

Remoras can live a free-swimming existence, but their particular speciality is hitching a ride by attaching themselves to the body of larger fish, especially sharks and rays. They will also travel attached to turtles, cetaceans and even inanimate objects, such as ship hulls or diving gear. The attachment is made by a modification of the dorsal fin, which forms a large suction disc just behind the head. The disc is made up of stout, flexible membranes that can be raised and lowered to generate suction. The remora 'pays its fare' by picking off any parasites clinging to the host's skin – mainly copepods. It may also detach from the host in order to pursue free-living prey. Remoras are not parasites and appear to be tolerated by their hosts.

Distribution: Tropical, sub-tropical and warm-temperate oceans and seas worldwide.
Habitat: Reef and pelagic zones as passengers of larger animals.
Food: Parasitic crustaceans and small, free-living planktonic invertebrates.
Size: 85cm/33.5in.
Breeding: Details not known.
Status: Common; not listed by IUCN.

Identification: Elongate body, large, slightly forked tail fin. Pectoral fins are rounded, second dorsal fin is a low triangle. First dorsal fin is modified into an oval-shaped suction disc on head. Colour variable from dark grey or brown to off-white.

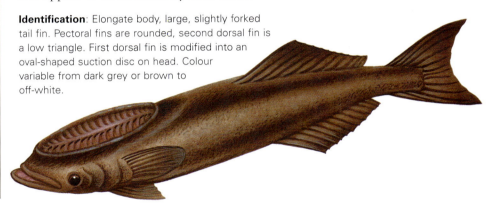

Dorado/dolphinfish

Coryphaena hippurus

This large, boldly coloured fish is known from coastal and open oceans. It lives in schools and frequently shelters under pieces of flotsam. Dorados are a prized food fish, often sold simply as 'dolphin', to the confusion and consternation of non-locals. Dorados are themselves active predators – as larvae and juveniles, they feed mainly on small crustaceans, graduating on to fish as they grow larger. As adults, they will tackle almost anything of suitable size. They are quick swimmers, able to make darting pursuits of even other swift species, such as flying fish. They themselves fall prey to other speed specialist, such as tuna and billfish.

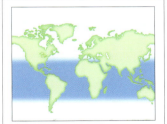

Distribution: Tropical and sub-tropical waters of Atlantic, Indian and Pacific Oceans.
Habitat: Open ocean, and coastal areas, occasionally brackish water; surface waters down to 85m/280ft.
Food: Small fish and zooplankton.
Size: 2m/6.6ft.
Breeding: Oviparous; breeds several times a year in its 5-year lifespan, associating in pairs to spawn.
Status: Commercially fished; not listed by IUCN.

Identification: Body tapers from a large head and upper body to a large forked tail. Down-turned mouth. A single dorsal fin runs the length of the body, pectorals and pelvics large, anal fin long and low. Males have conspicuous bony head crest. Body is vibrantly coloured: green, blue and yellow on back and flanks, white and yellow underside. Fins are blue and green.

TUNAS, MACKEREL AND BARRACUDAS

With their torpedo-shaped muscle-packed bodies, these perciforms are built for speed and endurance.
They are among the most voracious hunters in the seas, but also among the most hunted – their meaty,
oily flesh makes them enormously popular, and they support large fishing industries. Over-fishing, plus
the increasing levels of pollutants being accumulated in the flesh – are arousing serious concern.

Northern bluefin tuna

Thunnus thynnus

This is probably the largest of all the tuna species. The largest known individual was 4.58m/15ft in length and weighed 684kg/1,508lb. This size is achieved through an insatiable appetite for smaller fish and invertebrates, which the bluefin hunts day and night outside the breeding season. Bluefins live in schools often containing a mix of species, but all members of the school will be of similar size to avoid accidental cannibalism. These 'warm-blooded' fish migrate north in summer and spend winter in the tropics, where they breed. Their huge swimming muscles make them exceptionally meaty. There is real concern that the species is being over-fished.

Identification: Large, torpedo-shaped fish, two dorsal fins followed by series of finlets on tailstock. Pectoral and pelvic fins short, anal and second dorsal fin highly falcate (sickle-like), caudal fin a stiff, symmetrical crescent with darkly pigmented lobes. Body counter-shaded – bluish-grey above, silvery below.

Distribution: Northern Atlantic, Mediterranean and Black Sea. Sub-population off coast of South Africa. American range extends from Canada to Brazil.
Habitat: Oceanic, usually in surface waters, occasionally down to 3,000m/9,800ft; visits coastal waters.
Food: Smaller fish and pelagic invertebrates; will also take benthic animals and kelp close to shore.
Size: 4.5m/14.7ft.
Breeding: Oviparous, spawning up to 10 million floating eggs a year.
Status: Listed as Data Deficient by IUCN.

Albacore

Thunnus alalunga

Identification: Body rotund but highly streamlined with pointed snout and tapering tailstock. Eye is large. Two dorsal fins and dorsal and ventral rows of finlets. Pectoral and anal fins are small; dark-blue caudal fins form a shallow crescent-shaped tail with pointed tips. Pectoral fins are very long. Body steely blue above, silvery white below.

These fish move around their distributional range in schools, performing extensive migrations in search of food or to spawn in tropical waters in summer. They often congregate at thermoclines – depths where the water changes temperature, where upwelling currents bring nutrients up from below and prey is more abundant. Large albacore tend to live deeper than small ones. Albacore have a strong schooling instinct and often form mixed schools with other types of tuna. As with other tunas, over-fishing is a concern. The flesh is considered to be excellent and is sold as high-quality canned tuna. Also worrying from a consumer's perspective is the tendency of the species to accumulate high levels of mercury in the flesh.

Distribution: All tropical and temperate oceans and seas including Mediterranean. Very common off Australian coast.
Habitat: Pelagic in open ocean, mainly in surface waters to 600m/1,968ft.
Food: Smaller fish.
Size: 1.4m/4.6ft.
Breeding: Oviparous; spawn in tropical waters during the summer.
Status: Commercially fished; listed as Data Deficient by IUCN.

Wahoo (*Acanthocybium solandri*):
up to 2.5m/8.2ft
A close relative of tunas and mackerel, the wahoo (above) is a long, narrow-bodied predatory fish known from the surface waters of warm, tropical and sub-tropical oceans and seas worldwide. It can be solitary or schooling, and is fished commercially and for sport.

Skipjack tuna (*Katsuwonus pelamis*):
up to 1.08m/3.5ft
A small, cosmopolitan species of tuna. Skipjacks live in schools, and hunt smaller fish and pelagic invertebrates. In turn, they are important prey for larger tunas and sharks. Skipjack tuna account for the majority of tuna consumed by humans.

Bonito (*Sarda chiliensis*): up to 1m/3.25ft
A pelagic schooling tunafish of tropical and temperate oceans, the bonito is also an important commercial and game species.

Spanish mackerel (*Scomberomorus maculata*):
up to 90cm/36in
A streamlined, silvery mackerel of Atlantic and Pacific surface waters. Spanish mackerel form huge schools that are targeted by highly commercial fisheries. Like other scombrids, they are fast swimmers and prey on smaller fish and zooplankton.

Atlantic mackerel
Scomber scombrus

Schools of this species tend to remain in deep water in winter, but in summer feed close to the surface, travelling in search of suitable prey. Plankton, crustaceans and fish larvae make up the bulk of the diet, but the mackerel is also well adapted for pursuing small fish such as sand eels. Mackerel lack a swimbladder, and rely on lightweight oily musculature as well as continual, fast swimming to stop them from sinking. Their gills are ventilated by the force of water passing into the open mouth rather than by any kind of pump, so if they stop swimming they die. The species is highly commercial and supports large fishing industries.

Identification: Slender, near cylindrical body with pointed snout and tapering tailstock. Tiny scales; body is silvery green to white on belly, marked with vertical or slightly oblique black bands on back and flanks. All fins are small, tailstock bears tiny finlets, caudal fin forms a pointed crescent.

Distribution: Parts of northern Atlantic, also Mediterranean and Black Sea. Western Atlantic range is from Labrador to Cape Lookout, Oregon.
Habitat: Oceanic, in surface waters to 200m/650ft.
Food: Zooplankton and small fish.
Size: 60cm/23.6in.
Breeding: Oviparous; larvae feed actively and attain lengths of 25cm/10in in first year.
Status: Common and widespread but heavy exploitation may lead to declines; not listed by IUCN.

Great barracuda
Sphyraena barracuda

Distribution: Tropical and sub-tropical waters of oceans and seas worldwide.
Habitat: Surface waters down to 100m/330ft; most often recorded near shore, but performs extensive migrations into open ocean.
Food: Fish.
Size: 2m/6.6ft.
Breeding: Oviparous; spawns offshore in deep water during spring.
Status: Not listed by IUCN.

Unlike most tunas and mackerel, the great barracuda is a largely solitary species, though juveniles may form small schools and adults will gather at rich food resources. Barracudas are opportunistic or ambush predators of other fish, capable of short bursts of rapid acceleration. Their sharp teeth easily snag prey, and the jaws are powerful enough to bite fish in half that are too large to be swallowed whole. They are curious of divers and swimmers, but despite a bad reputation pose little serious danger. Attacks on humans do occur, but these usually consist of a single lunge, and although painful, a barracuda bite is unlike to be fatal. The species is fished for sport and sometimes for eating, although it is frequently contaminated with dangerous levels of toxins.

Identification: A long, slender, cylindrical body with a long, pointed head and large eyes. Very sharp teeth. Lower jaw extends further than upper jaw. Body is silvery green, marked on upper flanks with dark bands and also black blotches of variable size and shape. Dorsal and anal fins can be raised and lowered to aid steering.

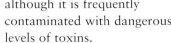

BILLFISH

*These spectacular members of the order Perciformes rank among the most glamorous of marine fish –
their speed and athleticism is legendary and their dramatic fins and colouration make them the
ultimate trophy for many game fishermen. All billfish possess a bony, sword-like extension of
the upper jaw, which is used to strike down prey.*

Blue marlin

Makaira nigricans

The largest and most spectacular of the billfish, the blue marlin is well adapted for
sustained, high-speed swimming. Its extremely muscular body is superbly streamlined, and
its powerful tail generates enormous thrust, allowing it to swim fast and tirelessly. The pelvic
and pectoral fins fold into grooves in the body to enhance streamlining. The species is also
highly acrobatic, sometimes leaping a metre or more clear of the water surface. These
qualities make is a very popular gamefish. It also makes good eating and is heavily fished in
many parts of its range. Marlin are generally solitary and hunt by day in surface waters.
Certain populations appear to show a marked preference for open, deep water. Swipes of the
bill are used to stun prey. Marlin sometimes
work cooperatively when hunting and in the
excitement some of the colours on the body
appear to 'light up' as the pigment cells glow
under nervous stimulation.

Identification: Cylindrical body tapers from
the back of the head to the tail. First dorsal
fin is long and tall, second much smaller;
pelvic and pectoral fins are small. Tail fins
form a slender crescent; bill is less than a
quarter of body length and stout. Dark
blue or black dorsal area; below
lateral line
is silvery-
white with
15 vertical stripes on
each flank, each bearing pale-blue spots.

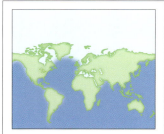

Distribution: Range shown
here is pantropical in Atlantic,
Indian and Pacific. However,
there is some debate as to
whether Pacific and Indian
dwellers constitute a
separate species, *M. mazara*.
Habitat: Pelagic; open ocean
down to 200m/660ft.
Food: Smaller fish,
cephalopods.
Size: 5m/16.4ft.
Breeding: Oviparous; no
parental care.
Status: Highly commercial;
not listed by IUCN.

Black marlin

Makaira indica

A slightly smaller and less decoratively marked relative of the blue marlin, this species is
only slightly less athletic and occupies a wider ecological niche. Its use of deeper water
enables it to take a greater diversity of prey than blue marlin, and it is fast enough to
specialize in hunting small tunas. The bills of all marlins are rounded in cross-section and
thus make crude weapons compared with the blade-like bill of the swordfish, but they are,
nevertheless, sometimes used to slash at prey. Black marlin have been recorded in the
Atlantic Ocean, but these are thought to be vagrant individuals and there is no evidence that
they breed there. Female marlin spawn anything up to 40 million eggs, which hatch as
larvae that develop in mid-water. The maximum lifespan of this species is not yet known.
Heavy commercial and sport fishing exert serious
pressure, and monitoring is needed to ensure it
does not become threatened.

Identification: Body shape much
as blue marlin, but usually lacks
obvious stripes; pectoral fins
stick out from sides of body and
cannot be folded away (unlike
blue marlin).

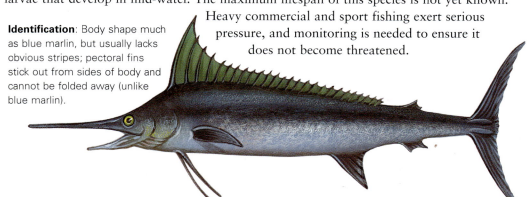

Distribution: Tropical,
sub-tropical and warm-
temperate waters of
Indo-Pacific Ocean.
Habitat: Pelagic, surface
waters of open ocean,
occasionally down to
900m/2,950ft; frequently
visits near-shore habitat.
Food: Fish, cephalopods,
crustaceans.
Size: 4.65m/15.25ft.
Breeding: Oviparous; spawns
in warm water.
Status: Highly commercial,
possible risk of over-
exploitation, but not listed
by IUCN.

Pacific sailfish

Istiophorus platypterus

This is the world's fastest swimming fish and can attain speeds of 100kmph/62mph plus. It is distinguished by a long, slender but muscular body and a sail-like first dorsal fin that is taller than the body is deep, and runs three-quarters the length of the back. Like the marlin, the sailfish lights up with bright blue vertical stripes when it becomes agitated. Sailfish migrate long distances on an annual basis to spawn in the tropics, sometimes in schools with similar-sized individuals, but they may also cruise the oceans alone in search of aggregations of prey.

Identification: Long, slender body, dark blue above, pale silver-white below, with faint vertical bars on upper flanks made up of blue spots; clearly visible lateral line. Huge, dark dorsal fin. Caudal fins form a large, slender crescent; pectoral fins large; pelvic fins each modified to a single spine.

Distribution: Tropical and temperate waters of Indian and Pacific Oceans.
Habitat: Pelagic, warm surface waters of open ocean to 200m/660ft.
Food: Fish, pelagic crustaceans and cephalopods.
Size: 3.5m/11.5ft.
Breeding: Oviparous; spawns in summer; juveniles grow rapidly, reaching 3kg/6.6lb in 6 months.
Status: Not listed by IUCN.

Swordfish

Xiphias gladius

Distribution: Tropical and temperate oceans and seas worldwide.
Habitat: Pelagic in midwater from 200–800m/650–2,600ft.
Food: Fish, cephalopods, crustaceans.
Size: 4.55m/15ft.
Breeding: Oviparous; spawns in spring; larvae grow rapidly.
Status: Listed as Data Deficient by IUCN.

The scientific names *gladias* means 'sword', as in gladiator. The bill of the swordfish is flat with sharp edges, and is used as a deadly weapon, to kill and slice prey into pieces small enough to swallow. Swordfish tackle a wide variety of prey, mostly other fish, but also pelagic invertebrates. They travel long distances, overwintering and spawning in warm waters in spring, then heading for cooler waters to take advantage of seasonally abundant prey over the summer. Juveniles have a fully developed sword by the time that are 1cm/0.4in long, and begin hunting immediately. Females grow slightly faster than males and reach a larger size. Swordfish is a tasty food fish; however, the species' position at the top of the food chain means it has a tendency to accumulate dangerously high levels of certain marine pollutants, especially mercury, so frequent consumption is not recommended.

Identification: Body tapers from head to tail, which bears long caudal fins forming a crescent. Pelvic fins are absent, pectorals are long and low slung. Single dorsal fin is tall and single anal fin is small – both are falcate. Head is large with large eyes and the upper jaw is modified into a long, blade-like bill.

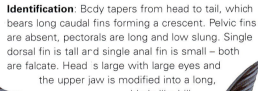

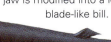

REPTILES OF THE OPEN OCEAN

The relatively few reptiles adapted to life at sea include some of the world's great ocean nomads. Marine turtles, including the enormous leatherback, may travel thousands of miles a year in search of food, but must return to land to breed. The pelagic sea snake, however, is wholly aquatic and unusual among marine serpents for its open water distribution – even its young are born at sea.

Yellow bellied sea snake

Pelamis platurus

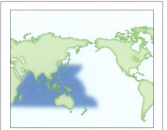

This is the only sea snake that ventures into truly open waters and it is often found hundreds of miles offshore. It is also known as the pelagic sea snake, and its wide-roaming habits have earned it the distinction of being the world's most widespread snake species. It can actively swim by wiggling its body – much as a terrestrial snake would move on land – but spends much of its time drifting idly near the surface, usually with head hanging slightly down. The sea snake feeds mainly on small pelagic fish and invertebrates, such as shrimp, which it catches with sudden, darting movements. Highly potent venom is injected into the prey on the first bite, and once immobilized the meal is swallowed whole, head first. The venom is sufficiently potent to kill a human, but the snakes are not aggressive and will not normally bite unless they are provoked.

Identification: Long narrow head and slender body with smooth scales; striking yellow and black colouration serves as a warning to potential predators that this species is toxic.

Distribution: Tropical and sub-tropical waters of Indian and Pacific Oceans.
Habitat: Surface waters of open ocean, also in coastal waters and reefs.
Food: Small fish.
Size: 90cm/35in.
Breeding: Mating occurs at the surface; live young born in water.
Status: Common; not listed by IUCN.

Leatherback turtle

Dermochelys coriacea

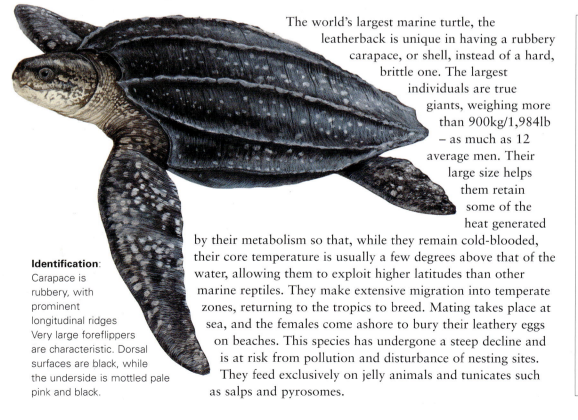

The world's largest marine turtle, the leatherback is unique in having a rubbery carapace, or shell, instead of a hard, brittle one. The largest individuals are true giants, weighing more than 900kg/1,984lb – as much as 12 average men. Their large size helps them retain some of the heat generated by their metabolism so that, while they remain cold-blooded, their core temperature is usually a few degrees above that of the water, allowing them to exploit higher latitudes than other marine reptiles. They make extensive migration into temperate zones, returning to the tropics to breed. Mating takes place at sea, and the females come ashore to bury their leathery eggs on beaches. This species has undergone a steep decline and is at risk from pollution and disturbance of nesting sites. They feed exclusively on jelly animals and tunicates such as salps and pyrosomes.

Identification: Carapace is rubbery, with prominent longitudinal ridges Very large foreflippers are characteristic. Dorsal surfaces are black, while the underside is mottled pale pink and black.

Distribution: Tropical to cool-temperate waters of oceans worldwide.
Habitat: Surface waters from coasts to open ocean, sometimes diving to more than 500m/1,640ft.
Food: Jelly animals.
Size: 2.8m/9ft.
Breeding: Mates offshore; eggs laid in batches of 60–100 on sandy beaches; no parental care after laying, although nesting sites are selected with great care.
Status: Listed as Critically Endangered by IUCN.

Olive ridley turtle

Lepidochelys olivacea

Distribution: Tropical waters of the Atlantic, Pacific and Indian Oceans.
Habitat: Surface waters from coasts to open ocean.
Food: Fish and marine invertebrates.
Size: 75cm/30in.
Breeding: Females breed every few years, mating offshore and crawling up beaches in order to lay 2–3 clutches of up to 120 eggs over the course of a breeding season.
Status: Listed as Endangered by IUCN.

Adults of this species spend much of their time in open sea, feeding on fish and squid. They return to the coasts to breed. The mass arrival (or *arribada*) of females at breeding beaches and the subsequent mass hatching of offspring are one of the world's great natural history spectacles. Up to 150,000 females may arrive simultaneously, climbing over one another in an effort to find a patch of sand in which to lay their eggs, and often digging up those of other females as they excavate a nest. Mass egg laying leads to the synchronous hatching of hundreds of thousands of young and a feeding frenzy for terrestrial and marine predators. But force of sheer numbers works in the turtles' favour – by making the dash for the sea together the youngsters gain at least some degree of protection.

Identification These diminutive marine turtles have an olive-coloured, heart-shaped carapace. The carapace is distinct in that there are more than five scutes, or plates, down each side.

Hawksbill turtle
(*Eretomchelys imbricata*): up to 1.12m/3.7ft
A relatively small sea turtle of tropical and sub-tropical waters, with a carapace made up of overlapping scutes, and a beak-like mouth. Feed mainly on sponges, jelly animals and seaweed. Listed as Critically Endangered by the IUCN.

Green turtle (*Chelonia mydas*): up to 1.5m/5ft
Endangered turtle named for the colour of its flesh. The populations of the Atlantic and Pacific Oceans are regarded as separate subspecies. Green turtles may travel thousands of kilometres a year at sea but return to their natal beaches to breed. As adults, they are strictly herbivorous, feeding on algae and seagrasses.

Kemp's ridley turtle (*Lepidochelys kempii*): up to 80cm/31.5in
This is a close relative of the olive ridley turtle. It is the world's most threatened marine turtle, with a breeding population estimated at just two or three thousand individuals. It nests only in Mexico.

Loggerhead turtle

Caretta caretta

Considered the most migratory of all sea turtles, loggerheads have been known to make crossings of both the Atlantic and Pacific Oceans. Even young animals spend long periods far out to sea, drifting along with clumps of sargassum weed or other flotsam. The heavy, powerful jaws and associated muscles that earn the species its name are able to demolish the shells of large crabs and molluscs. Thousands of loggerheads are killed annually when accidentally entangled in fishing nets, and since they develop and mature slowly, populations are slow to recover from these losses. Most damaging of all, however, is the effect of human disturbance at nesting beaches.

Distribution: Tropical to warm-temperate waters of oceans worldwide and adjoining seas.
Habitat: Surface waters, from coasts to open oceans.
Food: Marine invertebrates.
Size: 1.2m/4ft.
Breeding: Females breed every 2–3 years, and may produce several clutches of eggs, up to 100 at a time, in a single breeding season.
Status: Listed as Endangered by IUCN.

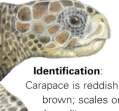

Identification: Carapace is reddish brown; scales on front flippers reddish fringed with yellow; ventral surface (plastron) is yellow.

OCEANIC DOLPHINS

*The cetacean family Delphinidae includes several species that are equally at
home in coastal waters or far out to sea. Most are highly social and athletic
and they have a natural curiosity that means they often approach boats,
providing a welcome spectacle to break the tedium of long sea voyages.*

Spinner dolphin

Stenella longirostris

Spinners are among the most conspicuous ocean-going dolphins.
They are social, and groups sometimes converge to create schools
several thousand strong. The species is named for its unique aerial
displays, which involve leaping up to 3m/10ft clear of the water
and rotating the body three or four times along the long axis.
Spinners are closely associated with schools of tuna and they were
the species most severely affected by careless fishing techniques
during the second half of the 20th century, when tens of
thousands were drowned in nets. Four subspecies are
recognized, each with very distinct physical characteristics.
Spinners hunt mainly at night in offshore waters, but may
visit shallow waters around tropical islands by day. Males are
larger in size than females.

Identification: Head tapers to a characteristically long and narrow beak
and melon (or domed forehead) has low profile. Body is slender with
erect falcate (sickle-shaped) or triangular dorsal fin set half way back.
Tail often has a pronounced ventral bulge. Body is predominantly grey,
but the belly is pale in some subspecies.

Distribution: Tropical
and subtropical waters
of oceans worldwide.
Habitat: Open ocean.
Food: Small fish, squid
and crustaceans.
Size: 2.35m/7.7ft long.
Breeding: A single calf
is born approximately
every 3 years, after a
10–11-month period of
gestation; calves weaned
at 1–2 years of age.
Status: Not listed by IUCN.

Risso's dolphin

Grampus griseus

Risso's dolphins are gregarious, typically living in groups of 20 or so individuals, but
occasionally coming together in large schools of several hundred. They are often seen from
ships, and occasionally from the shore, and appear curious and playful – apt to leap and
breach in a very acrobatic manner. At other times, whole schools seem to disappear
completely – presumably migrating in search of food, but the details of these movements
and many other aspects of the species' behaviour remain a
mystery. Mass strandings occasionally happen. The
scars that make the species particularly
distinctive are thought to be the result of
tussles with other dolphins and with
large squid. In older individuals,
the scarring may be so dense
that the body appears
to be almost
completely white.

Distribution: Patchy
distribution in tropical,
sub-tropical and temperate
waters in oceans worldwide
and many adjoining seas.
Habitat: Open oceans,
typically above steeply
sloping continental slope.
Food: Mainly squid and
other cephalopods.
Size: 3.8m/12.5ft long.
Breeding: Virtually unknown.
Status: Not listed by IUCN.

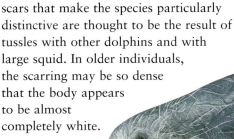

Identification: Blunt head with a square profile and
no beak. Body is stout and robust, with long, falcate
pectoral fins, a tall falcate dorsal fin and a slender
tail. Skin is a variable shade of grey to brown
dorsally, pale on the belly.

Atlantic white-sided dolphin

Lagenorhynchus acutus

Distribution: Temperate and sub-polar North Atlantic and Arctic Oceans.
Habitat: Open waters over deep slopes, canyons and steep ocean-floor topography.
Food: Fish, especially herring, hake and mackerel, squid and other invertebrates.
Size: 2.8m/9.2ft long.
Breeding: Single calf born every other year after an 11-month gestation period; weaned at about 18 months.
Status: Common; not listed by IUCN.

This distinctive species is easily recognized by its consistent flank markings. It is very gregarious, forming schools of anything from a handful of individuals to several hundred. Large numbers form around abundant food sources or when migrating in search of food. Members of a group work together to round up schools of prey fish, especially Atlantic herrings, forcing them into a tight ball, which is then attacked. White-sides often associate with other species, in particular white-beaked dolphins and larger cetaceans, such as fin and humpback whales. They are athletic and playful, and are commonly seen riding the bow waves of ships.

Identification: A stout, torpedo-shaped body; a tall, sharply pointed, falcate dorsal fin; broad, falcate pectoral fins; and a thick tailstock. The head is short with a short, thick beak and a low, tapering profile. The back, fins and flukes are black, while the flanks are grey with a white flash and broad stripe that is creamy-yellow in colour. The belly is white.

Pantropical spotted dolphin (*Stenella attenuata*): up to 2.4m/7.9ft
The pantropical spotted dolphin is probably the most abundant dolphin species, with a population numbering several million worldwide in most tropical and temperate oceans. It is highly gregarious and athletic, and huge schools have been seen performing spectacular displays of leaping and riding the bow waves of boats.

Striped dolphin (*Stenella coeruleoalba*): up to 2.65m/8.7ft
This is a familiar species of dolphin, common in tropical and temperate waters worldwide. It is a highly gregarious species and individuals are usually to be found in large schools of several dozen animals up to several hundred. They prey on small, schooling fish.

Rough-toothed dolphin (*Steno bredanensis*): up to 2.65m/8.7ft
An off-shore specialist of tropical and sub-tropical oceans with a long beak and tapering head profile. The teeth are finely grooved. Members of the species typically live in small groups of 10–20 individuals, and they appear to be highly intelligent and cooperative. Animals perform deep dives, lasting up to 15 minutes, in the search for squid and fish. Large prey, when caught, may be shared out among the group.

Common bottlenose dolphin

Tursiops truncatus

The bottlenose dolphin is known from a wide variety of marine habitats. There are distinct coastal and offshore forms. Popular with people because of their playful nature and apparent 'smile', bottlenoses are also considered to be among the most intelligent of mammals. The species has recently been separated from its close relative the Indo-Pacific bottlenose. Groups may number up to several hundred animals. Aggression is relatively common, especially towards other similar-sized cetaceans. Bottlenoses act cooperatively when hunting or in defence, and they communicate using a highly refined repertoire of body postures and sounds. Prey is detected by echo-location using pulses of sound focused through the melon.

Identification: Long, slender body with tall falcate dorsal fin and short falcate pectorals. Head has pronounced melon and short cylindrical beak. Mouth is slightly curved in what appears to be an appealing smile. Skin is fairly uniformly grey, slightly darker on the dorsal surface.

Distribution: Tropical and temperate oceans and adjoining seas worldwide, except High Arctic.
Habitat: Open and coastal waters.
Food: Pelagic and bottom-dwelling fish and invertebrates.
Size: 3.8m/12.5ft long.
Breeding: Single calves are born at intervals of 3 years or more; the young are weaned at 18–20 months, but they may then remain with their mothers for several more years.
Status: Some populations are thought to be in decline, but not listed by IUCN.

TOOTHED AND BEAKED WHALES

Larger members of the Delpinidae are commonly referred to as whales rather than dolphins. The beaked whales of the family Ziphiidae include many of the least known cetacean species. Adult males of the latter group often have just a single pair of teeth which erupt from the lower jaw outside the mouth. It appears these may be used for fighting. Adult female and juvenile beaked whales lack any functional teeth.

Pygmy killer whale

Feresa attenuata

Identification: Stout torpedo-shaped body and rounded head with pronounced melon and no beak. There is a large falcate dorsal fin half way along the back and moderately long pectorals. The skin is dark grey to black, with white markings on the belly and throat and around the mouth.

Pygmy killer whales, also known as slender blackfish, earn their common name through their similarities to orcas – both species have black and white colouration and a large dorsal fin. They are, however, much longer-bodied than true killer whales and are closer in appearance to pilot whales. They are reported to be unusually aggressive when cornered, but in open water they are apparently gregarious and live in groups of up to 50 individuals. While they are certainly capable of killing large animals, including other small cetaceans, there is no evidence they actively hunt them. Examinations of stomach contents suggest that they eat mainly squid. They are relatively slow moving, only rarely performing the athletic leaps associated with other dolphin species. They appear to be rather rare animals, and they may be at risk from accidental entanglement in fishing nets.

Distribution: Tropical and sub-tropical waters of oceans worldwide.
Habitat: Open ocean.
Food: Squid and fish.
Size: 2.6m/8.5ft.
Breeding: Virtually unknown.
Status: Appears to be relatively rare and there are some conservation concerns. Listed as Data Deficient on IUCN.

Cuvier's beaked whale

Ziphius cavirostris

Despite being among the best-studied of all ziphiids, detailed knowledge of Cuvier's beaked whale is still lacking. This deep-diving species may go 30 minutes or more without surfacing for air, and when it does it keeps a low profile – breaching is rare. Hence, sightings are relatively few and far between. The species is either recorded alone or in small groups. Cuvier's beaked whales hunt a variety of deep-water prey, mostly soft-bodied squid, which are sucked into the mouth and swallowed whole as the whale has no functional teeth. Mass strandings of these whales are a concern, since they seem to be related to military exercises involving underwater explosions and other loud noises. It seems likely that these disturbances affect their ability to navigate.

Identification: A large, cylindrical body, with a small falcate dorsal fin set well back, and small rounded pectorals. The head is large and tapers steeply but smoothly to a short beak. Skin is dark grey to black, sometimes flushed with pink around the face and marked with white spots and scars. In adult males, two small teeth protrude from the tip of the lower jaw.

Distribution: Tropical and temperate oceans and adjoining seas worldwide.
Habitat: Offshore specialist favouring deep water.
Food: Mainly squid, some pelagic fish and shrimp.
Size: 2.7m/8.8ft.
Breeding: Details unknown.
Status: May be in decline but listed as Data Deficient by IUCN.

Blainville's beaked whale

Mesoplodon densirostris

Distribution: Patchy distribution in tropical and warm temperate waters of oceans worldwide and some adjoining seas.
Habitat: Open waters, particularly those above continental slopes.
Food: Squid and small pelagic fish; possibly also bottom-dwelling crustaceans.
Size: 4.4m/14.4ft and perhaps longer.
Breeding: Details not known.
Status: Listed as Data Deficient by IUCN.

This medium-sized toothed whale occupies a very large distributional range, but reliable sightings are relatively infrequent outside three main areas close to the Bahamas in the Atlantic and Hawaii and the Society Islands in the central and South Pacific, where most research has been conducted. Dives are prolonged, up to 20 minutes or more, and probably take the animal into deep water in search of its prey – squid. On surfacing, Blainville's beaked whale breaks the surface beak first, takes a breath, then rolls forward with very little splashing, and is therefore difficult to spot. The bones of this species are among the densest of any mammal and the teeth are bizarre – they erupt from the side of a strangely stepped jaw, and are usually encrusted with tufts of barnacles.

Identification: Spindle-shaped body with small falcate dorsal fin and short pectorals. Head has a long, narrow beak and a strongly arched lower jaw with a large emergent tooth on each side. The skin is dark above and paler on the belly and usually covered with pale scratches and circular scars, the result of attacks by cookiecutter sharks, squid and other whales.

Baird's beaked whale (*Berardius bairdii*): up to 12.8m/42ft
The largest member of the Ziphiidae, also known as the giant bottlenose whale. Females are slightly larger than males. The species is restricted to deep waters of the northern Pacific Ocean. Little is known of its ecology and behaviour, though detailed anatomical studies have been made as a result of Japanese whalers using International Whaling Commission regulations that allow them to take whales for 'scientific purposes'.

Sowerby's beaked whale (*Mesoplodon bidens*): up to 5.5m/18ft
A little-known species found in the North Atlantic, Sowerby's beaked whales live in small schools of fewer than 10 individuals. Males have two tusk-like teeth erupting from halfway along the lower jaw. They are thought to eat mostly squid and perhaps certain groundfish, such as Atlantic cod.

Strap-toothed whale (*Mesoplodon layardii*): up to 6.2m/20ft
A medium-sized beaked whale restricted to the cool-temperate waters of the Southern Hemisphere. Both sexes are black with extensive white markings at the front of the body and a dark facial mask. Males have long, laterally flattened tusks protruding from either side of the lower jaw.

Northern bottlenose whale

Hyperoodon ampullatus

Among the largest-beaked whales, the northern bottlenose was previously subject to intensive hunting, but is now protected. Resident populations appear to inhabit deep water off Nova Scotia and off the Bay of Biscay, while other populations appear to be more nomadic or migratory. They live in small groups of fewer than 10 individuals, usually about four. Feeding dives are typically quite short, around 10 minutes, but they can perform extended dives of an hour or more, especially when frightened, and may reach depths of 1,500m/5,000ft. They appear to favour one species of squid (*Gonatus fabricii*) above all other food, but they may also opportunistically take fish and other invertebrates. Despite a history of hunting, they remain curious animals and will sometimes approach boats.

Identification: Cylindrical body with small pectoral fins and a dorsal fin set two-thirds of the way back. Has a prominent, rounded melon and pronounced beak. Skin is dark grey. The melon and beak are white (grey in females).

Distribution: North Atlantic Ocean and into Arctic Ocean.
Habitat: Deep water, often close to pack ice. Dives to depths of 1,500m/4,920ft.
Food: Mostly deep-water squid.
Size: 9.8m/32ft.
Breeding: Calves born singly in spring after a gestation lasting at least 12 months.
Status: Species is protected internationally and listed as Lower Risk, Conservation Dependent by IUCN.

SPERM AND OCEANIC BALEEN WHALES

These giant whales include the largest members of the animal kingdom. Most undertake vast migratory journeys in a lifetime, and some may live for more than 100 years. They may communicate with others of their species over hundreds of miles via 'songs'. The slow reproduction rate means that populations are unable to recover rapidly from the impact of past commercial exploitation.

Sperm whale

Physeter macrocephalus

The largest of the toothed whales and the largest predatory animal on Earth, sperm whales tackle prey up to 10m/33ft long. They are also the deepest-diving mammals, able to descend an estimated 3,000m/10,000ft. Sperm whales mature slowly – calves begin taking solid food at 2 years, but may continue to supplement this with milk for 10 years or so. This slow reproductive rate makes them vulnerable to over-exploitation, and they suffered heavy losses before hunting was banned in the 1980s. The oil inside the head, known as spermaceti, was used as a high-quality lubricant. In life, the spermaceti is thought to control buoyancy and focus sound. Also of value are the teeth, used in scrimshaw, and ambergris – a grey substance voided from the gut and used in perfume making.

Identification: Massive head, which contains spermaceti organ, is one-third body length. Teeth present only on lower jaw, which is very narrow. Skin of body is often wrinkled. Dorsal fin is very small and set well back, followed by several small bumps. Pectoral fins are short and broad; tail flukes are very wide.

Distribution: All oceans except ice-bound polar waters, although may be seen close to pack ice.
Habitat: Deep water; dives to 3,000m/10,000ft.
Food: Giant squid and other deep-water cephalopods.
Size: Up to 18.3m/60ft.
Breeding: Single calf born every 4–6 years after a gestation period of 15–18 months; calf weaned at 2 years. May live for more than 70 years.
Status: Protected by IWC ban on hunting. Listed as Vulnerable by IUCN.

Bowhead whale

Balaena mysticetus

Identification: Very large, deep-bodied whale with a massive head, and enormous, highly arching jaws which support 600 or more strips or plates of baleen up to 4m/13ft in length. There is a ridge on top of the head, in front of the blowholes. Dorsal fin is absent, pectorals are broad and triangular and tail flukes form a notched triangle. Males vocalize a haunting and highly varied song in the spring, in order to attract females.

This giant of Arctic waters spends its life close to the edge of the sea ice. It can travel considerable distances under ice and, if necessary, can ram air holes in ice almost 2m/6.6ft thick. There is some evidence that this species uses echo location to help them navigate around ice floes and bergs. Vocalizations, or 'songs', are common. The massive head and bowed jaw support hundreds of strips, or plates, of a horny material known as baleen. These plates act as strainers, filtering planktonic life from the water as the whale swims. The discovery of 19th-century harpoon tips in individuals alive at the end of the 20th century suggests the species is long-lived.

Distribution: Circumpolar waters of the North Atlantic, North Pacific and Arctic Oceans.
Habitat: Deep water, close to pack ice.
Food: Mainly krill and copepods, as well as other planktonic invertebrates.
Size: Up to 19.8m/65ft.
Breeding: Single calf born every 3–4 years; weaned from about 12 months, but may stay with mother several more years. May live for over 200 years.
Status: Listed as Low Risk, Conservation Dependent by IUCN.

Blue whale

Balaenoptera musculus

Distribution: All oceans, with three major populations in North Pacific, North Atlantic and Southern Hemisphere.
Habitat: Open ocean, may also visit coastal waters.
Food: Krill.
Size: 33m/108ft.
Breeding: Single calf born every 2–3 years after a gestation period of 11 months; development is rapid, young are weaned and independent within 8 months. May live for up to 70 years.
Status: Listed as Endangered by IUCN.

Identification: The largest of the the baleen whales. Head broad and flattened. Mouth contains up to 800 baleen plates. Throat folds into about 60 pleated furrows. Dorsal fin is tiny and set well back; pectorals are long and tapering; tail flukes are large and triangular. The skin is mottled grey, appearing blue in water. The underside is often coated in a sulphur-yellow growth of diatoms (single-celled algae).

The blue whale is the largest animal ever to have lived on Earth. Even a newborn calf is over 7m (23ft) long. It is difficult to assess to what extent these giants might be social – they are usually seen apparently alone or in small groups that disperse rapidly, but for animals of such size, with calls that carry vast distances, several whales spread out over, say, 200 miles or several hundred kilometres might still constitute a cohesive group. There appears to be a southerly migration in the austral summer, when travelling whales may consume up to 4 tonnes of krill per day. The species suffered severely from commercial whaling until it was protected in the mid 20th century and doubts remain over its ability to recover.

Fin whale (*Balenoptera physalus*): up to 27m/89ft
Second only to the blue whale in size, this species has strange, asymmetrical colouring on the sides of the head – black on the left and white on the right. Cosmopolitan in all oceans, it can swim at speeds of up to 47kmph/29mph. Feeds on krill and schooling fish such as herring.

Southern minke (*Balaenoptera bonaerensis*): up to 10.5m/35ft
Southern relative of the 'common' and dwarf minkes, but actually more closely related to the large, fast-swimming sei whale. Distinctive for their flat head, pointed snout, very curved dorsal fin and pale grey pectoral fins.

Northern right whale (*Eubalaena glacialis*): up to 17m/56ft
The northern right whale and its southern counterpart (*E. australis*) are closely related, but live at opposite ends of the Earth, with no apparent overlap. They look very similar, with a massive head and arched jaw. However, the northern species has white belly patch and facial calluses often encrusted with barnacles.

Minke whale

Balaenoptera acutorostrata

Distinguished by its pointed snout, the minke is the smallest and most common of the great whales. These whales are apparently migratory, but movements are difficult to follow. It seems that pregnant females travel to the tropics in winter to give birth, and the young are independent in time for the return journey. Minkes were intensively hunted in the mid 20th century and are still taken by Norway and Japan in defiance of an international ban on whaling. The so-called dwarf minke, regarded as a subspecies of *B. acutorostrata*, lives only in the Southern Hemisphere but should not be confused with the southern minke (see left).

Identification: Streamlined with a pointed snout and a ridge along the midline. There are 500–700 short pale plates of baleen and 50–70 pleated furrows on the throat. The skin is black dorsally with a grey chevron on its back; white on the throat and belly, with a white patch on the pectoral fins.

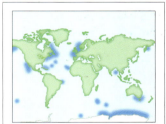

Distribution: Tropical, temperate and polar waters of North Atlantic and North Pacific Oceans (dwarf subspecies occurs in Southern Hemisphere).
Habitat: Open ocean, often over continental shelves and sometimes coastal waters.
Food: Mainly small fish, such as herring, sandlance and capelin, as well as some swarming planktonic crustaceans.
Size: 10.5m/35ft.
Breeding: Single calf born every 1 or 2 years after a gestation period of 10 months, weaned at about 6 months and independent soon after. May live for up to 50 years.
Status: Listed as Low Risk by IUCN.

GLOSSARY

Acanthopterygii The largest superorder of bony fish within the class Actinopterygii

Actinopterygii Class of bony fish, which accounts for about 96% of all fish. Distinguishing features include fins supported by rays (spiny fins) and the presence of a single dorsal fin

Agnatha Superclass of jawless primitive fish, of which only the lamprey and hagfish exist in the present day

Amoebocyte A cell capable of amoeboid movement; found in vertebrate body fluids such as blood

Amphibian A cold-blooded vertebrate which usually spends part of its life on land and part in water; includes frogs, toads and salamanders

Amphipod Member of the order Amphipoda (small crustaceans, including sand hoppers and ghost shrimps)

Ampullae Membranous anatomy usually associated with the semi-circular canals of the inner ear

Ampullae of Lorenzini Sensory organs forming a network of jelly-filled canals within the anterior part of sharks and rays, penetrating the surface of the skin as pores and usually visible as dark spots

Annelida Phylum containing wormlike creatures (annelids) with segmented bodies

Anterior At, or towards, the front

Anthozoa Class of cnidarians including hard and soft corals, sea pens and sea anemones

Aperture An opening, as for example, in a gastropod mollusc's shell

Aplacophora Worm-shaped marine molluscs lacking a shell

Appendage Broadly used for an external, protruding body part, ranging from (for example) the limbs of a vertebrate, or the antennae or mandibles of an invertebrate

Appendicularia Class within the phylum Urochordata or Tunicata

Arthropoda Phylum consisting of invertebrates with an exoskeleton and segmented bodies, to which are attached

pairs of jointed legs. Includes the insects, arachnids and crustaceans

Ascidiacea Class within the phylum Urochordata or Tunicata. Adults may be solitary, sessile zooids, or form colonies by budding

Asteroidea Class of echinoderms containing the sea stars

Atoll A circular or ring-like coral island enclosing a lagoon

Baleen Horny plates growing from the upper jaw of baleen whales and used in feeding by straining tiny food items, such as krill, from the water

Barbel A sensory, tentacle-like structure found around the mouth of certain types of fish

Barrier reef A long, narrow, coral reef usually found in shallow water and running close to the shore

Benthic Bottom dwelling

Bioluminescence The emission of light by a living organism that occurs as the product of a chemical reaction

Bivalve A shell consisting of two halves, or valves.

Brachiopoda Small phylum of ancient molluscoidal creatures, with a long, often spiral bivalve shell. Includes the lampshells

Branchiopoda Class or subclass of primitive crustaceans, predominantly freshwater

Bryozoa Small phylum of coral-like moss animals that form colonies by budding

Bycatch The unintentional harvest of commercial fisheries

Calcarea Class within the phylum Porifera, containing sponges with calcareous skeletons

Calcareous Chalky; term used to describe the shells of crabs, for example

Carapace The shield-like, dorsal part of the exoskeleton of various crustaceans; also used to describe the domed part of the shell of tortoises and turtles

Catadromous Describes a species which migrates from fresh water to the sea to breed

Cephalaspidomorphi Class of primitive jawless fish, most of which are now extinct

Cephalocarida Class or subclass of primitive crustaceans. Living members usually exhibit paddle-like appendages on the thorax

Cephalopoda Class of often highly-evolved molluscs including octopii and squid. Typical features include a large head, large eyes and, in some

cases, an ink sac

Chaetognatha Phylum of small, almost transparent wormlike creatures with bristles around the mouth.

Chela A pincer-bearing leg of a crustacean

Chelicera One of the pair of pincer-like mouthparts in front of the mouth opening in chelicerates (animals such as the horseshoe crab)

Chelicerata A subphylum of arthropods, members of which are known as chelicerates

Choanocyte A type of ciliated cell found in sponges

Chondrichthyes Class of cartilaginous, jawed fish whose members include sharks, skates and rays

Chordate An anima belonging to the phylum Chordata, having a single, hollow dorsal nerve cord, a notochord, gill slits, and a postanal tail at least during some part of its development; chordates include the vertebrate animals

Chromatophore A pigment-containing cell which can change its size or colour

Chrondrocyte A specialized cell in chimeras, sharks and rays that produces the gel-like substance chrondromucoprotein, which forms the basis of cartilage

Cilium A tiny, hair-like structure growing out from some cells; its whip-like beating action produces movement

Circumglobal Distributed around the world within a fairly specific latitudinal range

Cirripedia Class of marine crustaceans including barnacles

CITES The Convention on International Trade in Species; an agreement between nations that restricts international trade

Class A taxonomic level between phylum and order

Clupeid Member of the order Clupeiformes; includes herrings and anchovies

Cnidarian Member of the phylum Cnidaria (the hydroids, jellyfish, anemones and corals)

Cnidocyte One of the stinging cells found in most cnidarians

Comb-row Part of the sensory equipment of comb jellies, which is lined with cilia

Copepoda Class or subclass of crustacean. Members typically have six pairs of appendages on the thorax; many exist as parasites and plankton

Costal Concerned with the ribs

Crenulated (Of shells, especially bivalves) indented or scalloped

effect at edges of shell

Crinoidea Class of echinoderms containing the sea lilies and feather stars

Crustacea Subphylum of arthropods including lobsters, crabs, shrimps and barnacles

Ctenoid A fish scale with a toothed posterior edge; found in perciform (perchlike) fish, for example

Ctenophora Phylum of invertebrates commonly known as comb jellies

Cubozoa Class of cnidarians with a cube-shaped medusa and a highly venomous sting.

Cydippid Larval phase associated with ctenophores

Delta An often triangular, low-lying deposit of sediment at the mouth of a river

Demospongiae The largest class of sponges within the phylum Porifera, which have typically soft, spongy bodies

Detritivore An organism that feeds on detritus, or decomposing organic material

Deuterostome A member of a group of multicellular animals in which the mouth is formed as a secondary opening, and the original embryonic opening (blastophore) becomes the anus

Dimorphism Having two distinct forms (for example, different colours or sizes) within a species; sexual dimorphism refers to a marked difference in physical characteristics between males and females of the species

Dioecious Having separate sexes

Ecdysozoa One of the major groups of protostome animals, including the phylum Arthropoda

Echinoderm Members of the phylum Echinodermata

Echinodermata Phylum of exclusively marine creatures with radially symmetrical bodies formed around a central disk, in which the mouth is located. May be star-shaped, cylindrical or spherical

Echinoidea Class of echinoderms containing the sea urchins and sand dollars

Echiura Phylum of wormlike creatures, commonly known as spoonworms. Have various features in common with the annelids, but lack a segmented body

Elver A young eel

Ephyra Larval phase associated with medusoid animals

Epidermis The outermost layer of cells of an animal or plant

Errant Describes a species that actively hunts for food, such as some kinds of marine worms

Esca The lure, or bait, at the end of the angling apparatus (see ilicium) of anglerfish and frogfish (order Lophiiformes)

Eukaryote A cell which has genetic material contained within the nuclear membrane

Eumetazoa Subkingdom of multicellular organisms, members of which are called Metazoans

Eversible Describes a structure which can be everted, for example, the pharynx of some marine worms

Exoskeleton Hard, external, shell-like structure that supports and protects the body of some invertebrates, including the Arthropods

Falcate Sickle-shaped; as found in the dorsal fin of some sharks and dolphins, for example

Flagellate Refers to the whip-like portion (flagellum) of cells connected with feeding or reproduction, within simple multicellular organisms such as sponges

Flotsam Floating refuse or debris, usually the result of a wreck at sea

Fringing reef A coral reef occurring in the shallow water just off-shore

Gastropoda The largest class of molluscs, with representatives in terrestrial, freshwater and marine habitats. Members include slugs, snails, limpets and cowries

Gill An organ found in fish and many aquatic invertebrates, such as molluscs, which is used to absorb oxygen from water and to remove carbon dioxide

Gnathostomata Superclass of vertebrates with jaws and paired appendages, in contrast to the more primitive agnathans

Gnathostomulida Small phylum of microscopic marine worms

Hermaphrodite Organism possessing functioning male and female sex organs

Heterocercal Describes a tail fin in which the upper lobe contains some of the vertebrae of the backbone and is usually longer than the lower lobe

Hexactinellida Class within the phylum Porifera containing sponges with siliceous, or glassy, skeletons

Holothuroidea Class of echinoderms containing sea cucumbers

Homocercal Describes a tail fin in which both lobes are of equal length

Hyaline Clear or transparent; in animals it is a glassy substance usually associated with cartilage and skin

Hydrozoa Class of cnidarians where generations typically alternate between a colonial polyp (hydroid) phase and a medusoid phase. Medusae may form from individuals budded off by the colony. Includes the Portuguese Man-o-war

Ilicium The extensible part of the angling apparatus of anglerfish and frogfish (order Lophiiformes) formed from modified tissue on the first dorsal fin ray, which terminates in a 'lure', used to attract prey close to the mouth

Invertebrate An animal lacking a backbone

Instar A larval stage in the life cycle of some invertebrates

Intertidal Between the tides

IUCN The International Union for the Conservation of Nature; responsible for assigning organisms to agreed categories or rarity

IWC International Whaling Commission

Jetsam Traditionally referred to cargo and objects from a ship that was washed ashore; now largely used in the same way as flotsam

Kingdom A major grouping within the living world; for example, the animal kingdom

Krill Shrimp-like crustacea that form part of the plankton and are an important food source for many animals, including fish and whales

Lamella A thin, membranous plate-like structure; also part of the delicate, blood-rich tissue in a gill

Laminarian One of several types of large brown seaweed or kelp

Lophotrochozoa One of the major groups of protostome animals, including the phyla Mollusca and Annelida

Lower shore The part of the shore that is only normally fully exposed by the lowest level of the spring tides.

Malacostraca Class of crustaceans that includes krill, mantis shrimps, sand-hoppers and sea slaters

Mammal A warm-blooded vertebrate animal which suckles its young

Mammalia Class of jawed vertebrates whose members are mammals

Mandible One of the pair of jaw-like mouthparts found in some in crustaceans and insects

Mantle The folded tissue covering the body of molluscs; its outer layer secretes the shell

Marsupium The 'pouch' developed by some animals to brood their young – and which gives marsupial mammals their name; however, may also be present in creatures as tiny as sea lice

Maxillopoda Class of crustaceans including barnacles, copepods and ostracods

Medusa (pl. medusae) Free-swimming, bell-shaped cnidarians with a fringe of tentacles; may be a phase of sexual development in some jelly animals

Medusoid Relating to the medusa form or phase

Melon The lump of fatty tissue that forms the characteristic 'domed forehead' of many dolphins and whales

Metazoan A multicellular animal, that is one with cells that are differentiated into tissues and organs

Microtubule A very small protein filament found in cells

Middle shore The part of the shore that is covered and uncovered every 12 hours

Mollusca Phylum of bilateral invertebrates with unsegmented bodies and a mantle. Includes terrestrial and aquatic snails and slugs; also octopii, squids, clams, mussels and oysters

Molluscoid Of, or resembling, the molluscs

Monoplacophora Ancient class of molluscs whose few living members include the species Neopilina galathea

Morphology The study of the physical structure of an organism

Mucous Bearing mucus

Mucus The slimy, viscous fluid produced in the body of certain animals; used variously for lubrication and protection

Myxini Class of primitive jawless fish (agnathans) including the hagfish

Negative buoyancy Where an inanimate object or living creature is more dense per unit volume than water and will sink

Nematocyst A type of cell found in cnidarians which discharges a thread in order to sting or snare prey

Nematoda Phylum of simple, unsegmented worms found in terrestrial, freshwater and marine habitats

Nematomorpha Phylum of simple-bodied, parasitic worms with physical similarities to the nematodes. Commonly known as horsehair worms

Nemertea Phylum of unsegmented marine worms including ribbonworms, or proboscis worms

Neutral buoyancy Where an inanimate object or living animal is equal in density to the same volume of water and will therefore suspend in the water

Nictitating membrane Transparent 'third eyelid' found in some species of cartilaginous fish

North Atlantic Drift A warm sea current

Notochord A rod of cells running along the back in the early stages of development in chordates; in most chordates it is later replaced by the spinal column, but in primitive forms it is retained in adult life

Nuda Class of ctenophores lacking tentacles

Nudibranch A gastropod mollusc of the order Nudibranchia that lacks a shell and often has a beautifully coloured body

Operculum The gill cover found in many bony fish; also the lid that closes the shell of some invertebrates

Ophiuroidea Class of echinoderms containing the brittle stars

Organelle A specialized structure found in a living cell, for example, the ribosomes and nucleus

Ossicle A small bone in the ear of vertebrates; also the plate-like structures in the skin of many echinoderms

Ostracoda Extensive crustacean group of generally small members, whose shape has given rise to common name 'mussel shrimps'

Otolith A small calcium carbonate granule found in the vertebrate inner ear; vital for balance

Over-winter To survive over the winter period, often in a state of dormancy

Ovigerous (Of legs) bearing eggs

Oviparous Reproducing by eggs which hatch outside the mother's body

Ovoviviparous Reproducing by eggs which are retained inside the mother's body until hatching

Palp One of the sensory structures found around the

mouth of various invertebrates

Pantropical Distributed throughout the tropics

Parapodium One of the many paired, paddle-like structures found on the side of polychate worms; used for locomotion in free-living types

Parasite An organism that lives in, or on, another organism at its expense, and depends on it for food

Parazoa Subkingdom of multicellular organisms, including sponges (Porifera), with lessspecialized cell arrangement that metazoans

Parthenogenesis The growth and development of an embryo without fertilization by the male

Pedicellariae The tiny, pincer-like grooming and defensive structures on the bodies of starfish and urchins

Pelagic Living in the surface waters of the ocean

Peristome The area around the mouth in some invertebrate animals; the edge of the aperture of a spiral shell

Phoronida Small phylum of hermaphrodite marine worms that live in the substratum

Photophore A light-emitting organ often evolved by creatures living in habitats where little or no light penetrates

Phylogeny The evolutionary history of a group of organisms

Phylum One of the major subdivisions of a kingdom, consisting of one or more classes

Pinna The external ear flap of a mammal such as a sea lion

Plankton Microscopic plants and animals, including algae, protozoans and larvae, that drift in marine or fresh water

Planula A larval stage in the life cycle of some marine organisms such as cnidarians

Platyhelminthes Phylum of creatures commonly known as flatworms; also includes parasitic tapeworms and flukes

Pleopod One of the paired abdominal appendages found in crustaceans modified for swimming and, in females, for carrying eggs

Podia The rows of suckerlike appendages on the underside of the arms of echinoderms, associated with gas and water exchange; also movement and manipulation of prey

Pogonophora Tubelike, benthic

creatures that usually dwell in deep-sea habitats. Also known as beardworms

Poikilothermic Describes an animal whose body temperature fluctuates with the temperature of the surrounding environment

Polychaete A type of marine worm characterized by bristle-like appendages (chaetae) along its body; includes ragworm.

Polyplacophora Class of molluscs bearing a shell composed of overlapping calcareous plates.

Porifera Phylum of invertebrate animals including the sponges

Positive buoyancy Where an inanimate object or living creature is less dense per unit volume than water and will rise

Posterior At, or towards, the rear

Proboscis A feeding tube

Prokaryote A cell which has genetic material lying free in the cell cytoplasm instead of contained within the nuclear membrane

Protostome A member of a group of multicellular animals in which the original embryonic opening (blastophore) becomes the mouth.

Pycnogonida Class of marine arthropod within the subphylum Chelicerata, consisting of sea spiders

Radial symmetry Of anatomy repeated around a central axis, like the arms of a starfish

Ray A small spine that supports the fin membrane in a fish

Reef A ridge of rock, sand or coral, usually in shallow water

Remipedia Class of cave-dwelling crustacean lacking pigmentation and eyes

Reptile A cold-blooded, vertebrate animal with a dry, scaly skin

Rorqual Type of baleen whale of the genus Balaenoptera, such as the blue whale

Rotifera Small phylum of minute worms with whiplike cilia on the head, giving the appearance of revolving wheels.

Sarcopterygii Class of primitive fish with rounded (lobed) fins, including lungfish and coelacanths

Scaphopoda Class of mollusc, with cylindrical shells open at both ends

Sclerospongiae Extinct class of fossil marine sponges

Scutes Plates on a turtles shell; may be costal (on the side) or vertebral (across the back)

Scyphozoa Class of cnidarians that usually alternate between sessile polyp and free-swimming medusae forms

Semelparous Of an organism

that reproduces just once in its lifetime

Sequential hermaphrodite Organisms born as one sex but which later transform into the other, in contrast to Simultaneous hermaphrodites

Sessile Attached in one place; non-moving

Simultaneous hermaphrodite A species which has male and female reproductive organs that mature at the same time, making self-fertilization a possibility. May also be referred to as a synchronous hermaphrodite

Siphon Tubular organ in various invertebrates, usually connected with the sucking in and/or expulsion of water

Sipuncula Phylum of unsegmented wormlike creatures. Commonly known as peanut worms due to their tendency to retract into the anterior part of the body whenever disturbed

Sister group Closely related taxa; usually those appearing adjacent to each other in a typical family tree style classificatory diagram

Spermatophore Essentially a 'packet' of sperm

Spicule Minute crystalline fragment used as a skeletal support in sponges, for example

Spine The backbone of an organism; also a long, narrow structure – often venomous – such as the spine of a stingray

Spongin Interlocking, collagen-like fibrous material found in sponges

Spongocoel Central cavity of a sponge

Subkingdom A major subgrouping of living things within a kingdom

Sublittoral Area below the littoral, or tidal, zone. Equivalent to lower shore

Subphylum A major subgrouping within a phylum

Substratum The place where an organism is attached or situated, such as the seabed

Superclass A grouping between a phylum and a class

Suture Spiral seam or joint marking the junction of whorls of a gastropod shell

Symbiosis A relationship between different organisms in which each benefits from the association

Symbiont An organism taking part in a symbiotic relationship, for example, the photosynthesizing algae found in the cells of giant clams

Symbiotic A relationship in which symbiosis occurs

Taxon Any grouping within the

system of classification, such as a phylum, class or species

Teleost A member of the Teleostomi, the largest group of bony fish; includes most living species except for primitive types such as sharks and rays

Tentacle One of the tactile or prehensile appendages found around the mouth in various invertebrates, such as squid

Tentaculata Class of ctenophores with retractable or reduced feathery tentacles

Test The 'shell' of a sea urchin or sand dollar

Thaliacea A small class of pelagic tunicates

Thorax The section of an animal's body situated between the head and abdomen

Tube foot A hydraulic appendage found in echinoderms, used in locomotion; part of the water vascular system

Tunicate A member of the phylum Tunicata, such as a sea squirt

Umbo (pl. umbones) One of the 'hinges' of a bivalve shell

Univalve Describes a shell consisting of one valve

Upper shore The part of the shore that is only normally covered by the highest level of the spring tides

Varix One of the prominent ridges or ribs traversing the whorls of a univalve shell

Urochordata Phylum also known as Tunicata, containing the tunicates

Vertebrate An animal with a backbone

Water vascular system The hydraulic system found in echinoderms comprised of structures such as tube feet, and used for functions such as locomotion

Zooid An individual animal within a colony; usually used to describe cnidarians and ectoprocts (bryozoans)

Zooplankton Small invertebrate animals that feed on other plankton; zooplankton also includes the eggs and larvae of larger animals

INDEX

Pogonophora 154
Pollachius pollachius 82
  virens 82, *82*
pollock 82
Polychaeta 154
Polyplacophora 154
Pomatoschistus minutes 47, *47*
Porania pulvillus 29
porcelain crabs:
  broad-clawed 65, *65*
  long-clawed 23, *23*
Porcellana longicornis 23, *23*
  platycheles 65, *65*
Porcellanidae 23
porcupine fish, blotched 99
Porifera 154
Poroderma africanum 32, *32*
porpoises: common 49, *49*
  finless 49, *49*
  spectacled 49
Portuguese man-o-war 106, *106*, 138
poutings 83, *83*
prawns 20–1
  Aesop 21, *21*
  chameleon 21
  common 20, *20*
  snapping 20, *20*
Prionace glauca 120, *120*
Prionotus carolinus 43, *43*
Pristiophorus cirratus 75, *75*
Pristis microdon 76, *76*
  pectinata 76, *76*
Psenes cyanophrys 105
Psetta maxima 96, *96*
Pterois volitans 87, *87*
Pteroplatytrygon violacea 117, *117*
pufferfish, fugu 99, *99*
Pycnogonida 115, 154
Pycnogonum littorale 27, *27*

Pygoplites diacanthus 92, *92*

rabbit fish 116, *116*
Raja clavata 79, *79*
ratfish, spotted 117, *117*
rattails 132, *132*
rays 116, 117
  Atlantic torpedo 77, *77*
  blind electric 116, *116*
  Cortez electric 77
  southern 79
  spotted eagle 54, 79, *79*
  spotted torpedo 77, *77*
  thornback 79, *79*
Regalecus glesne 131, *131*
Remipedia 154
remoras 139, *139*
reptiles 100–1, 144–5
  see also individual species
Reptilia 155
Rhincodon typus 120, *120*
Rhinobatidae 78
Rhinobatos lentiginosus 78, *78*
Rhinomuraena quaesita 37
Rhynchocinetes durbanensis 65, *65*
ribbonfish, scalloped 131
rockling: five-bearded 38
  shore 38, *38*
  three-bearded 38
Rotifera 155
royal gramma 88, *88*

sable fish 87
sailfins 131, *131*
sailfish, Pacific 143, *143*
saithe 82, *82*
Salmo salar 81, *81*
  trutta 80, *80*
salmon: Atlantic 81, *81*
  kokanee 81, *81*
  sockeye 81, *81*
Salvelinus alpinus 80, *80*
sand gapers 61
sand-smelt 85
Sarcopterygii 155

Sarda chiliensis 141
Sardina pilchardus 124, *124*
Sargassum fish 134, *134*
Sargocentron rubrum 87, *87*
sawbellies 136
sawfish 76, 77
  great-tooth 76, *76*
  knife-tooth 77, *77*
  small-tooth 76, *76*
scallops: great 61, *61*
  queen 18, *18*
scampi 64, *64*
Scaphopoda 155
Scarus guacarnaia 95
Scatophagus argus 91, *91*
scats 91, *91*
Sclerospongiae 155
Scomber scombrus 141, *141*
Scomberomorus maculata 141
Scopelengys tristis 131
Scorpaenichthys marmoratus 43
Scorpaenidae 42
Scorpaeniformes 42–3, 86
scorpionfish 87
Scyliorhinus canicula 33
Scyphozoa 155
sea anemones 12–13
  beadlet 12, *12*
  black coral 12, *12*
  dahlia 13
  opelet 13, *13*
  plumose 13, *13*
  red-speckled pimplet 13, *13*
  snakelocks 13, *13*
sea bass, giant 89, *89*
sea bream, common 90, *90*
sea cows 52, 53, *53*
sea cucumbers 31, *31*
sea devils: giant 134, *134*
  toothy 135, *135*
sea dragon, leafy 41, *41*
sea lice 111, *111*
sea lions
  Australian 11, 53
  California 52, *52*
  steller 53
sea potato 31, *31*
sea robin, northern 43, *43*

sea snakes
  banded 101, *101*
  olive 101
  turtle-headed 101
  yellow bellied 144, *144*
sea spiders 27, *27*
  giant deep 115, *115*
sea stars: giant 29
  six-armed Luzon 69, 69
sea urchins 30
  black 30, *30*
  edible 30, *30*
  Savigny's 31
sea wasps 56, *56*
seahorses: longsnouted 41, *41*
  shortsnouted 41, *41*
seals 50–1
  common 50, *50*
  crabeater 51, *51*
  grey 51
  harbour 50, *50*
  harp 51, *51*
  leopard 50, *50*
  northern elephant 10, 51, *51*
  northern fur 52, *52*
  Weddell 51
seamoth, slender 40, *40*
Sepia officinalis 63, *63*
sergeant major 93
Seriola lalandi 138, *138*
Serranidae 88
shanny 47
sharks: Atlantic angel 35, *35*
  basking 70, *70*
  blue 120, *120*
  bonnethead 72, *72*
  botchy swell 33, *33*
  bramble 119, *119*
  brown-banded bamboo 75
  bull 32, *32*
  bullhead 34
  California horn 34, *34*
  common angel 35, *35*
  common thresher 71, *71*
  cookiecutter 119,

119
  frilled 118, *118*
  goblin 119
  great hammerhead 72, *72*
  great white 70, *70*
  Greenland 119, *119*
  grey nurse 71, *71*
  grey smooth hound 33
  ground sharks 32–3
  Japanese angel 35
  leopard 33, *33*, 75, *75*
  longnose saw 75, *75*
  mackerel 70–1
  megamouth 121, *121*
  night 121
  nurse 74, *74*
  oceanic white tip 121, *121*
  Pacific angel 35, *35*
  porbeagle 71
  Port Jackson 34, *34*
  pyjama 32, *32*
  requiem 72–3, 120–1
  saw 74
  scalloped hammerhead 73
  shallow water 74–5
  shortfin mako 71, *71*
  silky 121, *121*
  six-gilled 118, *118*
  sleeper 119, *119*
  small-tooth sand tiger 71
  smooth hammerhead 73, *73*
  soupfin 33, *33*
  spined pygmy 119
  spinner 121
  striped cat shark 32, *32*
  tiger 73, *73*
  whale 120, *120*
  whitetip reef 73, *73*
  zebra 75, *75*
sheep's head minnow 85, *85*

INDEX **159**